Sovereignty and Intelligence

*Spying and Court Culture in
the English Renaissance*

JOHN MICHAEL ARCHER

Sovereignty and Intelligence

*Spying and Court Culture in
the English Renaissance*

STANFORD UNIVERSITY PRESS

STANFORD, CALIFORNIA   1993

Stanford University Press
Stanford, California
© 1993 by the Board of Trustees
of the Leland Stanford Junior University
Printed in the United States of America

CIP data are at the end of the book

For my father,
   &
in memory of my mother

Acknowledgments

THIS book began as a dissertation in the English Department of Princeton University. I owe a special debt of gratitude and affection to my supervisor, Earl Miner, for his wise counsel, good humor, and astonishing promptness in commenting upon rough drafts. David Quint offered, and continues to offer, innumerable and invaluable suggestions for further thought and reading. The support of the Social Sciences and Humanities Research Council of Canada made my graduate career possible, and a fellowship from the Whiting Foundation enabled me to bring it to a close. A grant from the Columbia University Council for Research in the Humanities encouraged me to continue with my spies and speculations. All those who recommended me for these awards have my sincere thanks.

I discussed this project in its initial stages with David Bromwich, Andrew Barnaby, Lawrence Danson, Margaret Anne Doody, Deborah Esch, Michael Goldman, Alvin Kernan, Ron Levao, Jayne Lewis, and Thomas Roche. Portions of the original manuscript were read by Hans Aarsleff, Ian Balfour, and Victoria Kahn. I have traded ideas with Fraser Easton and Chris GoGwilt from the start; they continue to provide endless conversation and boundless good fellowship. Dorothea von Mücke, Susan Winnett, and Karen Van Dyck have helped me place my work in perspective. Gayle Cadzow, Madeleine Brainerd, Gary Burnett, and Nick Holman have been particularly generous, in intellectual and more important ways. To Siobhán Kilfeather I owe more than I can say.

I have benefited immeasurably from Hunter Cadzow's warm friendship and rare understanding: every page that follows tacitly registers a kinship of ideas that I wish openly to acknowledge here. Jean Howard helped me settle on the final form of the book; her guidance and support have been crucial over the last few years. David Scott Kastan and Margaret Ferguson offered much encouragement along the way. David Riggs provided crucial assistance during the project's later stages. The chapters on Marlowe and Jonson profited considerably from Richard Burt's attentive reading, as I have from his friendship. The Marlowe chapter was also improved by the advice of Mario DiGangi. Peggy Knapp, Gabrielle Bernhard Jackson, and another, anonymous reader at *Assays* spurred me to recast the *New Atlantis* section of the final chapter. The entire book has been strengthened by the skill and patience of my editor, Helen Tartar, and my copy editor, Bud Bynack.

I am grateful for the interest and advice of all. Any mistakes, of course, are my doing: I have exercised as much discretion in following instructions as any ambassador or agent of the Renaissance.

J.M.A.

Contents

Sovereignty and Intelligence

*Spying and Court Culture in
the English Renaissance*

Introduction

FRANCIS Bacon's *New Atlantis* (ca. 1625) tells of an ideal commonwealth on the other side of the world, dedicated to the gathering of information. Salomon's House, an institution founded by the ancient King Salomona to discover knowledge about the natural world, periodically sends agents abroad in disguise to report on scientific discoveries and provide "knowledge of the affairs and state" of various countries.[1] Salomon's House is a state apparatus of scientific investigation that depends partly on techniques of political intelligence gathering that were familiar to Bacon from his early career as a servant of Elizabethan sovereignty. With the *New Atlantis*, to adapt Milton's verdict, knowledge about nature begins to be "sequestered out of the world" into a scientific sphere separate from politics.[2] The links between politics and knowledge are still visible in Bacon's utopia, however, and they become clearer when the *New Atlantis* is read against other fictional writings touched by espionage during the preceding half century.

The conjunction of sovereignty and intelligence in these works complicates Bacon's well-known linkage of power and knowledge, while suggesting that Michel Foucault's concept of *pouvoir-savoir* ("power/knowledge") requires reexamination as well. Bacon's clearest coupling of the two terms occurs in "Of Heresies," the penultimate essay of the *Meditationes Sacrae* (1597). Heresy, he states, consists in denying the full extent of God's power, and finally in attributing "a wider range to the knowledge of God than to his power; or rather to that part of God's power (for knowledge itself is power) whereby he knows, than to that whereby he works and acts" (7. 253). Here, knowledge is power primarily for God, although Bacon is also suggesting that their identity is axiomatic, and that there is something divine about this.

Unlike the Baconian maxim that knowledge *is* power, Foucault's theory holds that knowledge and power produce one another: "there is no power relation without the correlative constitution of a field of knowledge, nor any knowledge that does not presuppose and constitute at the same time power relations."[3] I would add that power and knowledge were not identical in early modern England; they were separate domains joined through the mutually productive relationship between sovereignty and intelligence within a culture of surveillance. This relationship was actually obscured by Bacon's attempt to idealize knowledge by completely identifying it with a power that does not have to be produced, a divine power.

A brief sketch of the origins of Bacon's maxim in medieval political thought and its sequel in Tudor-Stuart England will help to demystify it. J. G. A. Pocock begins *The Machiavellian Moment* by analyzing the reinterpretation of the Platonic union of knowledge and power in John Fortescue's treatise *De laudibus legem angliae* (ca. 1470). Plato's philosopher-king possesses a perfect intelligence and knows reality directly, not through the imperfect senses, yet "in Christian Aristotelianism the direct apprehension of intellectual reality was possible only to angels, those created intelligences who sought knowledge of the Creator's works . . . immediately and intuitively."[4] One tradition in the political theology of the Middle Ages thus ascribed a *character angelicus* to the reigning monarch. The philosopher-king became in effect an angel, not quite divine but endowed with intellectual powers unattainable by other mortals.[5] Bacon's equation of power and knowledge within the divine sphere comes from this tradition of thought, as does his suggestion that the divine is penetrable by earthly rulers like King Salomona and the sages of Salomon's House.

But this strain of thought about sovereignty was problematic and self-limiting. Ernst Kantorowicz points out in *The King's Two Bodies* that Tudor jurists drew upon Fortescue's political angelology in developing their theory that the sovereign's physical body was conjoined with a corporate one, perfect, ageless, invisible, and ubiquitous. He maintains that the theology of sovereign intelligence could not work without some such "metaphor of perfection"; as Claude Lefort explains, in Kantorowicz's view "the *ancien régime* was made up of an infinite number of small bodies . . . [that]

fitted together within a great imaginary body for which the body of the king provided the model and the guarantee of its integrity."[6] Yet Kantorowicz admits that this legal fiction ultimately ran aground on the limited lifespan of the sovereign: "Without some *character aeternitatis* he could not have his *character angelicus*, and without some inherent value of eternity he could not have 'two bodies' or have a super-body distinct from his natural mortal body."[7] Furthermore, as Pocock shows, the related idea of the realm as *corpus mysticum*, a "super-body" composed of king and people, also worked against the successful ascription of a *character angelicus* to the ruler. If the king shared a body with his subjects, then his intelligence was tainted with their corporeality; the imperfect intelligences of both monarch and subject could either supplement or undermine one another. What Lefort calls the "disincorporation" of the individual within the body politic, in which "power appears as an empty place and those who exercise it as mere mortals who occupy it only temporarily or . . . by force or cunning," was a long process that began well before the democratic revolution to which he ascribes it, within the court of the double-bodied sovereign.[8]

For although angelic intelligence remained an ideal attribute of the sovereign, on the practical level political power was covertly joined with faulty human knowledge, an alliance that produced government by both council and (particularly in Jacobean England) manipulative statecraft. The king, as Pocock observes, "must perhaps know things about . . . [his subjects'] natures which they do not know themselves," yet "the arts of his statecraft [were] arcane even to him."[9] Intelligence in the sense of the sovereign's ideal knowledge became in practice intelligence as spying, a relation governed as much by opacity as by understanding. That is why in what follows "intelligence" denotes primarily spying and statecraft, although it also carries the deceptive promise of ideal political understanding. Following Foucault, I use the term "sovereignty" to signify a system of political power organized around the court of a single, personal ruler.

Sovereignty and intelligence were united in a culture of surveillance that was chiefly defined by life at court. Early modern intelligence gathering was ultimately in the hands of court aristocrats.[10] In addition, spying and surveillance were influenced by practices and habits of thought cultivated by life at court. Cesare Ripa, whose influential emblem book *Iconologia* contains an entry on the spy, took the courtly nature of espionage during his times for granted. His spy is a man "vestito nobilmente" in a cloak covered with eyes, ears, and tongues. We are told that the figure's ornate garments "mean that it is convenient for the Spy to have rich and noble clothes in order to practice among men of quality as well as commoners, for otherwise he would be driven from dealings with them, and not be able to deliver important news to the court." Expensive clothes are also appropriate because there are many courtiers who play the spy themselves; the Roman Republic forbade members of the senatorial class from trading in information, but Ripa tells us that it is the shame of the times that more nobles than plebeians become spies. They do so "per acquistar la gratia de i loro Patroni," and the eyes and ears on the cape "signify the instruments with which spies exercise such arts to please their Lords and Patrons."[11] Courtiers employ these "stromenti," base informers as well as their own faculties, to win grace from the greater nobles who act in turn as their patrons. The painter of Elizabeth's *Rainbow* portrait took up the eyes, ears, and tongues motif for the mantle that the queen wears, probably to indicate, in a less censorious vein, the many servants who provided her with intelligence.[12]

Many institutions and offices contributed to the culture of courtly surveillance. Informing on religious nonconformism was common in the countryside during the early stages of the English Reformation, and although as G. R. Elton has shown, it was not rigidly controlled from above, it was induced by an authoritarian church and addressed to a hierarchy, ecclesiastical or, increasingly under Elizabeth's rule, secular. Privy councilors and bishops alike employed pursuivants, special messengers with the power to execute warrants, in the hunt for Catholics.[13] The office of the spy also derived from two others, the *nuntius* (messenger) of medieval diplomacy and the *explorator* (scout) of medieval warfare.[14] The first was already a court figure, and the second became one by the sixteenth century as the feudal hierarchy of military command gave way to a system of service and favor directed toward the sovereign.

Elizabethan espionage, however, was far from the centralized ideal of the modern nation-state. There was no professional secret service, no systematic apparatus of surveillance at home or abroad. The field of intelligence was instead a particularly obscure sector of the greater field of patronage. The queen solicited information from her mightiest servants, rewarding them with prestige and authority. Rival officeholders like Burghley and Walsingham competed for whatever scraps of intelligence their own clients—spies in their pay, pursuivants, and occasional informers—discovered or invented. Information about the intentions of foreign princes often derived from domestic espionage, and spies abroad frequently reported on treasonous activities in England. Elizabeth had to decide upon the relative value of what she heard while weighing her servants' competing interests against one another.

Foucault's theory of the reciprocal relation between power and knowledge is more helpful than Bacon's equation of the two, but in his hands it fails to account for the intricacies of the court world of early modern sovereignty. For Foucault, "sovereignty" was primarily a legal structure based upon right and oppression. The medieval monarchy established a hegemony over feudal powers that had been in violent conflict with one another: "It made itself acceptable by allocating itself a judicial and negative function, albeit one whose limits it naturally began at once to overstep. Sovereign, law and prohibition formed a system of representation of power which was extended during the subsequent era by the theories of right: political theory has never ceased to be obsessed with the person of the sovereign."[15] Yet according to Foucault, sovereign hegemony did not continue to constitute the full range of political relations after the seventeenth century, if it ever had at all. This period saw the creation of "a new mechanism of power possessed of highly specific procedural techniques, completely novel instruments, quite different apparatuses, and which is also . . . absolutely incompatible with the relations of sovereignty."[16] This new form of power was the disciplinary power of surveillance.

What I call "intelligence" acknowledges disciplinary power as Foucault describes it, but it also involves a more complicated relationship between knowledge and power than Foucault allows or than Bacon admits in the theological discussion where he most firmly identified them. More than just an instrument of discipline within the juridical model of power, "intelligence" was an integral component in a broader configuration of knowledge and power in early modern Europe. In Foucault's *Discipline and Punish*, the main contrast between the power of the pre-Enlightenment sovereign and disciplinary power is phrased in visual terms: the power of sovereignty rests in the display of the sovereign's person, in making itself and the tortured bodies of its enemies visible to its subjects; by contrast, the power of the modern state rests in the discipline imposed by surveillance, which renders the majority of its subjects visible while keeping its own operations out of sight.[17] The model for the modern political field is Jeremy Bentham's proposal for the "Panopticon," a penitentiary whose inhabitants, inmate and guard alike, can be viewed from the center by their superiors at all times. The watcher at the center, however, no longer exists; instead, people are held in place by their sense of being watched, their mutual subjection in a structure of surveillance.[18] Foucault argues that the operations of surveillance in the modern state have been obscured by the survival into modernity of a centralized "theory of sovereignty," which "allowed a system of right to be superimposed upon the mechanisms of discipline in such a way as to conceal its actual procedures."[19] Consequently, Foucault claims, no theory based on the notion of sovereignty will explain the actual workings of surveillance.

But sovereignty and surveillance are more continuous than Foucault's dichotomous periodization suggests. If sovereignty is the mystifying survival of a medieval concept in the era of the Enlightenment, surveillance is equally a refinement of institutions and practices that enabled the creation of the modern state. The techniques of surveillance were firmly rooted in the court politics of the pre-Enlightenment state ruled by a personal sovereign. The culture of display that Foucault associates with the concept of sovereignty was supplemented by a corresponding culture of observation and surveillance in which sovereignty and intelligence were bound pragmatically together.

Foucault was aware that he had not solved the problem of whether sovereignty fully accounted for political life before the development of the modern state. Against the notion that power operates on the model of sovereign repression or centralized domination, he contemplated "a second hypothesis" that shows he may have glimpsed the culture of surveillance that lay behind the display of the Renaissance court. This hypothesis holds "that power is war, a war continued by other means. This reversal of Clause-witz's assertion that war is politics continued by other means . . . implies that the relations of power that function in a society such as ours essentially rest upon a definite relation of forces that is es-tablished . . . in war and by war."[20] According to this hypothesis, war, with the strategic systems and military organization that ac-company its brute force, constituted something like an earlier, more openly violent form of disciplinary power, contemporary with sovereignty but completely different from it.[21] War and sov-ereignty are brought together in the first volume of the *History of Sexuality*, however, where the king's power of life and death over his subjects is described in terms of his right to send them into bat-tle.[22] Clearly, sovereignty and war accompanied each other as mechanisms of power during the Renaissance; but between them we can already discern a third category, surveillance, which in the forms of reconnaissance in the field and diplomacy at court me-diated between these two systems of physical force.[23]

Foucault nevertheless rigidly separated sovereignty and surveil-lance, locating them in successive historical periods, and he never really grasped the practical conjunction of power as sovereignty with knowledge as intelligence. The work of Norbert Elias brings us closer to the concrete historical relationship between sover-eignty and surveillance, in part through his understanding of the connection between war and sovereignty among aristocrats in early modern society.[24] In a formulation similar to Foucault's re-versal of Clausewitz's aphorism, Elias asserts that "War . . . is not the opposite of peace . . . [for] wars between smaller units have been, in the course of history up to now, inevitable stages and in-struments in the pacification of larger ones."[25] In *Power and Civil-ity*, the second part of his study *The Civilizing Process*, Elias holds that the medieval monarch secured hegemony over warring ele-ments within the realm principally through monitoring their con-flicting interests and balancing them against one another.[26] The re-sulting monopoly of force not only allowed the king to conduct wars with other monarchs, it also influenced the behavior of pow-erful subjects within his own territory. Violence, to borrow Elias's metaphor, was stored behind the scenes of their dealings with the sovereign and each other, and it exerted a constant pressure on aris-tocrats to reflect upon their conduct and its consequences.[27] A degree of self-surveillance under the sovereign's watchful eye was introduced among the warrior nobility; it increased as nobles, more and more dependent on the sovereign for support and prestige, made their way to court.

Violence among aristocrats, and between aristocrats and the king, was sublimated in the courtly world: "If the sword no longer plays so great a role as the means of decision, it is replaced by intrigue, conflicts in which careers and social success are contested with words."[28] Diplomacy was required above all at the court of one's own prince, who created and encouraged differences and jealousies among his servants, differences that he observed, and that caused them to watch each other in turn. The king ruled his court by dividing and by monitoring his divisions, preventing one party from becoming significantly more powerful than another, and all parties from uniting against the throne. Elias realized that even within sovereignty, the figuration that Foucault opposes to surveillance, there existed versions of what Foucault calls "those disciplines that . . . are a modality of power for which individual difference is relevant."[29] The sovereign's watchfulness over the court reached its height during the rule of Louis XIV of France, who posted liveried spies in the corridors of Versailles to follow people and eavesdrop on their conversations.[30] Louis presided over an absolutist state, but less obvious forms of royal intelligence gathering existed in the English courts of Elizabeth and James I as well.

Continually under observation, courtiers attempted to deflect the gaze of their competitors and the monarch through splendid clothes and grand households. The king himself was not exempt from this regime. He was as dependent upon his courtiers for recognition and support as they were upon him, and was compelled to apply "constant vigilance" to his own words and actions as well as those of others.[31] The courtier's "compulsion to display," as Elias comments elsewhere, was the pattern for the king's own need "not only to exert his power but to demonstrate it constantly through symbolic actions, to see it ceaselessly reflected in triumphs over others."[32] Display occupies a similar place in Foucault's tableau of early modern sovereignty, but there it excludes the operation of surveillance. For Elias, however, display and observation are dependent upon one another; in conflating his insights with Foucault's, then, I am suggesting that some elements of surveillance and its characteristic forms of power developed within sovereignty, which concealed the practices of courtly observation just as the idea of the state was later to conceal surveillance itself.

Moreover, Elias links the new awareness of self and other among the nobility to an increasing "psychologization" of aristocratic culture, as courtiers began to attribute psychological depth to themselves and their rivals.[33] He calls for "a science that does not yet exist, historical psychology" to study this development, implicitly criticizing the psychoanalysis of his time for assuming a natural and unchanging human psyche detached from social conditions: "The libidinal energies which one encounters in any living human being are always already socially processed. . . . [T]he peculiarity of man discovered by Freud in men of our own time and conceptualized by him as a strict division between unconscious and conscious mental functions, far from being part of man's unchanged nature is a result of a long civilizing process."[34] Rivalry, with its practices of mutual observation, was the principal way in which social libido or desire was processed, perhaps even created, in court society.[35]

Elias claims that competitive practices of mutual observation generated a specific kind of individual consciousness during the Renaissance. He does not support this notion with a full-fledged "historical psychology" of his own, but the insights of other writers who touch on observation and self-formation suggest that he is right. In explaining his concept of "the gaze," Jacques Lacan pauses to consider Hans Holbein the younger's well-known painting *The Ambassadors*. This double portrait, painted in London in 1533, portrays the current French ambassador to England and his colleague, standing on either side of a table upon which astronomical, geometrical, and musical instruments and books are arranged. This display of learning is undercut by a diagonal shape at the feet of the ambassadors that forms an anamorphic image of a human skull, an ironic *momento mori* visible only at an oblique angle to the right of the picture. According to Lacan, "all this shows that at the very heart of the period in which the subject emerged and geometrical optics was an object of research, Holbein makes visible for us here something that is simply the subject as annihilated."[36] He cites Alberti, Dürer, and Descartes on the relationship between Renaissance perspective and the inauguration of the individual, "the

Cartesian subject, which is itself a sort of geometral point, a point of perspective."[37]

Yet at the moment of its constitution, subjectivity is also threatened with annihilation by the gaze—not its own gaze, but a gaze that is outside of it.[38] The laws of perspective made possible those of anamorphic distortion, which suggests that the point of view of another observer is necessary to reveal how the subject is really placed within the "scopic field" of the world it ostensibly views. In Lacan's allegory of Holbein's painting, insofar as this point is attainable, "it reflects our own nothingness, in the figure of the death's head."[39] Put another, admittedly non-Lacanian, way, one is fascinated by the anamorphic shape in the foreground of *The Ambassadors* because it signifies that only a second observer, someone or something who can gaze upon both the picture and its viewer, is in a position to understand the portrait's real, bleakly ironic relation to the viewer. It is telling that Holbein should have employed such a perspectival trick in a portrait of two diplomats, courtiers of a foreign prince whose job it was to watch the English king's servants.[40] Lacan does not remark upon this, but he does note that anamorphic distortion "may lend itself . . . to all the paranoiac ambiguities."[41]

Paranoia, in fact, is the psychoanalytic category that comes most readily to mind when we read the descriptions of early modern subjectivity in the work of Elias and Foucault, as well as Lacan. The position of the courtly observer is aptly summed up in a phrase that Lacan uses to invoke the gaze: "I see only from one point, but in my existence I am looked at from all sides."[42] In his discussions of paranoia and the "mirror stage" of early childhood, Lacan had already argued that the structure of paranoia is identical with the structure of knowledge in general, with "that which constitutes the ego and its objects with attributes of permanence, identity, and substantiality."[43] His later analysis of Holbein's *Ambassadors* suggests that the constitution of the subject in paranoia was first realized in the Renaissance.

History and social psychology were not Lacan's principal concerns. Max Horkheimer and Theodor Adorno, however, writing under the auspices of the Frankfurt Institute of Social Research, place the origins of modernity unequivocally within paranoia. The Frankfurt School's critique of the Enlightenment reflects back upon the Renaissance, and returns us from psychoanalysis to Foucault's account of the relationship between knowledge and political power.

Horkheimer and Adorno explore the bond between modernity and paranoia in the concluding section of their central work, *Dialectic of Enlightenment*. Granting the distinction between the subject and the object of perception in Enlightenment philosophy, they claim that all cognition depends upon a delusory projection of the subject's judgments upon the object; the ego itself, as in Lacan's nearly contemporary theory of the "mirror stage," is formed in such a manner.[44] Although they would not agree with Lacan's equation of paranoid knowledge with knowledge in general, Horkheimer and Adorno admit that "the weakness of the paranoiac individual is that of thought itself. . . . Paranoia is the dark side of cognition."[45] The self-critical element in Enlightenment culture counteracted the tendency toward false projection in the thought it fostered, but the reduction of thought to instrumental or practical reason under capitalism eventually commodified it. When knowledge becomes merely the acquisition of isolated facts, the modern subject is induced to accept the way authority orders such information into a coherent but incomplete and paranoid picture of the world. False projection has become socialized as "the normal member of society dispels his own paranoia by participating in the collective form."[46] The dialectic of enlightenment, according to which the rational critique of delusion becomes delusory itself, is fulfilled.[47]

The terms of this dialectical critique of enlightenment can be traced back to the Enlightenment itself. Of the paranoid inhabitants of modernity Horkheimer and Adorno remark: "The proverbial gaze into their eyes does not preserve their individuality. It merely fixes others and commands unilateral loyalties by pointing the way to the windowless monadic confines of their own personality."[48] In the fragment on punishment at the end of *Dialectic of Enlightenment* the "windowless" and discrete monads of the seventeenth-century philosopher Gottfried Leibniz are similarly evoked to describe "the rows of cells in a modern prison."[49] Leibniz's division of the world into atoms of consciousness becomes a paradigm for modernity, like Bentham's Panopticon.[50] In *Dialectic of Enlightenment* and *Discipline and Punish*, the subjection of modern life is traced back to the totalizing theories, the monadologies and panoptic principles, of an earlier Age of Reason.

Foucault's "surveillance" is a not too distant cousin of the Frankfurt School's Enlightenment; in German, *aufklärung* also denotes military reconnaissance. Foucault locates surveillance in the late seventeenth and eighteenth centuries, the era of Enlightenment, and Horkheimer and Adorno likewise assign the inception of modern reason, in both its critical and merely quantitative forms, to this period. But in the figure of the courtier the Renaissance had already bequeathed a model of rationality to later times, for the cultured, restrained, and calculating aristocrat was the paradigm of the "man of reason" for the emerging bourgeoisie. Courtly rationality, according to Elias, "played a no less important part, and at first an even more important one, than the urban-commercial rationality and foresight instilled by functions in the trade network, in the development of what we call the 'Enlightenment.' "[51] Reason was also reason of state, just as intelligence was coeval with political intelligence; both were part of the mutual observation and social competition of Renaissance court society.

The rationality that initially governed intrigue and diplomacy, however, was different from the commercial rationality that eventually overtook it. It was not lucid, efficient, methodical, or quantitative. It was opaque, prudent, improvisatory, and obsessed with degree rather than number. It developed, in fact, from symbolic interaction among people of various degrees; it did not seek to reduce exchange to equivalence. It was realized in contingent social relationships, not in philosophical frameworks or technological projects. Furthermore, the sovereign at the imaginary summit of society was not an absolute ruler, still less the puppet of some impersonal principle of power or domination. Instead, the monarch was partly dependent on other people in powerful positions, negotiating with and between them within the conventions of courtly rationality, making strategic but fallible use of its unwritten rules to gather as much information as possible. The modern state, insofar as it has inherited the sovereign's position, remains limited by this strategic relationship between knowledge and power. Horkheimer and Adorno's pessimism about modernity thus concedes too much to the founding myths of the Enlightenment they proposed to criticize and redeem. By shifting the origins of modern rationality and political intelligence to the sixteenth century, one circumvents the totalizing programs of a period that consolidated and commodified the fluid political culture of the Renaissance.

Like Horkheimer, Adorno, and other members of the Frankfurt School, Norbert Elias based his sociology upon an implicit narrative about the development of European rationality. Like them, he was influenced by Max Weber and spent a significant part of his early career teaching in Frankfurt before the Second World War. The Frankfurt School analyzed the rise of the bourgeoisie and its economic rationality. Elias, however, followed a different route, arguing that the origins of modernity lie in the aristocratic culture of the past as well. When read along with the writings of the Frankfurt School, Elias's work suggests ways in which Foucault's insights about the operation of power can be restored to a historical narrative more satisfying than the one Foucault provides for them.

The series of discussions that follow concern a number of Renaissance texts that were affected by surveillance and the culture it fostered. I end up where Horkheimer and Adorno begin the *Dialectic of Enlightenment*, with Francis Bacon and the image of the modern abstract state. My readings draw on Elias to provide the pre-history of the movements that the Frankfurt School and Foucault describe in different ways. Elias placed the origins of psychology in the court society of France, which other European aristocrats copied slavishly from the sixteenth century on.[52] In opening my book with a chapter on Montaigne's *Essais*, I am beginning with the psychological and phenomenological situation of the courtier within the French model of sovereignty. Montaigne, of course, repeatedly insists that he has retired from public life and royal service, yet his *Essais* embody the anxieties of the courtier who, like Lacan's subject, is looked at from all sides. The courtier's anxieties lead to his withdrawal into a private search for knowledge about the self, but Montaigne's description of this phenomenological quest as a form of self-spying reminds us that it remains informed by its political setting. Knowledge about the elusive self is implicated in sovereign power even when that power is conceived as a problematic absence at the center of society.

Chapter 2 turns to England, where I attempt to historicize the aristocratic psychology implicit in Montaigne's version of selfhood in terms of the courtly milieu in which Philip Sidney and his father-in-law, the spymaster Francis Walsingham, played out their differing careers. Elizabeth's court was an intimate, even domestic institution, in which the policing of sexuality—by the queen, and by rival courtiers watching their unmarried monarch as well as each other—was the dominant mode in which courtly observation evolved into a recognizably political intelligence by means of the patronage system. Sidney's *Arcadia*, particularly in its revised form, traces the development from the psychology of the courtier to the attitude of the state servant. The third chapter explores the place of Sidney's pastoral romance in this highly fraught environment.

The next chapter views the same world "from below," as it is represented upon the public stage in the work of Christopher Marlowe, who was both playwright and servant of the Elizabethan state. Marlowe's self-constructions in *Dido*, *Edward II*, and *The Massacre at Paris* play off his contemporary reputation as a lover of boys and his probable involvement in espionage. The accusations leveled against Marlowe by Kyd and the spy Richard Baines echo his own self-construction in a distorted, one might say anamorphic manner, suggesting that he was part of an urban subculture of intellectuals and travelers in which what we now call male homosexuality played a submerged and misrecognized role. Love between men and spying were also part of the patronage system, a "surculture" presided over by aristocrats that gave Marlowe some access to the court world and state service. In *Edward II* Marlowe uses Edward's relationship with his favorites to legitimate male love and, to some extent, espionage itself by authorizing both practices through the person of the sovereign.

Chapter 4 shows how two conflicting representations of the state in Ben Jonson's theater arose from the weakened remnants of the courtly ideal. Treating *Poetaster* as a prelude to the later Roman dramas, I go on to consider Jonson's negative depiction of an urban court under a regime of surveillance in *Sejanus his Fall*. Jonson's remote and omniscient Tiberius does not stand for James I; instead, his intangible relationship to power suggests that he is a transitional personification of the abstract sovereignty of the state. The logic of Jonson's representation of state power by means of the Roman example, as well as his own involvement in espionage, caused him to change his condemnation of surveillance. In *Catiline his Conspiracy* he attempts to rehabilitate espionage by associating the abstract state with the tradition of divine omniscience to which I referred at the beginning of this Introduction. The Jonson chapter looks back to the opening chapter on Montaigne, who theorized the dispersed early modern sovereignty that lay behind the centralized image of a court such as Elizabeth's, and that became apparent in the wake of her reign. By examining the effects of the culture of surveillance under fragmented and increasingly abstract forms of sovereign power, the chapters on Montaigne and Jonson frame and contextualize the formidable association of sovereignty and intelligence under Elizabeth. They help to explain how Bacon could ultimately formulate the possibility of the abstract, surveilling state from his experience within her government and court.

My fifth chapter begins by placing Bacon's *Essays*, counterparts in some ways to Montaigne's, in the context of Elizabethan court society and its psychology, and goes on to chart the consequences of his participation in the world of surveillance for Bacon's later representations of sovereignty and the state in his *History of the Reign of King Henry VII* and the *New Atlantis*. This concluding chapter recapitulates the narrative that structures the previous four, and takes the argument beyond the Renaissance to the Enlightenment and modernity. Bacon's experience as an intelligence-gatherer under Elizabeth's diffuse patronage system was far removed from his later ideal of clarity and centralization in the relation of knowledge to power, yet his *History* of Henry VII may have been intended as the blueprint for a centralized Stuart sovereignty based upon defensive political intelligence conceived on the Elizabethan model. With the *New Atlantis* we have a wholly idealized program for a society built on information gathering and secrecy; knowledge clearly supports social control in Bacon's utopia, and its identification with science and ostensible separation from politics have already begun.

I have set out in this book to explore the relationship between spying and court society by examining the representation of espionage in a selection of Renaissance texts. My examples are drawn for the most part from the Elizabethan period and its aftermath, for this was the age that saw the growth of both a complex court culture and the first large-scale intelligence networks in England. It was a violent era, but violent oppression was only the most visible expression of sovereignty, which had established itself as the defining mode of political power in part by monopolizing violence and then reorganizing relations of force. Other strategies of control, not incompatible with it, existed alongside sovereign violence. The monarchy, for all its judicial iconography of the sovereign body, was hardly a centralized structure. It maintained a constant and productive relationship with intelligence techniques that were deployed through patronage systems and aristocratic codes of mutual scrutiny, as well as through the vigilance of local religious authorities and the self-definition of a rising bourgeoisie. Diplomatic maneuvering, the creation and investigation of conspiracies, royal employment of unscrupulous servants—a number of obscure practices underlay the idealized intelligence of the ruler. Although more was involved in what I am calling "intelligence" than espionage, spying remains for me its emblematic activity—a dark, secretive activity, yet destined, it would seem, to illuminate the political field. But does it not destroy knowledge as rapidly as it creates it? Is spying then a rudimentary or "primitive" form of the open techniques of surveillance that Foucault has described? Perhaps, but if so, it has remained within disciplinary power, a vestigial but hardly useless organ. We have yet to escape from its faulty but effective political epistemology.

CHAPTER I

Ambassador at Delphi

The Servant of the Prince in Montaigne's 'Essais'

THE history of political power in early modern Europe is also the history of sovereignty and subjection. Michel Foucault divides that history into a period of display, in which power was enforced through its manifestation in public festivals and public executions, and a later period of surveillance, in which power was concealed from the sovereign's subjects, who were themselves rendered visible through a variety of apparatuses ranging from the education system to the military review.[1] Yet people at court were already under the sovereign's eye. The king engaged in a constant calculation of his courtiers' interests and secrets, a strategy that he likewise applied to other classes within the nation, and to other nations. "For him, therefore," Norbert Elias maintains, "the observation and supervision of people is indispensable in defending his rule," which depended on "encouraging and even creating breaches and tensions between people in both large and small matters."[2] Furthermore, the prince's servants watched each other, weighing the words and gestures of their rivals in a "courtly art of human observation."[3] As Maurice Merleau-Ponty remarks, at court "everyone puts in the place of his thoughts their reflection in the eyes and idle chatter of others."[4] The practice of mutual observation in the court world was the dark, obverse side of the culture of display. Observation often merged with organized political espionage, and both practices were forerunners of later mechanisms of surveillance. Thus, the origins of a culture of surveillance are earlier than the mid-seventeenth century, the earliest point at which Foucault places the transition from the first to the second mode of power, and the relationship between display and surveillance in the history of European political power is more complicated than Foucault allowed.

One way to recover the role played by surveillance in what has been regarded as simply an age of display is to examine the complex relations between sovereignty and the emergence of the subject in the *Essais* of Michel de Montaigne. Montaigne's *Essais* suggest the possibility of a phenomenology of perception specific to sixteenth-century court society. Indeed, Merleau-Ponty's depiction of the pre-Enlightenment court as a hall of mirrors was inspired by Montaigne. Elias relates courtly observation to the form of self-observation that it produced, and to an idiosyncratic writing practice, which comprehended the memoir, the aphorism, and the historical example.[5] Observation, whether of self or others, and its complementary writing practices constitute Montaigne's project. The *Essais* also describe the current state of the French polity and suggest a program for its improvement and stabilization under a single sovereign, advised by the faithful courtier or wise counselor.[6] In them the king is still a figure on display who cannot see into the breasts of his subjects, but the *Essais* also reveal a form of surveillance in the political sphere that served as a metaphor for self-fashioning introspection. The *Essais* are the product of a period in which individuality had not yet fully developed; they inscribe within the emerging concept of the self a primitive machinery of political surveillance that complicated the flow of information it solicited. The position of the subject, its self-knowledge, and its knowledge of others were destabilized at the very moment of their emergence.

The *Essais* intimate a world of political intelligence intersected with passageways linking the self, knowledge, and sovereign power, some of them unexpected. When Montaigne discusses the mind's assimilation and evaluation of knowledge, for example, he often uses metaphors drawn from the sampling and tasting of food. The very title of the *Essais* participates in this epistemology of taste, as Victoria Kahn demonstrates by drawing attention to a few sentences from "De l'experience": "I have lived long enough to give an account of the practice that has guided me so far. For anyone who wants to try it I have tasted it like his cupbearer [Pour qui en voudra gouster, j'en ay faict l'essay, son eschançon]."[7] Kahn notes "the implicit equation of tasting and writing, for the juxtaposition of *gouster* and *essai* activates one of the original meanings of the word *essai*. The word comes from the Latin *exagium* meaning 'weighing, weight, or balance.' . . . But the second definition which *Littré* gives is that of tasting, in particular the tasting of the king's food or wine."[8] The job of *eschançon* or royal taster was a hazardous one. It serves as the paradigm for all offices, including those of spy and ambassador, that involve the provision of an often dangerous knowledge to a sovereign who is always kept at one remove from experience. Taste in Montaigne is not simply a metaphor. It is one of the marks left on his text by the practices associated with being a servant of kings.

The appearance of the essayist as *eschançon* in "De l'experience" is directly connected with the passage immediately preceding it, in which the essayist casts himself as the ideal advisor of the king. His experience authorizes him to judge others as well as to study himself, and Montaigne claims that if given a chance he would use it to speak boldly to his sovereign and "watch over [contrerrolé] his conduct" (3. 13, 825, Villey 1077). But the attempt to *contreroller* the king, which means to guide or even manipulate him as well as watch over him, can be dangerous. Indeed, "most of the duties of true friendship toward a sovereign are hard and dangerous to attempt [en un rude et perilleus essay]; so that there is need, not only of much affection and frankness, but of much courage as well" (3. 13, 826, Villey 1078; translation modified). There is a parallel here between the counselor of the king, who tests royal conduct and policy against his own experience of affairs, and the taster in the following paragraphs, who has already tested certain techniques of living "pour qui en voudra gouster."

This similarity explains what would otherwise be too sudden a shift (even for Montaigne) from the ideal advisor passage to a discussion of bodily health in the next paragraph, which begins: "In fine, all this fricassee that I am scribbling here is nothing but a record of the essays [essais] of my life" (3. 13, 826, Villey 1079). The *Essais* themselves are a record of the experiences that would enable (and, in fact, did enable) Montaigne to become a counselor of kings. We are prepared for the introduction of the *eschançon* later on in the same (b)-text passage by the alimentary metaphor of the *fricassée*;[9] the reiteration of the word "essais" throughout these pages links writing not only with tasting the king's food for poison but also with the "rude et perilleus essay" of befriending and advising him.

The parallel between the king's servant as counselor and as taster in "De l'experience" is thrown into relief by a series of events that begins with a visit recorded in Montaigne's copy of the *Ephemeris historica* of Michael Beuther, a note dated December 19, 1584: "The king of Navarre came to see me at Montaigne, where he had never been, and was here for two days, served by my men without any of his officers. He would have neither tasting nor covered dishes [ny essais ny couvert], and slept in my bed."[10] Henri of Navarre, soon to become Henri IV of France, showed his faith in Montaigne by refusing to have his food essayed, but he also appears to have denied his host the opportunity to counsel him extensively at this point in their association. Nevertheless, Montaigne continued in the months that followed to bring Henri and the ostensibly loyalist comte de Matignon together, and within six months he had succeeded.

His mediation paved the way for the defeat of the French king, Henri III, by Navarre at Coutras. It has been suggested that the battle may have been lost by the French forces in part because Matignon arrived too late with reinforcements, in collusion with Navarre and on Montaigne's advice. Be this as it may, after Coutras, Navarre visited Montaigne once more, on October 23, 1587, and this time important discussions must have taken place. A mysterious mission from Henri of Navarre to Henri III, sponsored by Matignon, was undertaken by Montaigne a few months later. Sir Edward Stafford, the English ambassador at Paris, wrote to Sir Francis Walsingham about the sudden appearance on the scene of "one Montigny, a very wise gentleman of the king of Navarre. . . . I never heard of the man afore in my life."[11] He was more frank to his real patron, Walsingham's rival Lord Burghley: "I [have] written to Mr. Secretary in a letter in cipher—I cannot tell whether he will show it—of the coming of one Montaigne here from the King of Navarre . . . and how all the King of Navarre's servants here are jealous of his coming, being neither addressed to them nor knowing any tittle of the cause." The English feared that a concordat between the two Henris would finally exclude Queen Elizabeth, who "had in some kind still an oar in their boat," from French affairs.[12]

These dispatches, which show Walsingham and Burghley operating at cross-purposes and Stafford at a loss to help either of them, place Montaigne, the would-be essayist and royal counselor, in the dark and uncertain terrain of diplomatic intelligence. In France there was already a tradition of partially organized espionage dating from the time of Louis XI and his minister Philippe de Commynes in the middle of the fifteenth century.[13] Montaigne was an obscure figure in 1588, though soon to become perhaps the best-known person in Europe through the self-exposure of the *Essais*. His mysterious dealings nevertheless suggest that Montaigne was an experienced and trusted negotiator. Stafford suspected that he was really Henri III's agent: "the man is a Catholic, a very sufficient man; was once Mayor of Bordeaux, and one that would not take charge to bring anything to the King [of France] that should not please him." After Navarre's accession to the throne of France in 1589, however, Montaigne claimed in a letter to him that he had always acted in his interests and secretly considered him his king. He reminded Henri IV of his role in Matignon's services to him, and proceeded to give the new French monarch some advice about the conduct of his soldiers, the bluntness of which recalls the program for wise counseling in the recently written "De l'experience."[14] Stafford's guess at Montaigne's real allegiance in 1588 may simply have been wrong, but perhaps we should not underestimate the flexibility of this "very sufficient man" in such matters.

Montaigne's flexibility mirrored that of his royal patron. In a paragraph he added at the beginning of the ideal counselor passage in "De l'experience," Montaigne says that the erratic Macedonian king Perseus is like all people, in his "flighty and erratic character," but that he resembles one in particular, "another of his stature," who clearly represents Henri IV (3. 13, 825). The initial assertion that everyone is like the Protean monarch, however, is just as suggestive as the coded reference to Henri. Throughout the *Essais*, the monarch is implicitly defined as both the possessor of power and an unstable figure who should take advice and receive guidance. The counselor and the taster are both servants of the sovereign, and they are both similar to the essayist—in French, all three *essayent* in one sense or another. The taster and the counselor alike are to the king as the essayist is to the reader. The reader who picks up a volume of Montaigne voluntarily assumes the powerful but unstable position of the king, becoming a sovereign, capable of rejecting the knowledge it proffers, while remaining a psychological subject in need of its guidance. And Montaigne is capable of identifying himself as "I who am king of the matter I treat, and who owe an accounting for it to no one" (3. 8, 720). The metaphorics of sovereignty in this period mark out a zone in which persons and bodies multiply almost indefinitely.

It is a commonplace that the development of a concept of selfhood plays a large role in the writings of Montaigne.[15] What has received less attention is his repeated association of the emerging self or *moi* of the *Essais* with the figure, or rather with the multiplying and contagious figurations of the sovereign and his servant. The locus classicus for this connection in the *Essais* is found in "De la praesumption," where Montaigne recalls seeing a self-portrait painted by René, King of Sicily, and asks why everyone should not be permitted to portray themselves, with pen and paper if not on canvas (2. 17, 496). The figure of the monarch was the most obvious example of a single, even isolated, person whose role in society was defined and circumscribed by custom and law. As such, it readily served as the model for the growing sense of identity that emerged from the conflict between one's socially determined roles and one's awareness of being different from those roles, and from other people.[16] "Every degree of fortune," Montaigne remarks, "has in it some semblance of the princely" (1. 42, 194).

Yet the monarch's person or body was not "in-dividual" or undivided in law or iconography. Timothy Reiss has recently attempted to apply Kantorowicz's discussion of "the king's two bodies" to Montaigne's political thought.[17] According to Kantorowicz, by the sixteenth century, France had developed a political theology of the *corpus mysticum*, or mystical body of the realm, that paralleled the peculiarly English idea that the king possessed a second physical being, corporate and immortal, in addition to his individual body.[18] The body of the king was double, and in practice the power it embodied could fragment into even more persons. In Caesar's time, France was divided among *Roytelets* ("kinglets"), and Montaigne complained that princely power was still distributed among provincial lords who kept to their miniature royal courts and heard of the King but once a year, as if he ruled in Persia rather than Paris (1. 42, 194–95, Villey 265).

Reiss chooses the following (c)-text addition to an early essay as his prime example of the "king's two bodies" idea in Montaigne: "We owe subjection and obedience equally to all kings, for that concerns their office; but we do not owe esteem, any more than affection, except to their virtue. Let us make this concession to the political order: to suffer them patiently if they are unworthy, to conceal their vices, to abet them by commending their indifferent actions if their authority needs our support" (1. 3, 9).[19] The focus of attention here, however, is not the king, but the king's servant, who obstructs knowledge of the king's vices while he is alive, and (as the passage goes on to assert) must publish this knowledge after the monarch's death. The king is the object of knowledge as much as its master, and it is the subject who observes him, the courtier or servant of the crown, who determines the degree of his control over it. The ideal counselor, as we have seen, can in fact "contre-rolle" or monitor royal behavior, and it is in this sense that the Montaigne of the *Essais* is like a royal advisor and his reader like a king in council. Thus, while the monarch remains the model for a developing individuality in Montaigne, it is the king's servant—the counselor, ambassador, spy, or (on one occasion) taster—who assumes the role of active self-definition in the narratives and metaphors of the *Essais*.

If the sovereign provided Montaigne and his age with the multiple and unstable paradigm of the self, the observer or spy provided the figure of self-knowledge. Self-knowledge in Montaigne is frequently represented through metaphors drawn from the courtly culture of espionage. In the (a)-text of "De la praesumption," written in the late 1570's, for example, Montaigne writes: "The world always looks straight ahead; as for me, I turn my gaze inward. . . . I continually observe myself, I inspect myself, I taste myself [je me contrerolle, je me gouste]" (2. 17, 499, Villey 657; translation modified). *Gouster* and *contreroller*, two verbs that will reappear in later discussions of public affairs (*contreroller* also meant the visual inspection of account books) are here clustered together with *regarder* and *considerer* in the reflexive confines of self-examination. In French, the act of observing something often implies having power over it, as the double meaning of both *surveiller* and *controller* (Montaigne's *contreroller*) indicates. The *moi* of the *Essais* emerges as an object of knowledge, something to be tasted, watched over, and thus controlled, if only by itself.

Sovereign and self are both objects of a knowledge frequently described in terms of vision and observation, and both are involved in the power relations this knowledge creates. In an (a)-text passage from the "Apologie de Raimond Sebond," Montaigne describes himself as "I who spy on myself more closely, who have my eyes unceasingly intent on myself, as one who has not much business elsewhere [Moy qui m'espie de plus prez, qui ay les yeux incessamment tendus sur moy, comme celuy qui n'ay pas fort à-faire ailleurs]" (2. 12, 425, Villey 565). It is this meticulous spying upon himself, Montaigne implies, that allows him to claim he knows how unknowable and unstable his sovereign self really is.[20]

Such self-knowledge manqué frees him from any external authority—in the midst of this passage he inserts a quotation from Horace's *Odes* to celebrate his indifference to whatever remote king may rule the Arctic wastes.[21] Montaigne is at liberty to do as he pleases. In his remote skepsis he resembles those provincial lords who hear the monarch's name but once a year, and whom "le pois de la souveraineté" touches scarcely twice in a lifetime (1. 42, Villey 266). Yet it is significant that at his moment of greatest autonomy and instability Montaigne can resist neither a quotation from Horace nor a reference to a king, two external authorities from which he was not, in fact, completely free.[22] Montaigne's declaration of independent self-study is undermined from the outset by the political metaphor used to describe it.

Philippe de Commynes, in some ways Montaigne's major precursor as royal servant and memoir writer, had connected the instability of a decadent world and its inhabitants with the necessary use of spies a century earlier.[23] It is clear that Montaigne borrowed the language of spying from a milieu in which selves, however unknowable, are nevertheless subject to rudimentary mechanisms of surveillance and control. This is seen most clearly in "De l'utile et de l'honeste," where the instability of the self is transformed into a naturalness in behavior at court that devious statecraft cannot reproduce. Montaigne seeks to prove the uncontrollable frankness of his native self by inviting the surveillance of rival courtiers: "If anyone follows and spies upon me closely [espié de pres], I will concede him the victory if he does not confess that there is no rule in their school that could reproduce this natural movement" (3. 1, 603, Villey 795; translation modified). Early in the *Essais*, however, surveillance has already been internalized by the writing subject, who prepares himself for death, living as he does "at the very hub of all the turmoil of the civil wars of France," by minutely analyzing his experience of a nearly fatal accident: "This account of so trivial an event would be rather pointless, were it not for the instruction that I have derived from it for myself. . . . Now as Pliny says, each man is a good education to himself, provided he has the capacity to spy on himself from close up" (2. 6, 272). This "suffisance de s'espier de près" (Villey 377) is the distinguishing quality of the essayist as well as the courtier.[24]

The glimpses we catch of the world of Renaissance intelligence that Montaigne internalizes in the *Essais* further illustrate the problematic nature of a self fashioned in terms of self-spying in a culture of courtly surveillance. The original beginning of the essay "Des postes" presents us with King Cyrus receiving information from all parts of Persia by means of a system of couriers who travel by stages (2. 22, 515). This image of Cyrus at the center of an imperial communications network also appears in "Des coches" (3. 6, 690).[25] The essay that precedes "Des postes," "Contre la faineantise," likewise opens with Vespasian ruling the empire from his deathbed through dispatches (2. 21, 512). These classical examples represent an idealized system of government by information that the sixteenth century was far from realizing in practice. But riding post was a familiar component of administration, and one important enough in Montaigne's eyes to deserve a separate essay. He had himself experienced it at first hand, as he tells us in the new opening he added to "Des postes" after 1588: "I have been not of the weakest in this exercise, which is suited to men of my build, solid and short. But I gave up the business; it is too trying to keep it up for long" (2. 22, 515). Couriers during the Renaissance, such as those in the mail system established a century earlier in France by Louis XI, were as often as not also secret messengers or outright spies.[26] Montaigne wrote to Matignon in 1585 that Henri of Navarre had arrested his own wife's messenger to the court of France on suspicion of bearing intelligence about his affairs to his enemies there.[27] Whether or not the body of the sovereign was double, the identity of the spy was essentially duplicitous.

If Montaigne began his career of royal servitude as a messenger, he may also have been mixed up in the darker side of riding post. Later on, as we have seen, he was party to more important communications, and to the inevitable imputation of duplicity these entailed. The ethical qualities most associated with the prince's servant—integrity, frankness, discretion, and the ability to inspire friendship—prove equally subject to the subversive dynamic of a sovereign power founded on surveillance. In the essay "Des menteurs," where Montaigne claims his poor memory makes him unfit for negotiating (1. 9, 22), he tells the story of the Milanese ambassador who was caught out in a lie by Francis I. The French king, "in order to maintain some intelligence service in Italy, from which he had lately been driven out, and especially in the duchy of Milan, had decided to keep one of his own gentlemen near the duke, an ambassador in effect but in appearance a private person, who pretended to be there for his personal affairs" (1. 9, 24). This agent's situation recalls the ostensibly private capacity in which Montaigne himself seems always to have served his princes, at the court of Henri III in 1588, for instance.

The gentleman was put in place with the cooperation of the duke of Milan, but the duke had him executed when his presence was discovered by the emperor. It was on this point that the Milanese ambassador, sent to France to cover up the matter, was cornered by Francis I. Having denied that the duke knew the gentleman was a member of Francis's household, the ambassador then made the mistake of letting on that he was killed under cover of night to avoid as much embarrassment to the French as possible. In implying that he would be prone to similar mistakes because of his deficient memory, Montaigne is trying to distance himself from the duplicity attributed to diplomacy by advertising his singular potential for honesty in negotiation. But Montaigne, as Max Horkheimer realized, was a diplomat by disposition and class position.[28] From a recently ennobled family with distinctly bourgeois roots, he derived what prestige he had principally from his contact with princes. We have already noted his part in bringing Henri of Navarre and Matignon together, not to mention Henri of Navarre and Henri III; in the early 1570's, about the time this anecdote was written, Montaigne was at court as an unofficial mediator between Navarre and Henri of Guise.[29] As a diplomatic go-between, he had first-hand experience with the instability of sovereign selves, while living the double life that such dealings forced upon the courtly servant, ambassador, or spy.

"Des menteurs" closes with another story about a forgetful ambassador. This time the envoy acts on his own sense of sovereign integrity. He reveals that he does not approve of his master's plans for war, and is subsequently punished for undermining his own mission (1. 9, 25). Montaigne relates a similar tale of diplomatic creativity in "Un traict de quelques ambassadeurs." When the Emperor Charles V harangued a pair of French ambassadors in public, insulting the French army and challenging Francis I to single combat, they repressed most of his tirade, especially the insult and the challenge, in reporting the incident to their king. Montaigne says he finds such conduct strange; a servant should represent things exactly as they happened, for to judge what is or is not appropriate "seems to me proper for him who gives the law, not for him who receives it" (1. 17, 51). This observation brings the first version of the essay to a close. After 1588, Montaigne added a passage that begins by amplifying the original conclusion. Every servant has a natural desire to usurp authority, yet "we corrupt the function of command when we obey through discretion, not subjection" (1. 17, 51). But it is the prospect of a king kept ignorant of his own affairs that he particularly deplores: royal servants should be conduits for the flow of accurate information toward the monarch above all else.

It is a little surprising, then, when he performs a reversal in the next paragraph: "On the other hand, however, one might also consider that such constrained obedience belongs only to precise and stated commands. Ambassadors have a freer commission, which in many areas depends supremely [souverainement] on their judgment; they do not simply carry out, but also by their counsel form and direct [dressent] their master's will" (1. 17, 51, Villey 74; translation modified). Vague instructions create a considerable margin for discretion, and much is presumably permitted as long as the ruler knows what is going on within it. The use of the verb *dresser* in the last sentence, however, is arresting—it recalls Montaigne's ambition to *contreroller* the sovereign's conduct in "De l'experience." Ottaviano Fregoso's double bind in Castiglione's *Courtier* comes to mind: if the counselor is to instruct the prince, he must be superior to the prince.[30] To fashion oneself as the perfect servant of the sovereign is to usurp sovereign perfection. At this point the servant begins to take on the individuality of the king, fashioning his master's will and becoming the one who gives the law rather than the one who receives it.

The familiar example of the Persian empire appears once again at the end of the (c)-text of the essay, this time in a negative light. The kings of that country erred in giving their agents instructions so minutely detailed that constant recourse to them needlessly hampered administration (1. 17, 51). The lesson is clear: it is more important that information should travel from the bottom up than from the top down. The process is helped along when ambassadors are allowed to constitute themselves as subjects who act upon their own judgment, rather than remaining the self-erasing messengers of the first version of the essay. Diplomacy is not like speech. It does not disappear once its information has been passed on. Like writing, it remains behind in all its ingenuity and obscurity and continues to impress itself upon affairs. This is why a good memory is essential for negotiation. And this is why Montaigne recurs to examples from the reign of Francis I: he is able to do so because histories of diplomacy have been left behind by diplomats themselves (1. 17, 50, Villey 73). The "negotiations, *intelligences*, and diplomatic practices" of which they write seem to depend upon the transmission of correct information, but in fact they thrive in an atmosphere of vague commands and secret initiatives.

At the same time, however, the ambassador (or spy) is always implicated in his master's intentions. In "De l'utile et de l'honneste," Montaigne claims that when he is sent on a mission by a prince, he prefers not to know what its full import is: "If I am to serve as an instrument of deceit, at least let it be with a clear conscience" (3. 1, 603). Francesco Guicciardini had earlier commented upon this "need to know" principle in his *Ricordi*. Some princes tell their ambassadors only what they want the other prince to believe, for in order to deceive one's enemy it helps to deceive one's own instrument. Yet Guicciardini ultimately prefers it when envoys know all, for "it is impossible to give ambassadors instructions so detailed as to cover every circumstance; rather discretion must teach them to accommodate themselves to the end generally being pursued. But if the ambassador does not fully know that end, he cannot pursue it."[31] As in the first version of "Un traict de quelques ambassadeurs," the ambassador in this essay is presented as an instrument of his prince's will who merely follows orders. Montaigne admits, however, that he has served "princes who do not accept men halfway and scorn limited and conditional services" (3. 1, 603). The ambassador cannot implement secrecy without becoming absorbed by it.

Like the frankness Montaigne prized, discretion arises within a process of developing individuality in which ambassadors not only execute the prince's will but form it as well. In carrying out their commissions, "qui . . . depend souverainement de leur disposition" (1. 17, Villey 74), they also form their own wills by taking the singularity attributed to the sovereign as their model. This "usurpation," as Montaigne calls it (1. 17, Villey 74), involves the fashioning of one's own self and the self of the prince, and thus it governs the flow of information from above in the form of instructions by allowing for improvisation upon these instructions and influence upon their author.

The unstable self of the ambassador also determines the flow of information from below, or from other princes, that constitutes intelligence. In "De l'institution des enfans," Montaigne relates that he once jokingly asked a French nobleman how often he had got drunk in pursuit of his king's interests in Germany; those who can't hold their liquor often founder when negotiating with that hard-drinking nation (1. 26, 123–24). Cleverness in extracting information during drinking bouts was a common boast of ambassadors and spies; Montaigne tells a similar anecdote about Josephus in "De l'yvrongnerie" (2. 2, Villey 341).[32] In "De l'institution des enfans" it represents a prudential adaptability to social situations that he wishes to encourage.[33] Montaigne says he would make his pupil like Alcibiades, whose wonderful nature easily changed itself to fit differing circumstances, all without damage to his health (1. 26, 124). He is writing principally about the education of the king's future servant, who must be made "fit for all nations and companies, even for dissoluteness and excess, if need be. . . . He will laugh, he will carouse, he will dissipate with his prince" (1. 26, 123).[34] The culture of intelligence that Montaigne internalizes in his descriptions of the self-spying subject was already bound up with nascent individuality in its turn; the controlled instability of the developing individual lends itself to any situation or set of customs.

"The art of what, with a characteristic narrowing of meaning, we call 'diplomacy' is thus cultivated in the everyday life of court society," Elias observes. "The qualities that are today required only from the external representatives of a country . . . are forcibly produced by hierarchical 'good society' in each of its members." Friendship among royal servants is a matter of constant negotiation and calculation, for "all these court people are . . . inescapably dependent on each other as friends, enemies or relatively neutral parties."[35] In "De l'amitié," Montaigne turns to the idea of friendship in order to erect an individual sphere set apart from public life. He tells us that the unique friendship between himself and Etienne de la Boétie began before their first meeting, in his admiration for la Boétie's treatise attacking the "voluntary servitude" of the group that surrounds the tyrant. Montaigne distinguishes friendship from the sort of relationships monarchy promotes, but like integrity, frankness, and discretion, friendship nevertheless turns out to be dependent upon sovereignty and the public world.

The tyrant's surveillance of the court poses the greatest threat to friendship in la Boétie's *Discours de la servitude volontaire*. "From whence has he gotten the eyes with which he spies upon you," he asks, "if you have not given them to him yourselves?"[36] In the *Politics*, Aristotle mentions sowing distrust among friends as one of tyranny's main stratagems.[37] Closer to la Boétie's time, Guicciardini had similarly warned that a tyrant "will have you observed by men he has ordered to become intimate with you," abusing good fellowship in order to discover your secret thoughts.[38] The self-surveillance of la Boétie's court on behalf of the sovereign is echoed by the self-spying *moi* of the *Essais*, although Montaigne presents the complete internalization of surveillance as an antidote to political subjection.

In la Boétie, self-surveillance is expanded beyond the lone subject in a way that threatens traditional intimacies: "The tyrant certainly neither loves nor is loved. . . . Friendship is not able to exist where there is cruelty, disloyalty, and injustice. When the discontented gather together, they form a conspiracy, not a company . . . they are not friends, but accomplices."[39] Aristotle describes the king's servants as his eyes and limbs. But he states in the same passage that the servants of the king must be his friends as well, for they are, in a sense, corulers with him.[40] The situation is different in la Boétie's *Discours*. Here the sovereign is friendless, and his friendlessness infects the society that revolves around the throne.

Montaigne partially confirms his friend's conclusions. In several places he maintains that kings cannot enjoy friendship because no one can compete or even converse with them on equal terms. The words of the sovereign, written and spoken, can be obscured by their grandeur and majesty, or rendered unjudgeable by the power of their author and the fear it induces. For the writing of the sovereign can also kill. Montaigne concludes "De l'incommodité de la grandeur" with this *mot*: "Augustus wrote some verses against Asinius Pollio. 'And I,' said Pollio, 'am keeping quiet; it is not wise to be a scribe against a man who can proscribe [d'escrire à l'envy de celui qui peut proscrire]'" (3. 7, 702–3, Villey 920). The language barrier appears at a key juncture of "De l'art de conferer" as well: "most of those who judge the speeches of the great ought to say: 'I did not understand his meaning, it was so obfuscated by gravity, greatness, and majesty'" (3. 8, 714). The very uniqueness that ensures the prince's power over those who would observe and judge him also confines him to the friendless solitude described by la Boétie.

In "De l'inequalité qui est entre nous" Montaigne cites Xenophon's King Hiero as an authority on the loneliness of the monarch: "But above all Hiero emphasizes the fact that he finds himself deprived of all mutual friendship and society, wherein consists the sweetest and most perfect fruit of human life. For what testimony of affection and good will can I extract from a man who, willynilly, owes me everything he can do? . . . The honor we receive from those who fear us is not honor; these respects are due to royalty, not to me" (1. 42, 195). This last sentence recalls the passage that Reiss quotes as an example of the "king's two bodies" doctrine. Royalty is separate from the *moi*, but the *moi* now writes as if it were a king. Once more we are within a zone of discourse about the sovereign in which selves multiply, or in which what we call "the self" is seen to be inherently multiple before the advent of a fully developed individuality. Thus Montaigne continues for the space of a paragraph to translate the king's thoughts into his own first-person voice: "No one follows me for any friendship there may be between him and me; for no friendship can be knit where there is so little relation and correspondence" (1. 42, 195).

The friendless monarch's solitude serves as the pattern for developing individuality, a pattern that Montaigne tentatively usurps. "De l'amitié" attests that the unique form of friendship he shared with la Boétie is possible under a monarchy, if not a tyranny, although Montaigne also insists that "among men of today you see no trace of it in practice" (1. 28, 136). He is equally adamant against confounding his type of friendship with what he calls "Greek love." But in a long passage that glances back at Plato's *Symposium*, Montaigne indirectly underwrites the object of such love in the transfer from older to younger men of "philosophical instruction, precepts to revere religion, obey the laws, die for the good of the country"—"all that can be said in favor of the Academy is that this was a love ending in friendship" (1. 28, 138, 139). "De la vanité" intellectualizes male friendship even further: Montaigne claims that the absence of his friend was much sweeter to him than his "bodily presence," for they had means of communication, presumably epistolary, through which "he saw for me, and I for him" (3. 9, 746–47). In "De l'amitié" this rarified exchange of intelligence between men is revealed to be part of a wider circulation of knowledge.

"It is in order to know himself as la Boétie knew him that Montaigne questions and studies himself," Merleau-Ponty observes. "Montaigne and the author of the *Essays* were born of this friendship, and . . . for him, in sum, existing meant existing beneath his friend's gaze."[41] To some extent, la Boétie's memory enabled Montaigne to internalize court society, where one's thoughts become their reflections in the eyes of others. In the conclusion of "De l'amitié," Montaigne feels himself obliged to excuse his late friend for the antimonarchical opinions of his youth by claiming that they were products of a rhetorical exercise, and that la Boétie was a conservative, law-abiding citizen (1. 28, 144). Earlier, friendship is extolled through an exemplary figure whose story evokes the political world of surveillance and informers—the faithful Caius Blosius, best friend of Tiberius Gracchus, who was persecuted along with "all those who had been in his *intelligence*" (1. 28, 139–40, Villey 189; translation modified). Here the word *intelligence* means "friendship" or "intimacy" as well as "conspiracy."

In a (c)-text addition that comes just before this paragraph in the essay, Montaigne applies the same word to his relationship with la Boétie: "He wrote an excellent Latin satire, which is published, in which he excuses and explains the precipitancy of our mutual understanding [nostre intelligence], so promptly grown to its perfection" (1. 28, 139, Villey 188). Montaigne is betraying here the public nature of his friendship with la Boétie: the satire was published, their *intelligence* required explanation, and we are also told that the two men met "en une grande feste et compagnie de ville" (1. 28, Villey 188). As Jacques Derrida has recently suggested, Montaigne's participation in the "double exclusion" of women from friendship—as friends of men and of one another—is related to "the movement that has always 'politicized' the model of friendship at the very moment one tries to remove this model from an integral politicization." "It would be necessary," Derrida goes on, "to analyze all discourses that reserve politics and public space for man, domestic and private space for women."[42] Friendship turns out to be a public institution for the circulation of knowledge and prestige among men. Thus, while the essay "De l'amitié" seemingly represents an attempt to show how the practice of private friendship can exist despite the demands of a public world and its practices, the stories Montaigne tells and the very language in which he tells them circumvent its apparent intention. Even an idealized friendship with a dead man is not free of political considerations.

Like the other ideals associated with royal service, the ethics of friendship are complicit with a public sphere overshadowed by sovereignty and shot through with surveillance. Ambassadors, for instance, should obey their instructions honestly, yet their honor ultimately depends on how discreet they are. Discretion creates a personal domain of judgment that serves a public function; the improvising self is born of policy, and discretion returns it to its shifting origin. All the essayist's gestures of detachment end in a similar swerve from the newly invented private realm back to the public sphere. Throughout, the autonomous self's self-examination is described in terms of espionage, a secretive, even private activity that is nevertheless a technique of political power. The reflecting subject, as Montaigne asserts in his gloss upon the Delphic "Know Thyself," may be "le scrutateur sans connoissance, le magistrat sans jurisdiction" (3. 9, Villey 1001), but its construction as *scrutateur* and magistrate in the first place reveals a debt to the self-defining roles of the public realm.

It might seem as if the king is the ultimate observer, the center of the world of public power, but for Montaigne he is largely an absent center. With the Reformation, Montaigne laments, the "unity and contexture" of the French monarchy was dislocated and broken, and more fragmentation will probably follow (1. 23, 87). The sovereign has withdrawn or been split apart, becoming an abstract sovereignty that is also the field of surveillance in which its servants dwell, and ultimately the battlefield of civil war. Unlike his contemporaries in England, for whom the overwhelming figure of Elizabeth at the apex of court society posed different problems of identity, Montaigne's selfhood was determined in part by an overtly divided and disseminated sovereignty; the problems he encountered, however, anticipate those we will uncover in the Jacobean political fictions of Ben Jonson and Francis Bacon. Montaigne writes continually of "nos rois" or "nos princes," not of a single ruler. In the France of his day the king possessed two bodies indeed; they bore the names Henri III and Henri of Navarre. The image of a single sovereign at the center of an intelligence system, like the image of a stable, autonomous self at the center of a system of knowledge, was a utopian idealization for Montaigne's contemporaries in France.

The essay "De l'inequalité qui est entre nous" (1. 42) sets the keynote for Montaigne's speculations on the equivocal position—not of "the" king, but of a king—within society in some of the later essays. "De l'art de conferer" (3. 8) in particular takes up some of its themes in an attempt to demonstrate that rulers are also victims of a culture of surveillance that paradoxically blocks the flow of information it elicits, just as it blocks fellowship and association. In "De l'inequalité," as we have already seen, the commonplace of the friendless monarch is featured (1. 42, 195), along with the statement that, as in Caesar's time, the petty lords of France are all *Roytelets* who are touched by the state barely twice in their lives. The passage continues: "The real and essential subjection is only for those among us who go seeking it and who like to gain honors and riches by such service" (1. 42, 195). Montaigne seems to be questioning whether a properly national sovereignty even exists apart from those who succumb to voluntary servitude by seeking a center of power to feed their own greed and ambition.

He reveals his fascination with sovereign absence by his focus on the throng of people who surround the monarch in both "De l'inequalité" and "De l'art de conferer." In the latter essay, he links healthy disagreement with friendship, and goes on to complain that the great, and, by implication, kings in particular, have an unfair advantage in argument because of their "authorité magistrale" among "une assistance qui tremble de reverence et de respect" (3. 8, Villey 924, 935–36). In "De l'inequalité," the king finds himself amid the same "annoying crowd," and Montaigne claims to feel more pity than envy of him (1. 42, 194). His tone is more ironic in "De l'art de conferer," where we learn that royal servants derive their authority from the external trappings of their rank, and not from any intrinsic worth. "What I myself adore in kings is the crowd of their adorers," Montaigne slyly adds (3. 8, 714). The adorers are to the king as the signs of their rank are to the adorers. The throng that surrounds sovereignty like a screen or covers it like a mask also constitutes it in some sense.

And, masked itself, sovereignty is powerless to penetrate the mask of appearances. Montaigne ends the paragraph in "De l'inequalité" where his first-person singular becomes the voice of the king with the complaint: "All they say to me and do for me is only powder and paint. Their liberty being bridled on all sides by the great power I have over them, I see nothing around me except what is covered and masked" (1. 42, 195). The picture of the king who cannot see through appearances appears again in a different form in "De l'art de conferer." People are wrong to criticize monarchs for distributing offices according to fortune rather than merit, Montaigne writes, "for nature has not given them a vision that can scrutinize a whole populace in order to discern preeminence and to penetrate our bosoms, where dwells the knowledge of our wills and of our best worth. . . . If anyone could find a way in which men could be judged by justice and chosen by reason, with that single stroke he would establish a perfect form of government" (3. 8, 712). Here, again, a mask conceals the subjects from the gaze of their king. In this passage Montaigne at once lays the groundwork for a program of power based upon the visibility of the subject, and disqualifies the monarchical system of his own day from putting it into practice.

The crowd of servants and courtiers that surrounds kings and forms their field of vision is also a chattering multitude of voyeurs whose ability to provide truthful counsel or accurate information is undercut by the very royal power they address (1. 42, 194). Princes, we are told in a (b)-text addition to "De l'inequalité qui est entre nous," must hide their vices more than other people because their indiscretions are taken for tyrannies, and indeed often do spring from the pleasure they take in transgressing public observances: "And often, for that reason, the public display of their vice gives more offense than the vice itself. Everyone fears to be spied on and watched [espié et contrerollé], and the great are watched even to their expressions and thoughts" (1. 42, 194, Villey 265). Here surveillance is suddenly expanded to encompass the public display of the great, and in the private or secret form of spying at that. Once more in the *Essais*, the private is implicated in the public, as everyone's fear of being secretly monitored is projected onto those who openly manifest an often abusive power. The vocabulary of intelligence is being used to describe the slow emergence of a transgressive self.

Both sovereign and subjects are concealed from one another by the mask of power. A cat may look at a king. But the people cannot see past the display of sovereign prestige and perceive a singular royal identity. Similarly, the sovereign cannot discern the best of his subjects—they are too many; he cannot pierce the disguises of the few who become his servants, nor trust their flattering counsel. Montaigne's meditations on the frustrating epistemology of the royal person find their clearest and most remarkable expression in "De l'incommodité de la grandeur": "That extraneous glare [lueur estrangere] that surrounds him hides him and conceals him from us; our sight breaks and is dissipated by it, being filled and arrested by this strong light" (3. 7, 702, Villey 919). The field of surveillance has become an incandescent haze about the sovereign, through which the monarch can neither see clearly nor clearly be seen. Its strong light disrupts and dissipates our sight, and may actually conceal the virtual absence of a single central authority.

In Montaigne's France, the body of the king was not merely double, but fractured almost to the point of absence. Henri III, Henri of Navarre, and the Guises (along with lesser factions and interests) all jockeyed for power and influence. Furthermore, the decentering of authority during Montaigne's time was the result not only of the chaotic political situation in France but of the nature of early modern sovereignty itself. The fifteenth-century jurist Jean de Terre Rouge's opinion that royal dignities were part of the kingdom's *corpus mysticum*, and thus publicly rather than privately owned, was published as an appendix to François Hotman's *Concilia* in 1586. In 1489 the Parlement of France had declared itself "a *corps mystique* . . . representing the person of the king," and identical with his attribute of majesty.[43] While Montaigne was looking forward to a strong personal ruler who would stabilize France with the assistance of the ideal counselor, constitutional developments continued to dissolve sovereignty into the larger body of the realm. Louis XIV put a stop to this trend, at least for a while, but in Montaigne's day it threatened to engulf a weak king like Henri III. The passage on the "extraneous glare" begins by describing how majesty "stifles and consumes [kings'] other real and essential qualities; these are sunk in royalty; and it leaves them nothing to recommend themselves by but . . . the duties of their office. It takes so much to be a king that he exists only as such" (3. 7, 702). The king's physical body almost disappears.

"Des coches," the essay that precedes "De l'incommodité de la grandeur," is in part an attack on the display of royal wealth and power: "it is a sort of pusillanimity in monarchs . . . to labor at showing off and making a display by excessive expense [despences excessives]" (3. 6, 687–88, Villey 902). This was the old regime described by Foucault, in which ceremony was "the excessive, yet regulated manifestation of power . . . a spectacular expression of potency, an 'expenditure' [dépense], exaggerated and coded, in which power renewed its vigor. It was always more or less related to the triumph."[44] But according to Montaigne, "it seems to the subjects, spectators of these triumphs, that they are given a display of their own riches. . . . For, to be precise about it, a king has nothing that is properly his own; he owes his very self to others" (3. 6, 688–89). Montaigne himself could appeal to the jurists' idea that royal dignities are public property. The materials of greatness were held in common among the king and his subjects, although it might seem more accurate to conclude that they owed their "very selves" to him.

Montaigne was caught between two worlds: attacking display, he was able to propose only that the perfect form of policy would be attained when someone discovered a way of opening the hearts of his subjects to the king so that only the best of them might be chosen for royal servitude. As it is, monarchs "endure a public life, and have to suit the opinions of so many spectators, that, since people have formed the habit of concealing from them anything that disturbs their plans, they find themselves, without realizing it, the object of the hatred and detestation of their people" (3. 13, 826). In other words, it is display itself that precludes the development of a full-fledged system of surveillance.

The *Essais* are suspended at a turning point in the history of sovereignty's relation to knowledge. When Montaigne writes about the public display of princes in terms of everyone's fear of being "espié et contrerollé" (1. 42, Villey 265), he is putting them on the level of the private subject. He reverses this movement on the following page, when his "I" assumes the identity of the lonely king. He likewise declares his independence at the end of "De l'art de conferer" by calling himself the king of the matter he treats, who owes an explanation of it to no one (3. 8, 720). Sovereignty, however, was not really the locus of a unitary and thoroughly autonomous power. Perhaps it became one of the prime models for individuality in the sixteenth century because it exemplified an instability and inscrutability similar to that ascribed to the developing self by a developing self-examination such as we find in the *Essais*.

Nevertheless, the principal figure for such self-examination was not the prince but his servant, the counselor, ambassador, or spy. An unsteady identity was formed in the opaque space between sovereign and subject, a process recapitulated in "De l'utile et de l'honneste," which introduces the third and final book of the *Essais*. In a long, contradictory passage, Montaigne attempts to explain how one can take a side and remain virtually neutral at the same time in the midst of civil conflicts. The tyrant Gelon of Syracuse kept an embassy at Delphi so that he could instantly catch wind of the victorious party in any foreign war and align himself with it. It would be "une espece de trahison" to do this in the affairs of one's own country, yet "not to involve oneself, for a man who has neither responsibility nor express command that presses him, I find that more excusable (and nevertheless I am not using this excuse for myself) than to keep out of foreign wars" (3. 1, 601, Villey 793). Discretion in the absence of a "commandement exprés" plays only a slightly different role here than it does as a trait of certain ambassadors. The tortured syntax and parenthetical disclaimer betray Montaigne's awkwardness. His dream of an engaged moderation ends only in the promise of personal safety and survival: "even those who espouse a cause completely can do so with such order and moderation that the storm will be bound to pass over their heads without harm" (3. 1, 601–2).

This note is taken up in the next passage. "I hold that it properly belongs to kings to quarrel with kings," Montaigne maintains. "Nothing keeps us from getting along comfortably between two hostile parties" (3. 1, 602; translation modified). The honest man can get along well enough between two kings, as Montaigne did between Henri III and Henri of Navarre—to the former's disadvantage. In subsequent pages he describes how to comport oneself within the dangerous field of sovereignty and intelligence between monarchs. Montaigne declares that he wants little to do with the burdensome secrets of princes, but the string of tales that follows attests to his fascination with the unsavory side of public life. The stories all concern spies and traitors who were eventually punished by the very rulers who commanded or suborned them to commit their treacheries in the first place.

In this way Montaigne, like the rulers whose double-dealing he commends, tries to purge royal servitude, and perhaps his part in it, of its necessary but dishonorable elements. In 1588, after all, one of his masters, Henri III, had seen to the assassination of the Duke of Guise, and it may have been this recent event—as well as the memories of St. Bartholomew's Day that it revived—that led him to add "et qu'on massacre" to the sentence "Le bien public requiert qu'on trahisse et qu'on mente" after the edition of that year (3. 1, Villey 791). Montaigne wished to keep clear of such expedients, and he closes his essay by asserting "that not all things are permissible for an honorable man in the service of his king, or of the common cause, or of the laws" (3. 1, 609). Again, "de son Roy" is a (c)-text addition.

It is in "De l'utile et de l'honneste" that Montaigne invites those who look upon his honesty as cunning to follow and spy on him closely (3. 1, Villey 795). His earlier self-spying is externalized in this passage; as Horkheimer intimates, he becomes the prototype for those inhabitants of modernity who do not resent the secret police because they "have nothing to hide."[45] Foucault similarly writes of "a gaze which each individual under its weight will end by interiorising to the point that he is his own overseer."[46] But the partial realization of this program of open surveillance was still far in the future. Even though self-spying already existed with Montaigne, it revealed only self-ignorance and self-mutability. The later sixteenth century already possessed a machinery of informants, spies, and ambassadors that had begun to provide an ideal pattern for government by information while remaining bogged down in the misinformation and discretionary uncertainties it in fact fostered.[47] Yet the obscurity and mutability uncovered by self-spying were not to prove useless to authority. We should keep this in mind even as we challenge the totalizing element in theories of power such as Foucault's. Ambassadorial discretion and the code of following orders in supposed ignorance of their intentions abetted the operation of power in Montaigne's time, and together they served as the crucible of a bureaucratic individuality that was prepared to act on its own initiative while refusing to accept responsibility for the results. The consequences of this particular form of self-fashioning are still with us today.

CHAPTER 2

Woman's Best Eyesight
Sexual Surveillance and Sidney's 'Arcadia'

I N the late 1570's and early 1580's, the period during which Philip Sidney wrote and rewrote his *Arcadia*, politics at the English court revolved around the sexual choices of the female sovereign. Elizabeth's protracted marriage negotiations with Francis, duke of Alençon, the youngest son of Catherine de Médicis and brother to the Catholic king of France, galvanized parliament and the court. In the absence of Henry VIII, these masculine domains attempted to act in place of the sovereign father, enjoining Elizabeth to marry but attempting to restrict her choice to an English, or at any rate a Protestant, consort. The queen had resisted these efforts at sexual control from the very beginning of her reign, insisting in 1559 that it was "altogether unmeet" for "those to appoint whose parts are to desire, or such to bind or limit, whose duties are to obey, or to take upon you to draw my love to your liking, or to frame my will to your fantasy."[1] She refused to become the means by which her male subjects might enjoy their fantasies of the perfect masculine ruler. Instead, she used such unfulfilled desires as a way to manage those who entertained them.[2]

Espionage was bound up with the marriage question and the political erotics it fostered. Courtiers and counselors on both sides of the French marriage dispute watched each other uneasily, and everyone watched the queen. Elizabeth, in turn, employed the system of royal patronage for intelligence purposes, and relied upon the espionage network constructed by Sidney's father-in-law, Sir Francis Walsingham.[3] English spies in France and the Netherlands monitored Alençon's contacts abroad. Foreign embassies, particularly Spain's, collected their own intelligence about the course of Alençon's courtship, the outcome of which would substantially alter the balance of power in Europe.⁴ At one point Mauvissière, the French ambassador, obtained copies of Elizabeth's correspondence with the duke—intercepted letters were not just a feature of romantic tales.⁵ The court, already a theater of desire and competitive observation, became overtly eroticized as spying and counterspying escalated.

Elizabeth's decision to take greater control of her foreign policy by encouraging the attentions of a foreign prince—an important shift in political strategy on her part, as Wallace MacCaffrey has argued—augmented and capitalized upon a pervasive paranoia among the members of her court.⁶ For male aristocrats at court during the last decades of the sixteenth century in England, the social field corresponded with particular fidelity to the "scopic field" of desire described by Jacques Lacan. The courtier, a man observing other men, and observed in turn, might indeed have remarked with the Lacanian subject: "I see only from one point, but in my existence I am looked at from all sides."⁷ Elizabeth was paramount within this field of scopic anxiety; her motto was *video et taceo*, "I see and keep quiet." In some respects, it was less a matter of the queen watching from the center, than of her image serving as the central representation of the paranoia that each member of court society felt before a general gaze. Yet Elizabeth did monitor and manage relationships and marriages among the men and women around her, as Leonard Tennenhouse has recently reminded us.⁸ The transformation of courtly observation into the organized surveillance of those within and without court society was thus shot through with sexual anxiety, an anxiety registered in Sidney's pastoral fiction, the *Arcadia*.

Unexpectedly, it was the pastoral genre that offered Sidney and other contemporary writers a way of coming to grips with the paranoid political and erotic anxieties produced by the culture of surveillance at Elizabeth's court. In the revised *Arcadia* of 1590, for instance, the lengthy description of the rustic nobleman Kalander is idyllic yet charged with political significance. A comfortingly paternal figure, he is "a man who for his hospitality is so much haunted, that no newes sturre, but comes to his eares; for his upright dealing so beloved of his neighbours, that he hath many ever readie to doe him their uttermost service, and by the great good will our Prince beares him, may soone obtain the use of his name

and credit, which hath a principall swaie, not only in his owne Arcadia but in al these countries of *Peloponnesus*."⁹ Kalander is associated with the ear that passively receives whatever intelligence
comes its way. His pastoral situation registers the intermixture of
court and country during Sidney's time, when courtiers still spent
the summer months at their estates, and the monarch still took the
royal entourage to visit them in her great progresses. Elizabeth's
power and prestige were distributed among different locations in
the country and its social hierarchy through the patronage system,
which made the court more a way of life than a place.¹⁰ An ideal
representation of the well-informed aristocratic patron, Kalander,
like Montaigne, is distanced from the court yet intimately connected with the sovereign.

When he shares intelligence of a recent event in Arcadia with his
guest, the shipwrecked Musidorus, Kalander's access to the secret
of the ill-advised "discourting" of King Basilius and his retirement
with his family to pastoral seclusion is far from accidental or in-
nocent.¹¹ "I will discover unto you, aswell that wherein my knowledge is common with others, as that which by extraordinary means
is delivered unto me" (19), he tells Musidorus. Kalander's son Clitophon had served as a gentleman of the bedchamber to Basilius.
When the court broke up and Clitophon returned home, he
showed his father, "among other things he had gathered," a copy
of a letter to the king from Philanax, his most trusted advisor. Basilius, assuming that no one would dare examine his correspondence, had set it down, "but my sonne not only tooke a time to
read it, but to copie it." "In trueth I blamed *Clitophon* for the cu-
riositie," Kalander assures Musidorus, "which made him break his
dutie in such a kind, whereby kings secrets are subject to be revealed: but since it was done," he blandly adds, "I was content to
take so much profite, as to know it" (23). Clitophon may represent
the realpolitik of a new generation, but he also suggests the mechanism of casual observation and informing among men at court
that has upheld Kalander's supposedly passive and pastoral omniscience all along.

It has long been recognized that the fictional letter Clitophon
intercepts echoes the letter that Sidney sent to Elizabeth to protest
her pending marriage to Alençon.¹² Basilius has superstitiously
heeded an oracle that predicts his elder daughter Pamela will be sto-

len by a prince, that his younger daughter Philoclea will love un-
couthly, and that he will be murdered by the men they marry (327),
so he has taken his wife Gynecia and their two daughters off to a
rustic hiding place where the elder princess is kept under the watchful eye of the peasant Dametas and his family. The letter from Philanax urges the sovereign to remain among his subjects and avoid
rash changes in policy. As for the princesses, if they are secluded
"I know not what strange loves should follow" (25).[13]

Complaint, both of unrequited love and of social corruption, is
the dominant mode of pastoral. Sidney's allusion to the Alençon
affair in the *New Arcadia*, as Tennenhouse has recognized, gives
shape to the anxieties of Elizabeth's courtiers about the consequences of female succession and the unpredictability of the
queen's sexuality.[14] Basilius would control the princesses by hiding
them among the shepherds; Philanax's letter implies that this end
can be better attained by keeping them at home, away from the
danger of strange pastoral loves.

There is some evidence that Elizabeth recognized the attraction
that pastoral held for her followers, and that she employed for her
own ends the reconciliation of political and erotic anxieties it permitted, sanctioning the image of herself as Eliza, queen of lovelorn
and powerless shepherds.[15] In addition, she staged her negotiations
with Alençon in the pastoral mode, receiving poems from the pen
of Alençon's agent Maisonfleur and openly dallying, first with
Alençon's new emissary Simier and then for two months with the
duke himself, through a series of feasts, tournaments, and entertainments.[16] This intensified courtliness parallels the pastoral re-
creations of the royal family in the *Arcadia*, who are entertained by
the eclogues that conclude each book in both versions of the text.

Thus, Sidney's *Arcadia* and the events of the Alençon crisis form
part of the same discourse of courtly surveillance. The surprising
association of political intelligence with the pastoral ideal existed
elsewhere in the period. Sir Francis Walsingham affected a preference for country life from the beginning of his career, for example,
and spent much of the 1580's at Barn Elms, his manor in Surrey,
communicating with Elizabeth's court at Whitehall by means of
the Thames. The poet Thomas Watson, a friend of Christopher
Marlowe, commemorated Walsingham's death in 1590 with a pastoral elegy entitled *Meliboeus*; he dedicated the Latin version to

Marlowe's patron Thomas Walsingham, a kinsman of Sir Francis who had served as one of his spies.[17] Meliboe is also the name given by Spenser to the hospitable old shepherd, disillusioned with the court life of his youth, who is generally supposed to represent Walsingham in the sixth book of the *Faerie Queene*.[18]

Walsingham maintained a long-standing tie with Sidney, the nephew of his own patron Robert Dudley, earl of Leicester. Sidney stayed with Walsingham for a time while the older man was ambassador in Paris in 1572, and witnessed the massacre on St. Bartholomew's Day. Throughout the rest of the decade, Walsingham and Sidney were allies in the Protestant cause at Elizabeth's court, and when Sidney married Walsingham's daughter Frances in 1583 he moved in with him at Barn Elms (3. 423–24). It is probable that at least some of the revised *Arcadia* was written there. The fictional Kalander, then, may be a tribute to Sidney's watchful father-in-law. If so, Kalander is a token of the patronage relationship between them. But the pastoral portrait of Kalander also conceals its origins in this relationship and the obscure channels that underlay it, the exchange of influence and information.

The constant circulation of compliments, services, and information constituted perhaps the most important social bond, after kinship ties, during the Elizabethan period. But patronage among aristocrats, and between aristocrats and those of lesser rank, did not form a neatly pyramidal structure controlled from the top by the monarch. It was instead a mountain with a ragged gradation of different peaks, although Elizabeth occupied the highest and her greatest subjects perforce looked up to her.[19] Court patronage reached from executive, ceremonial, and domestic posts in the royal household to administrative and legal posts, with their secondary offices for secretaries and hangers-on. Provincial offices such as lord lieutenancies were also connected to the crown through its mightier servants at Whitehall.[20] To this one must add the support that all persons connected with the court, from the most powerful magnate to the humblest secretary or messenger, could dispense among members of their own households and circles. Patronage, then, also denoted a special type of relationship between two people unequal in class and means; the patron exchanged prestige or money with a client who, it was understood, would offer some service in return.[21] Espionage was an inevitable product of this multilayered system of mutual obligation that rendered English society, and even the world beyond it, susceptible to the influence of various interests at court. "An aspiring place-seeker," as R. Malcolm Smuts puts it, "had to know how to gather news and analyze political intrigues, whether as an ambassador reporting on the inner workings of a foreign court or as a domestic 'intelligencer.'" In 1608, the resourceful courtier John Harington even boasted to Prince Henry that his dog Bungey had carried secret messages from his house at Bath to the court at Greenwich before falling into the hands of the Spanish ambassador.[22]

Elizabeth required access to a field of information that cut across class and territorial boundaries; it is therefore not too much to say that Walsingham's initial resort to intelligence practices was a result of her patronage system. His early policy toward Scotland, where the followers of Mary Stuart conspired against the queen with Spain and France, is an example. As a newly appointed principal secretary, Walsingham counseled a combination of military action and high-placed bribery, but Elizabeth repeatedly opposed the expensive use of either violence or persuasion. Along with Leicester and Hunsdon, he began to employ more and more spies, ranging from common messengers to sources in the French ambassador's household, as the best way of forestalling Scottish conspiracy and remaining in his mistress's favor.[23]

Walsingham's spy network was gradually generated to fill the space between his own desire for militant action against England's Catholic enemies and the queen's temporizing; it seemed the best compromise between open war and peace. Elizabeth's preference for privy practices does not seem to have been a consistent policy on her part, either. She took advantage of the role played by intelligence in the patronage system, but she did not set out to become a spy queen. Walsingham was a client supplying her with a service in return for her patronage; he held his office of principal secretary by virtue of the monarch's support and the network of interdependence that he managed. "Membership of court society or connections with people who frequent the court are in many cases conditions of access to such positions," Elias observes, "they assure an income, but at the same time entail obligations to display."[24] Walsingham's position entailed expenditure on secret intelligence as much as, or more than, self-display. He was forced to furnish the queen with intelligence out of his own pocket, although the amount of money she granted him for spying slowly increased after 1585. This money provided for one of the first substantial systems of informants, couriers, and salaried spies that Europe had seen, with agents everywhere from Calais to Constantinople.[25] In the early 1580's, however, Walsingham's intelligence patronage was less developed, and it can be argued that he was no more of a spymaster than Burghley, or even some other members of the Privy Council.[26] Nevertheless, he was Sidney's chief point of contact with the sphere of espionage, and the court society that begot Walsingham's career also served as the condition of possibility for the ideological representation of intelligence embodied in Sidney's Kalander. This pastoral representation mystifies political knowledge gathering, depicting it as passive and defensive, removed from the thick of power yet intimately allied with the prince, "courtly" rather than court-centered.[27]

Elizabeth's two rounds of marriage negotiations with the duke of Alençon during 1572 and 1579–83 instructed Walsingham and his young client Sidney in how difficult involvement with the erotic designs of sovereigns could be. Walsingham's correspondence during the earlier period, when he was the queen's chief representative in France, was published in 1655 as a sort of manual of diplomatic technique entitled *The Compleat Ambassador*. The introduction speaks of "how vigilant he was to gather true Intelligence; what Means and Persons he used for it; how punctual he was in keeping to his Instructions where he was limited; and how wary and judicious where he was left free."[28] Yet the intelligencers in this early network seem to have been unreliable or careless at times, and Walsingham was at a disadvantage from the start. At first it appeared that the French crown wished to prevent the courtship. Although he was a Catholic himself, Alençon was linked to the Protestant cause in France, and his name had come up in a phantom plot for a Huguenot uprising that Walsingham had previously investigated. His mother, Catherine de Médicis, it transpired, was keeping her youngest son under secret observation. Yet Walsingham soon began to suspect that all this was part of "a plain practice," and that the French court was trying to entrap and embarrass the English queen. The editor of *The Compleat Ambassador* speculates that the first Alençon proposal of 1572 was intended to draw Elizabeth into the St. Bartholomew's massacre, a plot that, "by reason of the close carriage thereof, could never be discovered by our quick-sighted Ambassador, with all his Spyes and Intelligencers, till he was almost overwhelmed in it him self."[29] Whether this sensational claim was true or not, Walsingham had little success in determining the intentions of Catherine de Médicis, Alençon, or their proxies.

He already had some experience in the erotics of contemporary politics. Walsingham had begun his career as a spy in the service of principal secretary William Cecil, and one of his first missions in 1568 was to conduct an investigation of the conspiracy surrounding the proposed union of Thomas Howard, duke of Norfolk, and Elizabeth's rival, Mary Stuart. Walsingham published a pamphlet condemning this match as a cynical ploy designed to place a Catholic queen on the throne. True marriages, he wrote, are bonded by love, "wch love is engendered by the eye and by the ear and cannot be perfect unless both states be satisfied in either party; which eyeliking in them cannot be, for that neither of them hath seene the other."[30] Walsingham used similar language four years later in 1572 when he was concerned with the marriage plans of his own queen. Cecil, now Lord Burghley, favored the French match, but Walsingham felt that "the delicacy of Her Majesty's eye" would prevent her marrying the unattractive and smallpox-scarred Alençon.[31] Elizabeth, who was as intent on surveying prospective spouses as her father Henry VIII had been, instructed Walsingham to report on Alençon's appearance and send her a portrait of the duke from France.[32] His earlier dealings with Mary Stuart's marital projects, however, had not prepared him for the complex relationship between "eyeliking" and expediency in Elizabeth's courtships.

Having begun in 1572, the negotiations ran aground by the middle of the decade. Then, in 1578, Walsingham was instructed by Elizabeth to plumb the depths of Alençon's conflicting motives, just as he had earlier been commissioned to provide a description of his physical appearance. Had Alençon been trying to keep English troops out of the Netherlands by courting Elizabeth and offering to act as her knight in defense of the Estates General? Could he be trusted to lead the fight against Spain, thus saving English money and soldiers? The queen told Walsingham to visit the duke and discover "the very secret of his mind and disposition in these affairs"; her curiosity was both conjugal and a matter of policy, as Leicester soon informed Walsingham in a letter advising him to tread carefully. "Hard it is," Walsingham informed his patron, "to discover the bottom of that matter for that affections are inward things and can hardly be deciphered until they grow to effects." Alençon might no longer hope to marry Elizabeth, but he would certainly be content to do so, "being as she is the best marriage in her parish." As for the suitor, Walsingham found him "not so deformed as he was," and certainly more crafty (Read 1. 395, 402–3). Alençon, working once again through courtly agents in London, soon persuaded Elizabeth to allow him to be her general in the Low Countries. "I am right sorry to see the indirect dealings at home," Walsingham wrote Leicester, "in the meantime it behoveth us to have an eye into their doings; especially seeing, besides the public, they do seek some advantage against your Lordship and me" (Read 1. 415–16). The surveillance of Alençon's intentions led to anxiety about their consequences for the political future of Leicester's party. But Walsingham remained unable fully to "decipher" the ends of either Alençon or his mistress.

The rituals of royal courtship used the affective language of romantic love, but most of the emotion was directed toward the continuity of the line and the good of the realm rather than toward the beloved. Consequently, a spymaster's sense of hidden erotic motivation was of little help in determining the aims of Alençon and Elizabeth. The delicacy of Elizabeth's eye would not prevent her from making the best match for her "parish," or from holding out the prospect of marriage to a suitor in order to persuade him to do something for her, like fight the Spanish in the Netherlands.[33] Walsingham and Sidney both belonged to a rising mercantile and professional class that favored the affective model of romantic and family relationships. They never fully grasped the motives of their queen.[34] But the genre of court pastoral provided a common language for both the conduct of the Alençon affair and Sidney's literary response to it in the *Arcadia*.

Sidney had stayed with Walsingham in Paris during the St. Bartholomew's Day debacle that brought the first Alençon proposal to a close; during the second set of negotiations he did not remain a mere observer for long. In the summer of 1579 Alençon secretly visited England to dally with Elizabeth and further his suit for a marriage alliance. He probably wanted to keep England out of the Netherlands and thus insure himself a free hand there as the sole defender of the Protestant Estates General against Catholic Spain. Yet Leicester, Walsingham, and Sidney feared the consequences of both his personal ambition and his Catholicism for English Protestantism should he become Elizabeth's husband.[35] A powerful faction, much in favor with the queen, supported the marriage, however; Burghley had been promoting it since the early 1570's, despite the St. Bartholomew's Massacre and Sidney's efforts to form a Protestant league with the German princes, which would make an alliance between England and France against Spain unnecessary. The French maintained a number of diplomats in London to sue for Elizabeth's hand.

"Thus stood the Court at that time," Fulke Greville later wrote of Sidney and his situation, "and thus stood this ingenuous spirit in it."[36] Soon after Alençon's visit, Sidney was accosted by Burghley's scapegrace son-in-law, the earl of Oxford. According to Greville, who may have been present at the scene, Oxford "abruptly came into the Tennis-Court" where Sidney was playing and commanded him to abandon his opposition to the marriage. There was an exchange of angry words. Sidney "seemed . . . to provoke in yeelding" to Oxford, and then refused to budge when the earl commanded him and his friends to leave the court. Sidney's reply that milder terms might have persuaded his party to withdraw further enraged his challenger, who called him a "puppy." "In which progress of heat," Greville recalls, "as the tempest grew more and more vehement within, so did their hearts breath out their perturbations in a more loud and shrill accent. The *French* Commissioners unfortunately had that day audience, in those private Galleries, whose windows looked into the Tennis-Court. They instantly drew all to this tumult." Sidney, aware of this and of the "mighty faction against him," provoked Oxford to repeat the epithet; "resolving in one answer to conclude both the attentive hearers, and the passionate actor," and despite his opponent's great superiority in rank, he then gave Oxford the lie, "impossible (as he averred) to be retorted; in respect all the world knows, Puppies are gotten by Dogs, and Children by men." The defensiveness here reflects Sidney's worries about his father, Sir Henry, whose ill fortune during his deputy governorship of Ireland had recently led Philip wildly to accuse the elder Sidney's secretary of spying upon their correspondence. Oxford, refusing in effect to call Sidney's father a dog and make violence unavoidable, merely stared at his enemy, "till Sir *Philip* sensible of his own wrong, the forrain, and factious spirits that attended; . . . tender to his Countries honour; with some words of sharp accent, led the way abruptly out of the Tennis-Court."[37]

Greville's account is highly stylized, from its sporting metaphors (Oxford encounters a "steady object" in Sidney, and his roughness meets with more steadfast "returns" of style) to the shock of Sidney's transgression of rank ("they both stood silent awhile, like a dumb shew in a Tragedy"). Yet the language of competition and theatricality, the intense consciousness of being observed while in conflict, the ambiguity in Oxford's demand that Sidney depart "the Court"—all accurately represent the paranoid condition of the courtier under Elizabeth, a way of life that Greville witnessed and took part in through incidents such as this. The anxiety over the presence of the French diplomats in particular rings true. Here the domestic "observation" of courtly honor (the following of its codes, and the witnessing of their enactment) was in danger of becoming the foreign surveillance of civil discord, as Sidney himself seems to have felt. The "court society" that Sidney and his biographer Greville inhabited was also a society of courts, among them tennis courts, open spaces defined by galleries or the walls of surrounding buildings, intended for public display but also convenient for covert observation from the margins.[38]

We have an example of courtly display a few years after the tennis court scene in the tournament of the Fortress of Perfect Beauty, which took place before Elizabeth and a new set of French marriage negotiators in 1581. This time the gallery, located at one end of the tiltyard, was made part of the show. It became the Fortress, and four challengers, among them Sidney and Fulke Greville, took on the queen's champions after threatening to storm it. A messenger addressed their formal defiance or "plaine proclaimation of Warre" to the queen "without making any precise reverence at all," as the contemporary account informs us.[39] The challengers successfully defeated the queen's champions; Sidney may be referring to this tourney in *Astrophil and Stella* 41 when he writes: "I obtain'd

the prize / Both by the judgement of the English eyes, / And of
some sent from that sweet enemie *Fraunce*."[40] But at the end of the
tilt they surrendered themselves to Elizabeth in a gesture explicitly
designed to show the French that internal opposition to the match
had been quelled.[41] Such spectacular combat, of course, also plays
a prominent role in the *New Arcadia*, where accounts of jousts and
battles invariably include detailed descriptions of the opponents'
accoutrements. Yet here display produces secrecy: when they are
not hiding their identities completely, the knights usually sport
some allegorical outfit that refers obliquely to their fortunes. Phalantus, infatuated with the disdainful Artesia, holds a tournament
in which he challenges all comers and demands their ladies' portraits should they lose. This event calls forth a black knight (Musidorus), an "ill apparelled" knight (Pyrocles), and a knight who
loves secretly and thus bears for his impresa "the fish called *Sepia*,
which being in the nette castes a blacke inke about itselfe, that in
the darknesse thereof it may escape" (107). The anxiety exposed to
the prying gaze of the French commissioners in Sidney's free-
wheeling confrontation with Oxford was similarly granted public
expression in a sublimated form through ritual and display.

There are other ways in which the *New Arcadia* and the Alençon
crisis can be seen as part of the same courtly discourse. Sidney's
celebrated letter to Elizabeth arguing against marriage with the
Duke was probably written at Walsingham's instigation.[42] This address, as I have noted, resembles the letter to Basilius from his
trusted counselor Philanax that Clitophon intercepted. "Let your
subjects have you in their eyes," Philanax advises his master, "let
them see the benefites of your justice dayly more and more" (25).
Sidney encouraged his queen to "lett your excellent vertues of pi-
ety Justice, & liberality daily, if it be possible more and more
shine," and he added, "Lett those in whome you finde truste & to
whome you have committed trust in your weighty affaires, be held
up to the eyes of your subjectes."[43] The pressure to display one's
power and magnanimity was also a constraint on rulers and aristocrats.[44] Elizabeth managed to follow the injunction to display
herself and her servants in her own fashion, as the tournament of
1581 shows.[45]

Citing Philanax's advice and its similarity to Sidney's letter to
Elizabeth, Alan Sinfield remarks that "the role of the state servant,

because of its structural specificity, may promote a distinctive political awareness. It is one of the positions from which the Elizabethan state might be criticized if not subverted."[46] Sidney and Walsingham exemplify the independent political consciousness of the royal servant within the patronage system. Yet when the sovereign is a woman, criticism of sovereignty from within often assumes forms that uphold rather than subvert another system of hierarchical relations, the gender system.[47] Women were traditionally the subjects of sexual surveillance by men, a control that was political as well as erotic where the marriage alliances of the nobility were concerned, doubly so when a question of royal succession was involved. One of Sidney's main contentions in his letter to the queen is that although she should display her virtues and her servants to her people, she will remain unable to display herself to herself. Once again, we see a royal servant faced with the delicate task of trying to reduce his sovereign to an object of knowledge as a means of control. Although "our eyes [are] delighted in the sight of you . . . your owne eyes cannot see yourself," and so she cannot judge her own place in the kingdom.[48] Sidney goes out of his way to flatter her (Elizabeth's matchless excellence makes it impossible to find an example with which to explain her situation to her by analogy), but the implication is that she is in no position to make up her own mind about the marriage.

Elizabeth was not a sovereign to be controlled in this way. It must have been passages like this that provoked her rage at the letter and led to Sidney's disgrace. Undoubtedly she was unimpressed by the conceit that her very uniqueness barred her from self-knowledge. Sidney's letter represents an attempt to resist the royal gaze by turning it back upon itself and revealing its supposed blind spot. But Sidney and Walsingham had to contend with a resourceful woman ruler who converted the conventions of the gender hierarchy to her own advantage.

During the negotiations of 1572, Walsingham had quickly become impatient with the ceremonies and games of dynastic wooing. He took a particular dislike to Maisonfleur and La Mole, Alençon's over-courtly representatives. "To disguise the matter," he wrote to Leicester, "they borrow certain names out of Amadis de Gaul, wherein they deal most aptly, to add to a feigned thing feigned names" (Read I. 249, 248). In 1579 Walsingham would also complain about Jean de Simier, another of Alençon's agents, who deflected demands that Elizabeth see his royal master in person with precedents drawn from "old histories," and used his subsequent debates with the queen on the matter as an excuse for more flirting.[49] The French recourse to precedents drawn from romance narratives, which runs throughout the courtship, was nevertheless important. It held a fascination for Elizabeth that drew her into the power game that Alençon, or perhaps Catherine de Médicis, was challenging her to play. The royal household of France understood Elizabeth better than the Protestant gentry who served in her government, and she understood them.

Sidney also knew what was going on, even if he did not approve of it. "Truly," he concedes in the *Defense of Poetry*, "I have known men that even with reading *Amadis de Gaule* (which God knoweth wanteth much of a perfect poesy) have found their hearts moved to the exercise of courtesy."[50] The play with "old histories" in the Alençon suit may have influenced his experiments with prose romance in 1580 when he completed the first version of the *Arcadia* in virtual exile from the court over his opposition to the marriage, and again when he revised it in the years immediately following. The French version of *Amadis de Gaule* contains a number of magic mirrors and enticing portraits that serve as the only means of communication between separated lovers. John J. O'Connor argues convincingly that the central story of the *Arcadia* is based upon two separate incidents in the French *Amadis*, in Books 8 and 9, in which a knight falls in love with the picture of a woman he has never met and then adopts an Amazon disguise to gain access to her. In Book 8 the woman's father, Bazilique, sultan of Babylon, promptly becomes enamored of the cross-dressed hero. There is a clear parallel here to Basilius's infatuation with the disguised Pyrocles, who has fallen in love with the painting of Philoclea that Musidorus shows him in Kalander's pleasure-house.[51]

The picture is described near the beginning of the story. It portrays Basilius, Gynecia, and their youngest daughter Philoclea, and seems to be an affective portrait of a family in private, pastoral retreat: "a comely old man, with a lady of middle age, but of excellent beauty; & more excellent would have bene deemed, but that there stood betweene them a young maid, whose wonderfulnesse tooke away all beautie from her" (*New Arcadia* 18).[52] Yet this is also a portrait of the royal household, "the painter meaning to represent the present condition of the young Ladie, who stood watched by an over-curious eye of her parents. . . . *Palladius* [Musidorus] perceived that the matter was wrapt up in some secresie" (18, my addition). The disclosure of this family portrait, like the production of Clitophon's copy of Philanax's letter that shortly follows, is in fact another device "whereby kings secrets are subject to be revealed" (23). Kalander interprets the emblematic scene explaining how Basilius's abdication was brought about. Thus the youngest daughter, Philoclea, is depicted beneath an "over-curious" sexual surveillance, while her sister Pamela is not represented at all because the rustic lout who watches over her would not have it (18).

The very representation of sexual surveillance does in fact bring about its undoing. As we have seen with Elizabeth and Alençon, examining the lover's portrait was part of the ritual of long-distance dynastic courtship, and Pyrocles similarly falls in love with Philoclea through her painted image before he sees her in the flesh. The picture of Philoclea and her parents is preceded in Kalander's gallery by a painting of Actaeon and Diana, "anticipating," as Jon S. Lawry notes, "Pyrocles' spying on Philoclea" as she bathes later in the story.[53] In taking up the *Amadis*, with its portraits, improbable liaisons, and disguises, Sidney is capitulating to both Elizabeth's policy and her symbolic order. Yet he is also resisting that order from within. He wrests *Amadis de Gaule* and romance in general from the French and uses them to work out his own ambivalence towards Elizabeth's rule.

Love can take on as paranoid and diabolical an aspect in the world of the *New Arcadia*, where social relations are defined in terms of vision, as it exhibits in the world of Elizabeth's court. Pamela, the elder princess, is guarded by the foul shepherd Dametas and his wife Miso, who stand in for Basilius and Gynecia. Miso claims that Cupid was fathered by Argus upon Io, and she describes him as he appeared in a picture she saw:

he had a paire of hornes like a Bull, his feete cloven, as many eyes upon his bodie, as my gray-mare hath dappels, & for all the world so placed. This monster sat like a hangman upon a paire of gallowes, in his right hand he was painted holding a crowne of Laurell, in his left hand a purse of mony, & out of his mouth honge a lace of two faire pictures, of a man & a woman, & such a countenance he shewed, as if he would perswade folks by those alurements to come thither & be hanged. (238)

This extraordinary emblem was Sidney's invention.[54] In an accompanying poem he stresses Cupid's Argus aspect:

> To open eyes all beauties he doth raine;
> Creeping to ech with flattering of desire.
>   But for that Loves desire most rules the eyes,
>   Therein his name, there his chiefe triumph lyes.
>   (240)

Sidney is parodying the traditional belief that beauty and love travel through the eyes. The locus classicus of this notion of "eye-liking" for Elizabethans was Hoby's translation of Castiglione's *Courtier*: "make the eyes the trustie messengers, that may carrie the ambassades of the heart. . . . For those lively spirits that issue out at the eyes, because they are engendred nigh the hart, entring in like case into the eyes that they are levelled at, like a shaft to the pricke, naturally pearce to the hart."[55] Sidney's use of the motif, here and throughout the frequent eye-play of the *Arcadia*, brings out its associations with, alternately, violence and diplomacy.

The two pictures that dangle from Cupid's mouth remind us of the part played by portraits in the diplomacy of dynastic courtship, as well as the alluring portrait that captured Pyrocles and the knights' paintings of their ladies in Phalantus's tournament. Book 8 of *Amadis de Gaule* describes how a Thracian giant infatuated with a cow begot a creature that was shaped like a bull from the waist down and like a horned man with four arms above.[56] Miso is hardly a reliable guide to the nature of love, but through her Sidney grafts a monstrous image of unnatural lust onto his pastoral and romantic narrative, and he may have resorted to a favorite text of the French marriage negotiators in doing so. "In his partly sought, partly enforced, pastoral retirement at his sister's estate at Wilton," Louis Montrose remarks, "Sidney wrote analytical pastorals . . . to cope imaginatively with necessities and to prepare for better times."[57] Given the interpenetration of court and country house life during the Elizabethan era, however, it is possible that Wilton provided Sidney with only an ironic distance from Whitehall. He had, at any rate, begun the *Arcadia* as early as 1577, working at it periodically throughout the thick of the Alençon affair; he began to revise his romance around 1582, when the duke, fighting for Elizabeth in the Netherlands, was by no means out of the picture. The *Arcadia* represents Sidney's parodic immersion in the scopic field of dynastic intrigue, not a pastoral alternative to life at court.[58]

In Ovid's *Metamorphoses*, Argus was set on Io after Juno transformed her into a cow to prevent her from coming once again to Jove's attention. Sidney's revision of the story, in which Argus raped his ward, suggests that sexual supervision can turn into the gaze of love or lust, and this is borne out in both the main action of the *Arcadia* and the inset story of Plangus, prince of Iberia. Pyrocles disguises himself as the Amazon Zelmane in order to approach Philoclea, and when he comes within range of her parents' over-curious eye, Basilius and Gynecia promptly fall in love with him. In the Plangus story, the King of Iberia discovers "by his spies (the necessarie evill servauntes to a King)" that his son is having an affair with the commoner Andromana. When he spies on Plangus and Andromana in the act, he falls in love with her himself and eventually marries her. The king and his state are soon governed entirely by his young queen, "A thing," Sidney quickly adds, with a glance at Elizabeth, "that may luckely fall out to him that hath the blessing, to match with some Heroicall minded Ladie" (278). But Andromana takes over her husband's necessary evil servants and uses them to discredit Plangus and delude the king about the true condition of his kingdom.

Basilius, another blind and foolish king, falls for Pyrocles because he cannot see through his disguise; as we are later told, he "was not the sharpest pearcer into masked minds" (324). But "the terrible wit of *Gynecia*, carried with the beere of violent love, runnes thorow us all" (94). Sidney repeatedly associates intellectual penetration with queenly figures at the expense of male characters, and this connection helps to explain the significance of male crossdressing in Sidney's two *Arcadias*. He appropriated this motif from *Amadis* to signal his adoption of a feminized and passive, if not pacifist, position while criticizing Elizabeth's prudentially scopophilic regime. Yet a certain paranoia in response to surveillance and the opacity of its objects overtakes this strategy in the *New Arcadia* and moves us beyond his intentions. This paranoia should be located not so much in any unconscious that Sidney may have possessed as in the political unconscious of Elizabeth's court, the product of what Elias calls the psychogenesis of social relationships at a particular time and place.[59]

Pyrocles's cross-dressing is directly related to the courtly suitor's consciousness of being watched and his desire to watch in turn. He gains some access to a world of feminine vision through his Amazon mask, which allows him to watch his true love disrobe before bathing (217). Musidorus remains a man and is not so fortunate in his pursuit of Philoclea's sister Pamela. She discovers his identity, but refuses for a while to give an outward show of her affection: "what did that helpe poore *Dorus*? whose eyes (being his diligent intelligencers) coulde carrie unto him no other newes, but discomfortable" (180). Castiglione's trusty messengers are not very effective here. Musidorus first comes across the transformed Pyrocles in a bower of trees "whose branches so lovingly interlaced one the other, that it could resist the strongest violence of eye-sight"; he does not recognize his friend until he hears his voice (76).

Gynecia's penetrating eyesight makes her the principal example of feminine power early in Sidney's story. "I perceive you know ful little," she tells Pyrocles, "how percing the eyes are of a true lover" (149). Kalander describes Gynecia as "a woman of great wit, and in truth of more princely vertues, then her husband: of most unspotted chastitie, but of so working a minde, and so vehement spirits . . . it was happie shee tooke a good course: for otherwise it would have beene terrible" (19–20). Her pursuit of Pyrocles almost turns her into another Andromana. She sees through his disguise and realizes that he has assumed it out of love for her daughter—"But if it be so, the life I have given thee (ungratefull *Philoclea*) I will sooner with these handes bereave thee of, then my birth shall glory, she hathe bereaved me of my desires" (146). Gynecia's jealousy explodes once again when she confronts Philoclea with Pyrocles after Miso, acting as her spy, informs her that the two are alone together (309–10).

It is significant that rebellion breaks out in Arcadia at this important erotic juncture, putting an end to further conflict between mother and daughter. The unrest, we soon learn, has been instigated by Cecropia, the wife of Basilius's dead brother. Cecropia is Andromana's counterpart in the main plot of the *New Arcadia*, and the ultimate focal point for the anxieties produced by eroticized politics and courtly surveillance in its pastoral world. She raises the identification of physical love with manipulative vision to an even higher power, claiming that "mans experience"—sexual experience of men—"is womans best eie-sight" (380). Her son Amphialus is obsessed with Philoclea, and when Cecropia captures the sisters she tries to force both of them to return his love; the imprisonment and torture of Philoclea and Pamela at her hands is a grotesque realization and displacement of Gynecia's jealousy.[60]

Earlier in the narrative, Cecropia's pet lion and she-bear escape and attack Philoclea and Pamela, who are saved, of course, by the princes. Gynecia correctly suspects that her sister-in-law set the animals loose on purpose, "mistrusting *Cecropia*, because shee had heard much of the divellish wickednesse of her heart, and that particularly she did her best to bring up her son *Amphialus* . . . to aspire to the crown, as next heire male" (125). The incident of the wild beasts, as Ronald Levao points out, was an unmotivated accident in the *Old Arcadia*; in the new version it is the stratagem of a malevolent female will that secretly controls much of the action.[61] Sidney's rewriting of the *Arcadia* resembles the "secondary revision" that Freud associates with both the dreamwork and paranoia, whereby an explanatory coherence is imposed upon the original content of dreams and delusions. In paranoia, such reconstructions involve the projection of internal perceptions into some external, persecuting power.[62]

This process of paranoid projection can be seen most clearly in the revisions made in the rebellion episode, which becomes an attempted coup in the *New Arcadia*. In the first version the revolt is ascribed to the influence of wine upon a country rout (*Old Arcadia* 126–27); in the revision Sidney transferred the passage describing its drunken origins from the narrator to the spy and rumormonger Clinias (*New Arcadia* 321–22). Similarly, when Pyrocles pacifies the mob in the *Old Arcadia*, the narrator comes in with a conventional exclamation on the fickleness of the people: "O weak trust of the many-headed multitude, whom inconstancy doth only guide at any time to well-doing! Let no man lay confidence there" (131). In the *New Arcadia* this passage appears in the same spot as if spoken by the narrator, but is then attributed to Clinias as he spies upon the proceedings: "So said a craftie fellow among them" (319). Clinias turns out to be Cecropia's instrument. He "oft had used to be an actor in Tragedies, where he had learned, besides a slidingnesse of language, acquaintance with many passions, and to frame his face to beare the figure of them . . . in nature, a most notable Coward, and yet more strangely then rarely venturous in privie practices" (319). Despite the narrator's repeated assurances of his cowardice, Clinias's theatrical skills make him a threatening figure.[63] As with Kalander's production of an intercepted letter whose advice was delivered verbally by Philanax in the *Old Arcadia*, the absorption of expository functions by characters engaged in some form of espionage renders the narrative less reliable. Yet it also suggests the affinity of prose fiction with narratives produced by information gathering and intrigue in the first place.[64]

The *Old Arcadia* ends with an investigation and trial in which Philanax is detective and chief prosecutor. He places Pyrocles and Musidorus under surveillance as suspects in the murder of Basilius, examining them separately and then together "with espial of their words and behavior, that way to sift out the more of these forepassed mischiefs" (318). In the unfinished *New Arcadia* this orderly if misdirected process is replaced by Cecropia's incarceration of Pyrocles and the sisters, and the wild physical and psychological torments to which she subjects them, together and apart. She terrorizes Philoclea and Pamela, "sometimes with noices of horror, sometimes with suddaine frightings in the night, when the solitary darkenesse thereof might easier astonish the disarmed senses" (*New Arcadia* 470). The sisters are then whipped and tortured by Cecropia, while Pyrocles, both dressed and addressed as the Amazon Zelmane throughout, is helpless to interfere. Pyrocles's strategic access to a feminized scopophilic power ends up imprisoning him in the revised narrative. Arcadia has become a land of confusion dominated by an evil queen figure who uses spectacle and misinformation as well as violence in pursuit of her ambitions.

At one point Cecropia encourages the smitten Amphialus to force himself upon Philoclea, and the headnote to the chapter describes this as "his mothers ghosty counsell to a rape" (*New Arcadia* 450, italics removed). Ghostly (here "ghosty") counsel or advice, usually administered by a "ghostly father," quickly became a sarcastic code word for Catholic spiritual guidance and the confessional during the second half of Elizabeth's reign. The term complements the equivocating arguments and inquisitorial prying to which Cecropia subjects the captured sisters; once she even eavesdrops at Pamela's door (382). Without being precisely an allegorical figure like Spenser's Duessa or Lucifera, Cecropia gives form to fears about England's invasion by Jesuits and secular priests, which increased during the years in which Sidney composed his revision.[65] She holds that religious opinions are bugbears invented by "great Clerkes" to keep the people in line and make them hear in the thunder "some angrie body above, that spake so lowde" (*New Arcadia* 406). Cecropia's deft control of spectacular effects and the fear they induce is thus a parody of divine power. She drives Philoclea, Pamela, and Pyrocles-Zelmane to distraction by simulating the execution of each sister before the eyes of the other and the disguised prince. These juggling tricks take place in the hall of Amphialus's castle, the ultimate Elizabethan gallery or court. This multilevel prison-theater reverses the principle of Bentham's panopticon: its inward-looking cells are ranged on several tiers facing a scaffold covered with crimson velvet, like a Catholic altar, and it is designed to induce awe or terror, not self-discipline (476–77).

With the Elizabethan Settlement in religion, the queen took over the comforting attributes of the church traditionally associated with the Virgin Mary. Cecropia alludes to a host of evil female figures—historical as well as symbolic—that were carefully differentiated from Elizabeth and set against her. Catherine de Médicis, reputed architect of the St. Bartholomew's Day massacre and the finagling of the first Alençon marriage project, was a prominent Catholic woman who occupied the opposite pole from Elizabeth in English minds throughout the 1570's and 1580's. Sidney, normally so restrained in his description of the Catholic side, called Catherine "that Jezabel of our age" in his letter to Elizabeth on the Alençon match.[66] But pride of place here should perhaps be given to Mary Stuart. The Scottish queen had been placed under arrest in England since her flight in 1568, but she remained the center of a series of conspiracies to depose Elizabeth and return both kingdoms to the Church of Rome. Like Cecropia during the early action of the *New Arcadia*, she seemed to hover nearby but out of sight, working her mischief from a succession of prison strongholds through spies and noble sympathizers. The Queen of Scots's very imprisonment within England made her the mirror image of Elizabeth, an excluded double with a claim to the throne. For Walsingham and his militant Protestant friends, she represented the incorporation of conspiracy into the realm, Jezebel or the Whore of Babylon indeed.

Yet if Cecropia, like the whorish Andromana, is related to popular female personifications of the supposedly atheistic Church of Rome, her talent for manipulation through surveillance and spectacle also realizes the anxieties of men like Sidney under Elizabeth's unpredictable and strong-minded rule. She captures the sisters by having a band of pastoral performers—women who say they want to rival Basilius's shepherds—lead them to a place of ambush in the forest. Her lion and bear had earlier been released into another clearing set aside for rustic sports. Cecropia's invasion of the eclogues represents the female appropriation of a largely masculine form of entertainment. In this they recapitulate the history of pastoral display under Elizabeth.[67]

Cecropia recalls the reverence in which the Arcadians used to hold her in words that might also be used to describe Elizabeth's power of self-display:

Their eyes admired my Majestie, & happy was he or she, on whom I would suffer the beames thereof to fall. Did I go to church, it seemed the very Gods wayted for me, their devotions not being solemnized till I was ready. Did I walke abroad to see any delight? Nay, my walking was the delight it selfe: for to it was the concourse; one thrusting upon another, who might shewe him selfe most diligeant and serviceable towardes me. (364)

The gaze, as Lacan would say, shows as well as looks; in Cecropia's world, display is a form of surveillance.[68] Since women have great social, if not precisely political, power at court, the high-ranking Cecropia dominated court society in Arcadia after her marriage to Basilius's brother and heir apparent.[69] Yet her authority was short-lived, for Basilius went on to marry Gynecia and beget the princesses. In England, there was no male ruler to reassert his authority over the court.

Sidney presents another court presided over by a woman ruler in his portrayal of Queen Helen of Corinth, a figure obviously inspired by Elizabeth. The Corinthian court, as Helen herself tells us, "swarmed full of suitors" (*New Arcadia* 66). She kept these lovers at arm's length, "using so straunge, and yet so well-succeeding a temper," as we read later, "that she made her people by peace, war-

like; her courtiers by sports, learned; her Ladies by Love, chast"
(283). Yet the use of courtly sports and romantic love to enforce
chastity has a darker aspect. Our only glimpse of Kalander's son
Clitophon after the opening chapters is as a spurned suitor of
Queen Helen who loses his round in defense of her beauty at Philantus's tournament of portraits; a frustrated and angry man, he refuses to pay his respects to King Basilius (108–9).

The tournament episode in general reveals the idolatry behind
Helen's chivalrous court and its cult of chastity. Philantus intends
it as a tribute to Cecropia's lady Artesia, but the proud Artesia
"called her disdaine of him chastitie, and placed her honour in little
setting by his honouring her" (98). Helen herself carries a portrait
with her—a likeness of Cecropia's son Amphialus, with whom she
is hopelessly in love, much to his ambitious mother's delight (67,
98). Helen and Cecropia are united in their devotion to Amphialus.
Immediately after Cecropia's death and Amphialus's suicide, Helen
arrives at their fortress—it is as if Sidney's stage could not hold
both of these contradictory yet oddly similar emblems of women's
rule at once. Instead of sympathizing with the plight of the tor-
mented Philoclea, Helen blames her, saying "your want of pityie,
where the fault onely was infinitenesse of desert, cannot be ex-
cused," and wishing that Amphialus had enlisted her to plead his
suit for him, as in fact Cecropia had done (497).

Like Gynecia before her, Helen is absorbed by the figure of Cecropia, whom Levao aptly calls "an Elizabethan's nightmare of a
willful female ruler."[70] Helen seems a praiseworthy character, yet
through her Sidney is paying elaborate compliment to a regime of
compulsory passivism and sexual control for which he harbored
ambivalent feelings at best. Elizabeth herself supervised dynastic
alliances within her court by acting out the conventional roles of
jealous woman and watchful mother, and Sidney had felt the royal
gaze upon his own politic marriage plans. During the diplomatic
mission in 1577, it was first rumored that a match between Sidney
and the sister of a powerful German prince was in the offing; then
William of Orange offered his daughter to the young diplomat.
But both projects fell through because of Elizabeth's disapproval.[71]
Sidney eventually married Walsingham's daughter Frances in 1583,
and the queen objected to this humbler union as well.[72] In 1579 the
Alençon business only increased the politically competitive and

eroticized atmosphere at court. While in London, Simier discovered through a pair of Catholic courtiers that Leicester was secretly
married to Lettice Knollys; he revealed the match to the queen,
who confined Alençon's chief opponent to a tower in Greenwich
Park, an incident that may have caused Sidney's mother to leave the
court.[73] Elizabeth's willingness to accept such information from a
French agent set her against her own courtiers. Helen of Corinth
was in danger of becoming Cecropia.

After breaking off the *New Arcadia*, and immediately before setting out on his fatal commission to the Netherlands in 1585, Sidney
sent a coded message to Elizabeth with a cover letter that reads in
part:

This rude peece of paper shall presume becaws of your Majesties commandement, most humbly to present such a cypher as little leysure coold
affoord me. If there come any matter to my knowledg the importance
whereof shall deserv to be so masked I will not fail . . . to your own handes
to recommend it. In the mean tyme I beseech yowr Majesty will vouchsafe
legibly to reed my hart in the cource of my life.[74]

Sidney's gift of encrypted information was a conventional bid for
the renewed patronage of a queen who hungered for news. A few
months later, however, Elizabeth was blaming him for his uncle
Leicester's acceptance of the absolute governorship that the Dutch
had offered him. In 1586 she "put on a very hard conceypt" toward
him, and attributed his attainment of an infantry colonelship to
self-promotion.[75] Sidney wrote to Walsingham: "I understand I am
called very ambitious and prowd at home, but certainly if thei
knew my ha[rt] thei woold not altogether so judg me."[76] His consciousness of being talked about at home and desire that his heart
might be read like the rude piece of paper he had offered Elizabeth
manifest the regulated paranoia of the Elizabethan royal servant.
Affections are not easily deciphered, as Walsingham had remarked
in another matter, and Sidney was doomed to be misconstrued by
his mistress.

Freud claims that persecutory paranoia is a defense against
overly powerful homosexual impulses, which often have their origin in a fixation upon the father. Daniel Paul Schreber, whose persecutory anxieties were accompanied by the belief that he was
being transformed into a woman by the divine rays of a solar god,

is the paradigmatic case of this mechanism—he sought to adopt a woman's body in order to render his desire for the father a heterosexual fantasy.[77] Lacan similarly associates the gaze with the father; in his reinterpretation of the Schreber case, he upholds the orthodox Freudian view against Ida Macalpine, who contends that homosexuality is a symptom of paranoia rather than its cause.[78]

Such explanations do not account for the paranoia of Elizabethan court society and its representations, although the analogy between Pyrocles's feigned and Schreber's fantasized transformations of gender suggests that psychoanalysis is right to pose the question of paranoia in terms of sexuality. As we will see in the next chapter, homosexual practices, although probably quite common, did not have to be repressed or defended against in the everyday life of people during the sixteenth century because same-sex love did not exist as a clearly defined category of sexual activity in early modern England.[79] Musidorus associates "effeminacy" not with homosexuality but with the love of women, and puts Pyrocles's crossdressing down to an intensified heterosexuality (78). This reflects Sidney's view that to participate in Elizabeth's court of love and sanction the French marriage was to give up the prospect of a military campaign against Catholicism on the Continent, and with it one's manhood. Elizabeth imposed a compulsory "heterosociality" upon the homosocial court that she inherited from her father, Henry VIII.[80] Having toyed with the idea of marriage in the first decades of her reign, only to deny its necessity for herself, she regulated matches among her courtiers while making their status dependent upon their paying court to her as well. This reminded Francis Bacon of "the accounts we find in romances, of the Queen of the Blessed islands, and her court and institutions, who allows of amorous admiration but prohibits desire."[81] Philip Sidney constructed a more disturbing relationship, in fact a paranoid one, between sovereign surveillance and heterosocial romance.

According to Alice Jardine, paranoia is best defined as the reinforcement of sexual difference, just as hysteria is the confusion of its boundaries.[82] Homosexuality is neither a symptom nor a cause of paranoia; rather, it is an engagement with the cause of paranoia in the way modernity organizes sexuality and gender. Departing from Freud and Lacan, Jardine analyzes male paranoia, and the Schreber case in particular, less as a defense against homosex-

uality than as a response to the "woman who *knows*," "whether in
the European transition from the Middle Ages to the Renaissance,"
she goes on, "or, more visibly, in the nineteenth and twentieth centuries."[83] Under certain dispositions of sexuality it is not the father
but the mother who provokes feelings of frustrated love, perse-
cution, and surveillance.

Queen Elizabeth was a remarkable example of an authoritative
and knowing woman who produced a deep ambivalence in the
courtiers who surrounded her. Their feelings indicate not so much
an increase in social constraint as a change in the forms it assumed.
Elizabeth's reign witnessed the gradual transformation of the reciprocal scrutiny customary among courtiers into a competition to
provide the sovereign with all sorts of information. At the same
time, mutual observation lent itself to the deliberate supervision of
courtly manners from above. The anxieties that these alterations
generated accompanied a growing awareness of infiltration from
beyond England's borders, whether this intrusion manifested itself
as Simier, the French negotiators at the tennis court, or Catholic
priests from Douai and Rheims. Sidney's *New Arcadia* translates
this unease into the world of pastoral romance, where it gathers
itself into the monstrous and contradictory shape of Cecropia, the
would-be mistress of man's experience. Seen from outside the
court, however, the culture of courtly surveillance displayed a
somewhat different aspect. Its paranoia and sexual anxiety assumed
other guises in the drama of Christopher Marlowe—playwright,
reputed lover of boys, and probable spy.

CHAPTER 3

Marlowe and the Observation
of Men

AN episode in Thomas Nashe's *Unfortunate Traveller* (1594) caricatures the romantic rituals of Sidney's *Arcadia*. In defense of his lady Geraldine's supreme beauty, the earl of Surrey, ostensible hero of Nashe's historical fiction, enters the tiltyard costumed like an Arcadian knight who has allowed his invention to range a bit too freely. His armor resembles an unweeded garden and his helmet looks like a watering can; the drops that sprinkle from it nourish nettles along with flowers, just as his tears increase both his mistress's disdain and her fame. Surrey's mount is disguised as an ostrich, complete with wings that have crystal eyes on their pinions, inset with sharp diamonds, "as rayes from those eyes deriued, that like the rowell of a spur ran deep into his horses sides, and made him more eager in his course." The motto is: "I spread my wings onely spurd with her eyes."[1] The eye motif comes up again in Surrey's tournament of perfect beauty, adding some retrospective point to this device. There is a knight "who, being a person of suspected religion, was continually haunted with intellygencers and spies that thought to praie vpon him for that he had. . . . To obscure this, he vsed no other fansie but a number of blinde flyes, whose eyes the colde had closed." His device reads "Gold is the onley phisicke for the eiesight" (277). Despite the Florentine setting, these spies recall the pursuivants and Catholic-hunters of England, who were permitted to plunder their victims' goods. Nashe, who seems to have sympathized with Catholicism, is probably extending his veiled satire to the queen's surveillance of recusants, some of whom had fled England spurred with Elizabeth's eyes.[2]

The episode parodies Sidney by relating the exalted world of courtly display directly to the underworld of intelligencers and their unwanted "eyesight." The commonest spy, as Nashe's Jack Wilton observed, "must be familiar with all and trust none, drinke, carouse, and lecher with him out of whom he hopes to wring any matter, sweare and forsweare, rather than be suspected, and, in a word, haue the Arte of dissembling at his fingers ends as perfect as any Courtier."[3] Though at opposite ends of the social scale, the spy and the courtier employ the same strategy of simulation and dissimulation, as Bacon would call it. Sexuality forms part of the intelligencer's tactics as well as the courtier's; later, Jonson would link the two figures in Captain Hungry and the "yong States-men" who lie with him to get information.[4] The relation between knowledge and the body is more immediate for the common spy than for the chivalric performer, however, as Jack's ambiguous injunction that one must "lecher with" one's victims suggests.

Nashe's friend Christopher Marlowe can be viewed as Sidney's mirror image in the underworld of intelligencers, a writer situated at the margins of court society and its sexual anxieties rather than its center. Francis Meres claimed that *"Marlow* was stabbed to death by a bawdy Seruingman, a riuall of his in his lewde loue."[5] An inaccurate account of Marlowe's murder, Meres's statement is nevertheless a vestige of the contemporary gossip that associated an excessive sexuality with Marlowe and his way of life. In a careful reading of the spy Richard Baines's so-called "libel" or report on Marlowe's Catholic-leaning atheism, Jonathan Goldberg argues that accusations of sexual transgression, charges of blasphemy, and intimations of treason are signs of the "counteridentity" that Elizabethan society conferred upon Marlowe. A spy himself, Marlowe was allowed to enter an alternative realm of subversion otherwise inaccessible to those in authority. "The Baines libel," Goldberg explains, "records the *double agency* of society, creating the Other as it creates itself."[6] A Machiavellian attitude toward religion and royal authority coincided with the homosexuality imputed to Marlowe in the Baines document. Furthermore, as we shall see, Marlowe himself attempted to realize this self-construction through the characters he created within the licensed transgression of the stage.

Yet Marlowe was also negotiating his identity with Elizabethan society through the dispersed mechanism of the patronage system, the collective medium of the theater, and the often violent world of London's urban subculture. In a sense, all accounts of Marlowe's life, including the one that I have assembled below, are traces of his failed attempt to fashion himself as the intimate servant of the great. The ruins of this self-construction can be seen in plays like *Doctor Faustus*, *Edward II*, and *The Massacre at Paris*, where Marlowe described the combination of politics and sexuality at court as an outside observer, a servant of the servants of the prince.

Marlowe's career as a spy resembled in some ways that of Maliverny Catlyn, one of Walsingham's principal agents, though Marlowe did not share Catlyn's Protestant aversion to the theater. (The Catholics, Catlyn told Walsingham sometime in 1586–87, welcomed stage plays as a distraction from the Gospels: "when the bells toll to the lectors, the trumpets sound to the stages, whereat the wicked faction of Rome laugheth for joy."") Religious fervor may have joined with the need for ready cash to impel Catlyn, a soldier and something of a scholar, to become a spy, but he must have been a good actor himself. He had fought in the Netherlands, where he may already have been employed in spying of some sort. After a dispute with his commander, Catlyn fled to Rouen, and in 1586 he wrote to Walsingham offering his services as someone who had infiltrated English Catholic circles in France. Next he was placed in jail, first at Portsmouth and then, by his own request, in the Marshalsea, to spy on imprisoned priests and find out about future invasion plans. After Catlyn's release, Walsingham sent him among the Catholics of the northern counties at least twice; back in London, Catlyn claimed to have gained the confidence of a suspect nobleman before disappearing for good (Read 2. 327–30).

Like Catlyn, Marlowe was an educated man who seems to have been employed in France and the Low Countries, after which he returned to England, more than likely as a prisoner. He had already spent two weeks in Newgate in 1587 after a street brawl in which the poet Thomas Watson stepped in to kill his opponent. Marlowe "had thus an excellent opportunity of becoming acquainted with the prisoners," as Mark Eccles puts it, and it may have been at this time that he met "one Poole a prisoner in Newgate" who taught him how to counterfeit.[8] Marlowe probably had other prison experiences as well. In May 1593 the Privy Council had him arrested; he was released, but was killed in a fight a few weeks later. Catlyn had gone on to become one of Walsingham's better agents in England, but Marlowe somehow fell prey to the intelligence apparatus he had served on the Continent.

A clearer pattern emerges when the case histories of Catlyn and Marlowe are compared with those of other spies that Conyers Read and Lawrence Stone have documented. According to Stone, the typical intelligencer began as a stool pigeon. Thrown into prison, "the unfortunate would insensibly drift into offering himself as a spy. Cleared of his debts and given money for his journey, he would set out boldly on his travels to the enemy country." Where a journey to the Continent was involved, the agent would often be imprisoned by a Catholic power, "turned," and dispatched to England as the agent of a new master.[9] Walsingham avoided sending Catlyn back to Europe altogether; Marlowe seems never to have lost the taint, whether fact or rumor, of the early association of his name with Rheims, the site of a notorious Catholic seminary.[10]

This association cropped up in March 1587, when the Privy Council itself demanded that Cambridge grant him his M.A. degree despite the report that "Christopher Morley was determined to have gone beyond the seas to Reames [Rheims] and there to remaine." Although he had often been absent from Cambridge, the Council assured the university that Marlowe "had behaued him selfe orderlie and discreetlie wherebie he had done her majestie good service, and deserued to be awarded for his faithful dealing." Hearsay about his papist leanings should be put to rest "because it was not her majestie's pleasure that anie one emploied as he had been in matters touching the benefitt of his Countrie should be defamed by those that are ignorant in th'affaires he went about."[11] Marlowe was awarded his M.A. by the following September.

There is evidence that Marlowe continued in government service abroad after the controversy over his degree. In October 1587 a "Mr. Morley" is mentioned as one of Burghley's messengers in Utrecht, and "Mr. Marlin" evidently served the English envoy to Henri of Navarre in a similar capacity during part of 1591–92. In March 1592 one "Marlin" was employed as a courier between besieged Rouen and Dieppe, and then sent on to Robert Cecil in London.[12] If Marlowe was employed in some or all of these European missions, it is easy to see why he continued to be suspected of crypto-Catholicism by those who were ignorant of the affairs he went about, and perhaps by some who weren't. The most interesting, and most certain, escapade involved his only recorded encounter with Richard Baines, the spy who after Marlowe's murder submitted the report on his supposed beliefs. January 1592 found Baines and "Christofer Marly" in the custody of Sir Robert Sidney, who had succeeded his brother Philip as the commander of Flushing. We have Sidney's letter to Burghley describing the case: Marlowe and a goldsmith had been picked up for trying to counterfeit Dutch shillings after Baines, who shared lodgings with them, reported the plan to Sir Robert. Baines and Marlowe promptly accused each other of intending "to goe to the Ennemy or to Rome."[13] The Baines libel states that Marlowe claimed to have as good a right to coin as the queen, and that he knew a prisoner in Newgate who had taught him how to exercise this right.[14] The counterfeiting charge seems to have been scored from the original document, but it was not out of place: according to Mark Eccles, Elizabethan authorities "as a matter of course examined prisoners at the same time on coining and religion."[15] Marlowe was sent back to London by Sidney. But during the following March he may have been employed on the Continent again and then sent home with a message for Cecil. In May 1592 "Christofer Marle" was bound over by a pair of Shoreditch constables.[16]

If Marlowe was the Morley and Marlin mentioned above, he evidently did much of his work for Burghley and his son Robert Cecil rather than for Walsingham, even though he was also patronized by Thomas Walsingham, Sir Francis's relative and sometime agent.[17] Robert Sidney had written to Burghley, and Burghley may have interceded for his prisoner, just as the Council had intervened to get Marlowe his M.A. Unfortunately, Marlowe remained unlucky in his choice of roommates. When Thomas Kyd was arrested early in May 1593 on suspicion of circulating libels against the state, he probably offered to turn queen's evidence against the man with whom he had lived for a while a few years earlier.[18] Kyd was found in possession of a manuscript copy of a book called *The Fall of the Late Arian* that was deemed to contain heretical material. After Marlowe's death, Kyd wrote two letters to the lord keeper. In the first he claimed that the book was Marlowe's, and that their papers had become mixed together when they shared chambers; the second letter accuses his former acquaintance in some detail of mocking the Scriptures.[19] It is possible that Kyd had already denounced him under interrogation, leading to Marlowe's own arrest on May 20 at Thomas Walsingham's house near Greenwich by order of the Privy Council.

Despite the gravity of such charges, Marlowe must once more have been granted an early release, for at the end of May we find him in Deptford, a short distance away. The circumstances of his murder there by Ingram Friser have inspired several attempts to explain the killing as a political assassination.[20] Nicholas Skeres and the notorious Robert Poley were present at the death; although both spied on the Babington conspirators, Poley had been an agent of Francis Walsingham and remained associated with the Cecils, and Skeres was connected with Robert Devereux, earl of Essex.[21] In the early 1590's Essex was trying to establish secret contacts with James VI of Scotland as the most likely successor to the English throne; in his second letter to the lord keeper, Kyd later claimed that Marlowe had also been planning to go over to James, as his friend Matthew Roydon had done.[22] Essex and Robert Cecil were building rival espionage networks during these years; in some obscure way Marlowe may have been a minor casualty in the struggle for Elizabeth's intelligence patronage in the wake of Francis Walsingham's death in 1590.[23]

Doctor Faustus, a text that probably dates from Marlowe's later years, traces the course of his career from university man to spy. Scholars, with their command of languages and international contacts, often engaged in espionage during the Renaissance, as the dual careers of Guillaume Pellicier, Nicholas Wotton, and Thomas Randolph attest.[24] In *Faustus*, magic—another secretive activity that similarly involves hidden knowledge and cryptic writings— stands for both scholarship and spying. Faustus links sorcery to his previous studies through their common use of writing ("Lines, circles, sceanes, letters and characters"), and Mephostophilis gives him magic books, translating their lessons into theatrical spectacle: "The framing of this circle on the ground, / Brings whirlewindes, tempestes, thunder and lightening."[25] Yet Faustus aspires to command more than the elements. He would have the spirits "tell the secrets of all forraine kings" as well as read him strange philosophy (1. 18–19). When Mephostophilis takes him to the pope's private chamber, Faustus realizes the intelligencer's fantasy of becoming "inuisible, to do what I please unseene of any whilst I stay in Rome" (7. 875).

Earlier in the play he parades his geopolitical ambitions:

> Ile be great Emperour of the world,
> And make a bridge through the moouing ayre,
> To passe the *Ocean* with a band of men,
> Ile joyne the hils that binde the *Affricke* shore,
> And make that land continent to *Spaine*,
> And both contributory to my crowne:
> The emperour shal not liue but by my leaue,
> Nor any Potentate of *Germany*.   (3. 349–56)

Yet when he arrives at the Emperor Carolus's palace after his Italian adventures, Faustus becomes as sycophantic as a wandering scholar or mountebank looking for a handout. He presents the narcissistic emperor with an image of his putative ancestor Alexander the Great, and with Alexander's beautiful paramour; both, he explains, are devils in disguise (10. 1086–89). "Ifaith thats as true as *Diana* turnd me to a stag" (10. 1095), a jealous knight interjects. The antlers that Faustus fixes upon the knight's head indicate that he has supplanted him in Carolus's affections, politically cuckolding him. Faustus punishes his rival to please his patron the emperor, not to revenge a slight to his honor as an aristocrat would have done (10. 1125–29). Traditional feudal obligations have been defeated by clientage. But Faustus has become little more than an erotic entertainer at court, not unlike Gaveston, another one of Marlowe's upstarts, who as we shall see plans a sensual masque of Actaeon at the start of *Edward II*.

The oddest thing about the Faust legend is the way its protagonist fails to gain real power through the magic placed at his disposal for 24 years. Faustus's decline stands out in sharp relief in Marlowe's version, partly because his early ambitions are pitched so high in the play. His voluntary subjection to the emperor echoes his prior bond with Lucifer, and confirms its political character. The deal with the devil is a hybrid of feudal, commercial, and patronage relationships. Mephostophilis's "service" is bought with Faustus's soul, although at the end of his life he will become Lucifer's servant (5. 471–87). The overtones of patronage and clientage here are brought out by the previous scene in which his servant Wagner hires Robin. Robin is bound for seven years, and Wagner observes that the boy is so hungry he would sell his soul for a shoulder of "blood rawe" mutton (4. 371). He threatens to "turne al the lice about thee into familiars, and they shal teare thee in peeces" (4. 386–87). Faustus signs his deed of gift in blood, and faces the threat of dismemberment throughout the play should he violate it. Dismemberment is a feudal punishment, a sign of the lord's power over the body of the serf. It is not surprising that Marlowe's Faustus should substitute the emperor's approval for world dominion, becoming a flatterer, court entertainer, and (in the horse-courser scene) a trivial local trickster given to guilty ramblings. Magic, like espionage, authorship, and scholarship, remains trammeled in the class and patronage systems.

In *Faustus*, Marlowe partly adopted, partly created, a transgressive identity that was of a piece with his reputation as a sojourner on the outer fringes of court society. One of the items in the Baines report records "That on[e] Ric Cholmley hath Confessed that he was purswaded by Marloe's Reasons to become an Atheist."[26] Richard Cholmley had been employed by the Privy Council to spy out Catholics, but someone informed on him in turn, claiming that he led a band of 60 atheists who intended to set up their own king after Elizabeth's death, and in the meantime planned to expose the atheism of her ministers. Cholmley was arrested on these charges soon after Marlowe's death. A separate "remembrance" claims "That he saieth & verely beleveth that one Marlowe is able to showe more sounde reasons for Atheisme then any devine in Englande is able to geve to prove devinitie & that Marloe tolde him that hee hath read the Atheist lecture to Sr walter Ralegh & others."[27] Given Cholmley's supposed scheme to accuse prominent men of atheism, his linking of Ralegh's name with Marlowe's may not be particularly reliable. But there are other, more circumstantial, points of contact between the two figures. Ralegh famously replied to Marlowe's poem "The Passionate Shepherd to His Love," which he may have seen in manuscript. Known for his interest in an experimental natural history, he was rumored to be skeptical in matters of religion. The Jesuit Robert Parsons wrote that Ralegh headed a "school" of atheism and necromancy frequented by noble youths, and in 1594 his unorthodox views were investigated by a local commission near his country house in Dorset.[28]

It is true that Ralegh patronized scientists and mathematicians like Thomas Harriot and Walter Warner, as well as the writers Matthew Roydon, an old friend of Marlowe, and George Chapman, who completed *Hero and Leander*. Roydon, Harriot, and Warner are all mentioned as companions of Marlowe in Kyd's first letter. Kyd also told the lord keeper that his former chambermate believed "that things esteemed to be donn by devine power might haue aswell been don by observation of men."[29] A dramatist-spy like Marlowe knew that the observation of men and manners made their manipulation through spectacle possible; the scientific observations of Ralegh's circle created seeming miracles in another way. According to Baines, Marlowe "affirmeth that Moyses was but a Jugler and that one Heriots being Sir W Raleigh's man Can do more then he." Baines attributed to Marlowe the opinion that the sacrament "would haue bin much better being administered in a Tobacco pipe"; Ralegh was erroneously supposed to have brought tobacco to England from America, and its enthusiastic use among members of his circle was well known.[30]

Marlowe was also supposed to have maintained "That all they that loue not Tobacco and Boies were fooles." He said that St. John was Christ's bedfellow, and "that he used him as the sinners of Sodoma."[31] Kyd corroborated this allegation: "He would report St John to be our saviour Christes Alexis I cover it with reverence and trembling that is that Christ did loue him with an extraordinary loue."[32] Taken together, the accusations of Kyd and Baines suggest that the company of poets, scientists, and spies kept by the Marlowe of the London years constituted an urban subculture in which religious skepticism, a natural history that veered toward the occult, and homosexuality were all involved.

Yet Alan Bray has usefully questioned the applicability of the term "homosexuality," a clinical category from the late nineteenth century, to the early modern period. According to Bray, what we would now call homosexual practices may have been, in fact probably were, quite common, but they usually passed unrecognized as such by society at large, and even by the men who participated in them. Intimate sleeping arrangements were common at all levels in the Renaissance household. The laborer Meredith Davy's sexual relations with the boy he was sleeping with were eventually caught out by a third chambermate and reported to a magistrate, but Davy swore that he had no idea he was a sodomite and was allowed by the court and his employer to continue sharing the boy's bed.[33] "Sodomy" was the name for a terrible force outside the order of creation that could nevertheless erupt in everyone, a threat associated with Satan, witchcraft, and the Roman Catholic church.[34]

Most recent studies agree that a male homosexual subculture, with its own codes of behavior and mutual recognition, did not exist in England toward the end of the sixteenth century.[35] Yet if homosexual practice did not form the basis of a subculture in Renaissance England, it was nevertheless part of the "surculture" of aristocratic patronage that also produced the developing mechanisms of espionage and surveillance. I am coining this term to designate those overarching social practices that are at once "above" the threshold of visibility, and yet too large to be seen in full by their participants, too taken for granted. Patronage among aristocrats, and between aristocrats and their less well born clients, was the crown of such a surculture in sixteenth-century England. In a discussion of "paederastice" in Edmund Spenser's *Shepheardes Calander* and his "familiar letters" to Gabriel Harvey, Goldberg has demonstrated that male homosexual practice was fleetingly exposed when it was understood as a sign of subordination within the patronage relationship, and then only upon the moment when this relationship came to an end.[36] As "sodomy," it threatened society from without, or from deep within, but as "pederasty" it paradoxically served as the barely visible mortar that held the social framework together at its surface.[37]

Baines's implication that Marlowe was a lover of boys made him doubly subversive, then—not only was Baines's Marlowe a sodomite, but as a sodomite he assumed the dominant position within his relationships, thus usurping and parodying the role of patron. Yet Marlowe had already trumped such an imposed "counter-identity" by uniting patronage and sodomy in the person of the sovereign. In *Edward II* he explores the pattern of all patronage relationships in early modern England—that between the sovereign and the sovereign's favorite. Marlowe's own patron Ralegh was either Elizabeth's current favorite while the play was being written, or had just fallen out of her good graces because of his secret marriage to Elizabeth Throckmorton.[38] *Edward II* both underwrites the political erotics of Elizabeth's court examined above and criticizes its compulsory heterosociality by imagining a male monarch, courted by male suitors, and threatened by over-mighty male subjects. In doing so, it once again both conceals and reveals the paradoxical link between patronage and homoeroticism as subversive practice and social bond.

The parallel between Edward and Elizabeth is established in the soliloquy by Piers Gaveston that opens the play, where he proclaims: "The sight of *London* to my exiled eyes, / Is as *Elizium* to a new come soule."[39] Edward, like Elizabeth, is fond of courtly entertainments (I. 1. 54–56), and he tries to contain aristocratic resistance to his rule through a chivalric tournament. But the barons plan to bear emblems to the joust that attack Gaveston as an ambitious flatterer, comparing him to a flying fish or, in the younger Mortimer's device, a canker that creeps up a lofty cedar tree (II. 2. 16–18).[40] Edward's tenuous court society soon dissolves into concealed conspiracy, then open rebellion because of the barons' jealousy of his favorite, Gaveston. The new regime of Mortimer and Isabella, Edward's rejected queen, fails to control the unstable relationship between sexuality and power.

The shift from stability to antagonism, and from courtly display to secret observation, is foreshadowed in the first 100 lines or so of the text. First we witness the undermining of feudal bonds by patronage and the unstable relationships it fosters. Gaveston enters reading the letter from the newly crowned Edward that has summoned him back from exile in France. Subsequent events, like Gaveston's banishment, his recall, and Edward's murder, will be accompanied by less intimate documents and messages; sovereignty and its abuse are construed in terms of writing throughout this play.[41] The king's personal letter is a sign of Gaveston's new power. He will base his prestige solely upon physical proximity to Edward, rather than on the existing system of competition and compromise with the monarch's more aristocratic followers. "Farewell base stooping to the lordly peeres," he resolves, "My knee shall bowe to none but to the king" (I. 1. 18–19). Three "poor men" then enter and pay suit to the reinstated favorite, who mocks them but determines to "flatter these, and make them live in hope" (I. 1. 43). This piece of business again shows the audience Gaveston's position in the chain of royal patronage. He will serve as a self-interested intermediary between commoners and king, circumventing the feudal power of the magnates.

And yet, he concludes, "these are not men for me." Edward delights in display, in comedies and Italian masques, so Gaveston wants poets, musicians, and dancers for followers, men who "with touching of a string / May draw the pliant king which way I please" (I. 1. 49–53). The court itself is transformed into such a "pleasing show" in Gaveston's plans, for he next imagines Edward walking abroad and happening upon a scene suddenly populated by his favorite's men. Gaveston's pages will dress like nymphs, while his satyrs "graze" upon the lawn and dance an antic hay. Courtly display becomes identical with the display of the male body, as indeed it often was at Elizabeth's court. But here the sovereign's gaze is a homoerotic one, although it is constructed through a cross-dressing masquerade that simultaneously cancels and affirms heterosexual desire:

> Sometime a lovelie boye in *Dians* shape,
> With haire that gilds the water as it glides,
> Crownets of pearle about his naked armes,
> And in his sportfull hands an Olive tree,
> To hide those parts which men delight to see,
> Shall bathe him in a spring, and there hard by,
> One like *Actaeon* peeping through the grove,
> Shall by the angrie goddesse be transformde,
> And running in the likenes of an Hart,
> By yelping hounds puld downe, and seeme to die.
>
> (I. 1. 61–70)

Gaveston's fantasy about the observation of men resolves itself into a well-known emblem of the dangers that access to the sovereign's person and its secrets can bring, and immediately after the Actaeon set piece, we see how precarious Gaveston's position actually is.[42] Edward enters, pursued by the angry barons, the hounds who will eventually pull both the king and his darling down. Gaveston withdraws from his contemplation of erotic display to spy upon the argument, making comments upon the scene like a spectator in the theater. The movement from display to surveillance in the opening scene of *Edward II* informs the ensuing action. No sooner is Gav-

eston apprehended and killed than Edward adopts his more devious client, Hugh Spenser, in his stead (III. 1. 144).

When the feudal hierarchy is replaced by the exercise of royal
patronage it formerly tolerated and contained, the duplicity that
underlies all social bonds in court society is given free rein, and espionage becomes the prime way of dealing with these new political
relations. To some extent, Edward's relationship with his new favorite Spenser parodies his old love with Gaveston, yet there is little question of there having been any originary honesty in the earlier bond—Spenser's machinations retrospectively reveal the policy that lay behind Gaveston's rhetoric. Still, policy and affection
were more closely entwined for Gaveston than his successor, and
only after Gaveston's fall does it become possible to speak of honesty and dishonesty in royal clientage. When we first see Spenser,
he is a hanger-on in the household of the recently deceased duke of
Gloucester, whose title he will one day be granted. Spenser, who
is depicted as something of a university wit (see IV. 7. 16–19), is
asked by Baldock, his scholarly sidekick, which noble patron he
will now follow. "Not *Mortimer*, nor any of his side," he replies,
"Because the king and he are enemies" (II. 1. 4–5). Gaveston,
newly created "the liberall earle of *Cornewall*," is his man, Spenser
discloses, and he means to become not his "follower" but his
"companion," "for he loves me well, / And would have once pre-
ferd me to the king" (II. 1. 13–14). There is little of the spurned
lover in Spenser, however. Gaveston has been newly exiled, but

> A friend of mine told me in secrecie,
> That hees repeald, and sent for back againe,
> And even now, a poast came from the court,
> With letters to our ladie from the King,
> And as she red, she smild, which makes me thinke,
> It is about her lover *Gaveston*.   (II. 1. 17–22)

The lady here is the daughter of the dead duke of Gloucester,
whom Edward intends that Gaveston should marry.

Spenser already has at least one informant at court, and he is
clearly an adept at the courtly art of human observation, able to
read in his mistress's looks the news of her betrothed's return. He
also is an adept at "turning" others' spies. After Gaveston's death,
Spenser seeks to please Edward by employing Levune, Queen Is-

abella's spy in the French court, against the queen herself (III. 1. 60–65). Isabella escapes to the Continent with plans to invade England and place the young prince on the throne, but Levune successfully bribes the French not to aid her, and reports back her resort to Flanders in a message that Spenser reads aloud to Edward (III. 1. 262–71; IV. 1. 28–36). Marlowe may have served as a messenger between France and England during or shortly after the composition of *Edward II* sometime in 1591–92. The relics of his self-construction in the play are found in the scholar Baldock, in the agent Levune, and in Gaveston, the would-be homoerotic masquer of the first scene, but they may be seen in the ambitious Spenser as well.

With Spenser, a heightened sense of deceit and dissimulation enters the drama. "*Balduck*, you must cast the scholler off," he tells his friend,

> And learne to court it like a Gentleman,
> Tis not a black coate and a little band,
>
> . . . .
>
> Can get you any favour with great men.
> You must be proud, bold, pleasant, resolute,
> And now and then, stab as occasion serves.
>
> (II. 1. 31–33, 41–43)

Baldock assures Spenser that he is ready to follow this code of pretense and self-concealment; despite his "curate-like" attire, he is "inwardly licentious enough, / And apt for any kinde of villanie" (II. 1. 50–51). As the new favorite, Spenser appropriates the courtly conventions that Edward and Gaveston followed, taking up one of the mythological allusions that characterized their discourse. He tells Levune to bribe the French, so that "all enchaunted like the guarde, / That suffered *Jove* to passe in showers of golde / To *Danae*," they will refuse to help Queen Isabella (III. 1. 266–68). Edward had once greeted Gaveston by comparing himself to the lovers of Danaë who "Desirde her more, and waxt outragious" when she was confined in the brazen tower (II. 2. 52–56). Edward's figure of desire has become Spenser's Machiavellian conceit. The discourse of transgressive sexuality is re-absorbed opportunistically into quotidian politics as soon as its deeper function in court society is glimpsed.

Throughout *Edward II*, the homoerotic desire that cements social bonds between men is at once revealed and concealed, and the neoclassical parallels that pepper courtly language in the play aid this paradoxical effect. When Gaveston imagines himself as Leander and Edward, implicitly, as Hero, in the soliloquy that begins the action, there is no lascivious Neptune to intercept his channel crossing as there is in Marlowe's contemporary poem. Even Edward's comparison of himself to Hercules and Gaveston to Hilas, it could be argued, functions as a reference to an earlier and alien realm of sexual possibility remote from present realities.[43] Old Mortimer apologizes for Edward's relationship with Gaveston through classical examples that justify the homoerotics of power and knowledge. "The mightiest kings have had their minions," he says, "Great *Alexander* lovde *Ephestion* . . . And for *Patroclus* sterne *Achilis* droopt" (I. 4. 391–94). More examples follow, yet all this is seemingly beside the point. "Unckle, his wanton humor greeves not me," the younger Mortimer replies, "But this I scorne, that one so baselie borne, / Should by his soveraignes favour grow so pert" (I. 4. 402–4). Young Mortimer's complaint is repeated several times elsewhere in the play. The barons read Edward's relationship with his minion principally as an extension of the patronage system beyond the feudal hierarchy of mutual obligation that has heretofore contained it.

Yet young Mortimer himself sees more of a sexual threat in Gaveston than his initial response to his uncle lets on. As his choler builds, he dwells on the minion's appearance:

> I have not seene a dapper jack so briske,
> He weares a short Italian hooded cloake,
> Larded with pearle, and in his tuskan cap
> A jewell of more value then the crowne.
>
> (I. 4. 412–15)

This virtual blazon is followed by the complaint that Gaveston and the king "From out a window, laugh at such as we . . . and jest at our attire. / Unkle, tis this that makes me impatient" (I. 4. 17–19). Mortimer's paranoia under such observation, and his own close observation of Gaveston, reveals a confused perception of the dangers that homosexuality poses to the homosocial world of the feudal court, where king and nobles should "love" one another according to their rank. (See I. 1. 80, 100.)

One character who does seem to understand the erotics of

power is the spurned queen. She calls Gaveston "a bawd to his affections" before Edward (I. 4. 151), and tells the clueless peers of her husband's displays of devotion to him: "He claps his cheekes, / and hanges about his neck, / Smiles in his face, and whispers in his eares" (I. 2. 51–52). Old Mortimer, seemingly uncomprehending, can only reply "Is it not straunge, that he is thus bewitcht?" (I. 2. 55). When Isabella addresses the troops before the final battle (a rare example of overreaching rhetoric from a woman in Marlowe), she apostrophizes her husband as a king

> Whose loosnes hath betrayed thy land to spoyle,
> And made the channels overflow with blood,
> Of thine own people patron shouldst thou be
> But thou—   (IV. 4. 11–14)

She is cut off, typically, by a condescending remark from young Mortimer, who has become her lover. Mortimer may well feel that any reference to kings' patronizing their people, rather than sustaining their nobles, will merely perpetuate the threat that Gaveston and Spenser have posed. His subsequent speech to the soldiers emphasizes "All homage, fealtie, and forwardnes" to the prince, a return to feudal categories that also allows him to speak for Isabella, "That *Englands* queene in peace may reposesse / Her dignities and honors" (IV. 4. 20, 24–25). Yet Mortimer himself eventually turns to the practice of patronage, if not its public display, to consolidate the power he derives from his erotic link to the queen he claims to represent.

It is Isabella who comes up with the governing mythological symbol for the mutual involvement of patronage and physical love between men:

> Like frantick *Juno* will I fill the earth,
> With gastlie murmure of my sighes and cries,
> For never doted *Jove* on *Ganimed*,
> So much as he on cursed *Gaveston*.
>   (I. 4. 178–81)

Her allusion to Jupiter's cupbearer recalls the opening scene of Marlowe's *Dido, Queen of Carthage*, a play that can be related to *Edward II* through the figure of Ganymede in other ways.[44] "Come gentle *Ganimed* and play with me," Marlowe's Jupiter begins, "I love thee well, say *Juno* what she will" (I. 1. 1–2). Ganymede replies by complaining that Juno struck him for spilling the wine that day, and Jove resolves to hang her between heaven and earth again should she repeat the offense. Gaveston likewise sets himself up against the queen, informing Edward of her affection for Morti-mer (I. 4. 147–48). Marlowe's Ganymede, though dandled on Ju-piter's knee like a child, is very much the courtly gallant in Gav-eston's style. "I would have a jewell for mine eare, / And a fine brouch to put in my hat," he demands, "And then Ile hugge with you an hundred times" (I. 1. 46–48). At this point, Venus enters and upbraids her father for "playing with that female wanton boy, / Whiles my *Aeneas* wanders on the Seas" (I. 1. 51–52). Although they are defined against one another here, there is also an odd par-allel between Venus's "sweet boy" and Jupiter's. The Father of the Gods goes on to assure Venus that Aeneas will prevail despite Juno's hatred of him, "But first in bloud must his good fortune bud" (I. 1. 86), just as poor Ganymede is promised future protection from such blows "As made the bloud run downe about mine eares" (I. 1. 8). When Juno herself appears later on, she tells Venus that she raised the storm against Aeneas "for the hate of Troian *Ganimed*, / That was advanced by my *Hebes* shame, / And *Paris* judgement of the heavenly ball" (III. 2. 42–44). This not only reminds us that Ganymede is a Trojan like Aeneas, it also makes Jove's affection for Hebe's replacement as cupbearer one of the chief causes, if not the chief cause, for the action recounted in the *Aeneid* and staged by Marlowe.[45] Juno's resentment of Ganymede is displaced onto Aeneas; we do not hear about her rivalry with the minion again, but her designs against her other Trojan enemy are dwelt upon at length.[46]

The parallel between Ganymede and Aeneas is nevertheless lim-ited by their contrasting relationships with Jupiter and Venus. Ju-piter's affection for his boy is sexual, but Venus's is parental. This difference is significant in itself, however, for *Dido, Queen of Car-thage* charts the transformation of polymorphous desire into ho-mosocial affect sanctioned by the institution of the family.[47] As the play progresses, Aeneas and his son Ascanius replace Venus and Aeneas as the familial alternative to Jupiter and Ganymede. The substitution of the disguised Cupid, Venus's other son, for Asca-nius in the scene where Dido falls in love with Aeneas helps the transition along. In the meantime, Juno calls Ascanius "my hate,

Aeneas cursed brat" and an "ugly impe"—her ill will toward him absorbs her hatred of his father, and of Ganymede before them (III. 2. 1, 4).

Aeneas's attachment to his son displaces Jupiter's love for Ganymede, but it does not render it completely illegitimate. When we move from timeless and remote Olympus to Aeneas's Mediterranean world, affection between older and younger men enters history. It becomes the bond between father and son within the family, and here the family is to be understood as a dynastic unit that ensures the continuity of patriarchy through time. Women perform an indispensable but almost unacknowledged function here. The consummate emblem for the dynastic notion of the family is Aeneas, with "my father on my backe, / This young boy in mine armes," and his wife Creusa, whom he nevertheless soon loses, in tow (II. 1. 265–66). Dido's rival for Aeneas's attentions is not a woman, but a country: "he will leave my love, / And seeke a forraine land calde *Italy*" (IV. 4. 97–98). And although the name "Italia" may be construed as feminine in gender, for the Trojans it signifies the masculine heritage of "An ancient Empire, famoused for armes . . . Which we now call *Italia* of his name, / That in such peace long time did rule the same," the eponymous ancestor Italus (I. 2. 21, 23–24). In a sense, Ascanius is Dido's ultimate rival, for he represents the future of Italy. "Now lookes *Aeneas* like immortall *Jove*," Dido says as the Trojan spurns her, "O where is *Ganimed* to hold his cup" (IV. 4. 45–46). By abandoning the queen, Aeneas secures his manhood, assuming the role of Jupiter and leaving that of Ganymede to his son.

The Ganymede-Ascanius pattern is also present in *Edward II*, although in the later play the family becomes an affective unit rather than a means of legitimate dynastic continuity, and as such it fails to contain the tragedy's volatile blend of politics and sexuality. At first, the queen's urging of her son's claim to the throne seems to position the boy as an Ascanian rival to Edward's latest Ganymede. The prince goes along with this strategy, saying "I warrant you, ile winne his highnes quicklie, / A loves me better than a thousand *Spencers*" (IV. 2. 6–7). After Edward is captured and Spenser disposed of, the little family that Mortimer creates as a vehicle for his own power is an obviously artificial construction (V. 2. 1–20). He makes his affair with Isabella the means of reining in the prince's right as lord protector. "Let not that *Mortimer* protect my sonne," Edward rages, "More safetie is there in a Tigers jawes, / Then his imbrasements" (V. 1. 115–17). Aeneas's bond with Ascanius extended Jupiter's with Ganymede in *Dido*; Mortimer's attempt to control the prince is a failed imitation of Edward's position as father, patron, and lover of boys or young men. The displaced eroticism in his alternate embracement and coercion of the prince is signaled by Mortimer's own fantasy of schoolmasterly violence: "I view the prince with *Aristarchus* eyes, / Whose lookes were as a breeching to a boye" (V. 4. 54–55). But the nuclear family that Mortimer, self-appointed tutor and foster father, sets up is a fragile and inadequate alternative to older institutions like patronage, pederasty, and the dynastic household, all of which do a better job of managing the erotics of court power.[48]

Before his construction collapses, however, Mortimer consolidates his power by arranging the murder of the king. He does so through the well-known device of the "unpointed" Latin message *Edwardum occidere nolite timere bonum est*, which can be read by his agents the jailers to mean either "Kill not the king tis good to feare the worst," or "Feare not to kill the king tis good he die" (V. 4. 8–12). We have already seen sovereign power abused through language, particularly written language, and here the instability of writing would seemingly permit power to erase its abuse. If sodomy is a crime *inter Christianos non nominandum*, it seems that regicide is not to be named either. Both actions mark the ethical limits of the early modern moral field. Sovereign and sodomite are opposites; when brought together, one of them must die, the sodomite if power justly travels downward, the king if its course is reversed, *contra naturam*.

But what if sodomite and sovereign are the same? "In the darkest region of the political field," Foucault writes, "the condemned man represents the symmetrical, inverted figure of the king. We should analyse what might be called, in homage to Kantorowicz, 'the lesser body of the condemned man.'"[49] But placing king and *condamné*—each with his own legal body, ceremony, and theoretical discourse—at opposite poles from one another obscures the ritual similarities between these figures, similarities that persisted despite the late medieval attempt to separate the monarch from the risk of death. As Kantorowicz himself remarks of *Richard II*,

"Kingship itself comes to mean Death, and nothing but Death. . . . The king that 'never dies' here has been replaced by the king that always dies and suffers death more cruelly than other mortals."[50] These words apply equally to *Edward II*, the impossible memory of which Shakespeare was in some sense trying to obliterate in his play.

Edward's death is more cruel than other mortals', certainly more cruel than Richard's. The assassin Lightborn calls for a red-hot spit as well as a table and feather bed—it is not clear from the text that the spit was used on Marlowe's stage, but its presence betokens the chronicle tradition in which Edward was impaled in a tacit, but grossly parodic, specification of sodomy, as well as pressed to death. Both forms of execution were employed so as not to leave a mark on the corpse, and thus Edward's end embodies the unspeakability of regicide and of sodomy as well. As Gregory Bredbeck points out, however, Marlowe elides the tradition about the apparently woundless death in his version of the king's murder, and the brand-like spit "can be seen as an attempt to 'write' onto him the homoeroticism constantly ascribed to him."[51] Such writing remains unstable, perhaps partly illegible, yet Lightborn's initial approach and Edward's response, in which he gives his executioner a jewel, darkly rehearse the dynamics of his generous courtship of Gaveston and Spenser. But finally it is regicide and not sodomy that is fully recognized and punished.

For the conceit of the unpointed message fails—the prince, now Edward III, has Mortimer beheaded after identifying his handwriting. One of the jailers has escaped, rumor is afoot, and the barons back up the young king: popular voice, consensus, and sovereign hegemony outstrip mere writing and through his son's decision produce the truth of Edward II's murder, for "in me my loving father speaks" (V. 6. 41). The king's second body lives on in Edward III, confirming social hierarchies against excessive adulteration by patronage and the manipulative regime of writing that is linked to it in this play. Despite his use of feudal language in public, Mortimer's regime operated through patronage after all. He extended the principle of Gaveston's and Spenser's ascendancy, although without violating existing hierarchies of sexuality and gender, similarly basing his power upon his relationship with royal bodies—his sexual conquest of the queen and his paternal, but erotically tinged, relationship with her son. Mortimer unites the nuclear family, patronage, and rule by the pen when he vaunts:

> The prince I rule, the queene do I commaund,
> And with a lowly conge to the ground,
> The proudest lords salute me as I passe,
> I seale, I cancell, I do what I will.

"Mine enemies will I plague, my friends advance," he concludes, "And what I list commaund, who dare controwle?" (V. 4. 48–51, 67–68).

"Control" here carries a range of meanings similar to its French cognate *contreroller* in Montaigne; it can signify both domination and scrutiny.[52] When Edward's brother Kent asks the queen how the imprisoned king will be treated, Mortimer cuts in with "Tis not in her controulment, nor in ours, / But as the realme and parlement shall please" (IV. 6. 35–36). But the king's fate is controlled by Mortimer, as is Kent's—"tis good to looke to him betimes," he warns Isabella in an aside (IV. 6. 39). The king exercises his authority by bestowing favor on whom he pleases; thus "Triumpheth *Englands Edward* with his friends," as Edward himself rejoices before the fight, "And triumph *Edward* with his friends uncontrould" (IV. 3. 2–3). Yet Edward recognizes the limits of royal power in the deposition scene through a metaphor of opacity and light:

> But what are kings, when regiment is gone,
> But perfect shadowes in a sun-shine day?
> My nobles rule, I beare the name of king,
> I weare the crowne, but am contrould by them.
>
> (V. 1. 26–29)

The sovereign is watched over and to some extent controlled by his court after all, and he is eventually removed by that court from the presence chamber to the dungeon. Mortimer suffers a similar fate when the prince turns on him and regains control of the barons.

Bad as Edward's rule may have been, Marlowe depicts Mortimer's usurpation as worse. Edward resolves at one point to "Make *Englands* civill townes huge heapes of stones" in defiance of the nobles—"A desperate and unnaturall resolution," as Warwick exclaims (III. 1. 215, 217). His own brother, Kent, calls him an "Unnaturall king, to slaughter noble men / And cherish flatterers" (IV.

1. 8–9). It is Edward's violence and his trust in hangers-on, and not his desires, that Kent regards as unnatural or monstrous. But Edward is after all England's anointed monarch, and Kent resolves covertly to support his brother once he is defeated and captured. "Raigne showers of vengeance on my cursed head / Thou God," he prays, "to whom in justice it belongs / To punish this unnaturall revolt" (IV. 6. 7–9). The unnatural is now associated with bearing arms against "Thy lawfull king thy soveraigne" (IV. 6. 4–5). Marlowe's play renders any easy distinction between the natural and the unnatural impossible, opening a space for homoerotic desire that is seemingly tangential to transgressions of hierarchy.[53]

In Elizabeth's England, Edward's cause must finally appear to be the better one because he embodies legitimate sovereign power. But Marlowe's plays also contain an implicit challenge to Elizabeth's politics of heterosexual courtship. In *Dido,* Aeneas's sojourn on "this courteous Coast" (I. 1. 232) is clearly portrayed as a voluntary submission to the "female drudgerie" of court life, where "wanton motions of alluring eyes, / Effeminate our mindes inur'd to warre" (IV. 3. 55, 35–36). Here, as in Musidorus's tirade against love in Sidney's *Arcadia,* effeminacy is associated with heterosexuality, not with love between men.[54] There is an unmistakable reference to Elizabeth herself in *Dido,* which may have been performed before her by the Children of Her Majesty's Chapel. "O heare *Iarbus* plaining prayers," Dido's rejected suitor complains, "Whose hideous ecchoes make the welkin howle, / And all the woods *Eliza* to resound" (IV. 2. 8–10). "Elissa" is an alternative name for the Carthaginian queen in the *Aeneid.* That the echo of the name is "hideous" here may signal the play's subtle critique of Elizabeth's courtly reign. A sexuality "uncontrolled" by external powers became the hallmark of English sovereignty with Henry VIII's first divorce and the Reformation, and it remained so under his daughter Elizabeth. An uncontrolled homosexuality is the unspoken affirmation of sovereignty in *Edward II,* as it was to be when James I came to the throne a decade later.

In *The Massacre at Paris,* the monarch's sexuality once more becomes the hidden spring of the action. In a curious scene, the logician Ramus and his "bedfellow," Taleus, are killed during the St. Bartholomew's Day massacre by Anjou, the future King Henry III, while the diabolical Guise looks on. The pair then plan "To get those pedantes from the King *Navarre*, / That are tutors to him and the prince of *Condy*" (7. 426–27). Navarre's tutors, who recall Baldock and Spenser, are a dim anticipation of Henry III's own minions later in the drama, a group about the throne for whom physical intimacy and knowledge of a political kind are closely allied. Guise is determined to kill the clients of the enemy king, just as he manipulates first Charles IX and then Henry himself through their bodily pleasures.

Unlike Edward II's barons, the Guise has learned to manage the "pleasures uncontrolde" of his monarch, allowing him to weaken his body and his realm by treating him like a child (2. 127). So far the Guise has succeeded with the infantilized king where Mortimer failed to manipulate either Edward or his young son. But when Charles begins to regret the massacre, his mother Catherine de Médicis poisons him and places his brother on the throne. Henry III seems even more tractable than Charles, as Catherine assures the Cardinal of Lorraine:

> His minde you see runnes on his minions,
> And all his heaven is to delight himselfe:
> And whilste he sleepes securely thus in ease,
> Thy brother *Guise* and we may now provide.
>
> (12. 633–36)

Henry, unlike Edward II, is a monarch who can be controlled because of his favorites, not in spite of them.

Yet the Guise runs afoul of Henry because the sexual energy that surrounds the king breaks its bounds and invades his own household. One of Henry's principal minions is carrying on an affair with the duchess of Guise. "Sweet *Mugeroune*, tis he that hath my heart," she says, making the political parallel clear, "And *Guise* usurpes it, cause I am his wife" (13. 660–61). Her husband pries into the letter she is writing to her lover and arranges his assassination. When Henry makes horns at the Guise and teases him about the "the letter gentle sir, / Which your wife writ to my deare Minion" (15. 754–55), the jealous husband scorns the king's love for his favorites and openly threatens Mugeroun.

The violence that follows is set loose by the unstable combination of disruptive sexual desire and royal patronage. The Guise murders Mugeroun in a scene that is juxtaposed with Navarre's fair and open defeat of the minion Joyeux in battle. Henry's relationship with Epernoun, another minion, leads to his unexpected conversion to the side of Navarre and the queen of England. Epernoun informs upon the Guise, telling the king that he has raised an army to depose Henry for affronting the pope, and that he is funded by Rome and Spain. "I, those are they that feed him with their golde," Henry agrees, "To countermaund our will and check our freends" (17. 845–46). Henry's similarity to Marlowe's other minion-minded king is emphasized by his violent threat against the pope as he lies dying at the end of the play: "Ile fire his crased buildings and inforse / The papall towers to kisse the lowly earth" (22. 1201–2). These lines are almost identical with the words Edward speaks when he rails at Rome after the clergy side with the barons against Gaveston (*Edward II*, I. 4. 100–101). Henry is assassinated because he lured the Guise himself to his death at the hands of hired killers after entering into an alliance with Navarre.

Catherine de Médicis pines away and dies when she hears the news of the Guise's murder. Marlowe's handling of the queen mother exhibits the same anxieties over the mixing of political power with female sexuality that animate Sidney's depiction of Cecropia in the *New Arcadia*. Catherine dominates the stage in the early throne scenes, muttering in the first one that she will dissolve the celebration of Navarre's marriage "with bloud and crueltie" and calling openly for Guise's massacre plans in the second (1. 26, 4. 229). She is given to repeating resolutions like "Ile rule *France*" and "while she lives, *Katherine* will be Queene"; she murders one son and determines to kill another should he not follow her behests (9. 525, 12. 654). Yet it is the Guise who emerges as the active villain in the events Marlowe dramatizes, more strongly in the *Massacre* than the pamphlet literature that influenced it.[55] Amphialus eventually steps forth from behind Cecropia in a similar way, and his death is also linked to hers.[56]

After the Guise is done away with, an almost anonymous Jacobin friar volunteers to assassinate Henry III; the dying king interprets his own murder as a warning to Elizabeth (23. 23–25, 24. 50–51). This chain of antagonists—Catherine, the Guise, the friar—indicates the changes that had taken place in English anxieties about Catholic conspiracy during the period covered by the play. In 1572, the year of Navarre's marriage and the massacre, the dangers of a French marriage for Elizabeth were uppermost in people's minds. Fears of a dynastic Catholic plot embodied in Catherine de Médicis were carried over well into the mid-1580's as Alençon's negotiations with Elizabeth dragged on. In the mean-time, however, priests began to infiltrate Scotland and England, and with the Throckmorton Plot it finally became clear that Spain was allied with the Guisan faction in France rather than with the French crown. This realization was marked by Henri III's assassi-nation of Guise and Catherine's subsequent death in 1588, the year of the Armada. The murder of Henri by a clergyman in 1589, on the heels of the Babington Plot to kill Elizabeth and put Mary Stuart on the throne, confirmed English anxieties about a large-scale invasion of devious and regicidal Catholic agents. The con-nection between the Guise and Spain is stressed in *The Massacre at Paris* as if to revise the faults in Walsingham's actual intelligence of affairs in France before the mid-1580's (11. 573, 14. 701–13).[57]

The historical Guise had in fact established the college for priestly agents at Rheims, as Henry later discloses (19. 1030–32). Marlowe's character boasts that

> Paris hath full five hundred Colledges,
> As Monestaries, Priories, Abbyes and halles,
> Wherein are thirtie thousand able men,
> Besides a thousand sturdy student Catholics,
> And more: of my knowledge in one cloyster keeps,
> Five hundred fatte Franciscan Fryers and priestes.
>
> (2. 137–42)

Marlowe, as we have seen, may have attended Guise's seminary at Rheims sometime before 1587. The phrase "of my knowledge" sounds like something out of a spy's report rather than the Guise talking to himself; the public theater has become the forum for the display of secret intelligence, and for an admonition to the queen and her ministers. At the end of the drama, a taciturn "English Agent" is suddenly summoned by the dying king, who resolves: "Ile send my sister *England* newes of this, / And give her warning of her trecherous foes" (22. 1189–90).

H. J. Oliver tentatively identifies the Agent with Walsingham; this may be correct in a symbolic way, but Walsingham was am-

bassador to France during the St. Bartholomew's Day massacre in
1572, not in 1589.[58] Sir Edward Stafford filled the post the year
Henri was killed, yet he was visiting England at the time. His servant, one William Lyly, acted in his place. Lyly was a tireless dis-
patcher of intelligence reports, and his account to Elizabeth of the
murder and the role he played afterwards is remarkably similar to
Marlowe's dramatization. The friar, "in making him a monastical
reverence, with a knife which he held in his sleeve struck the King
under the short ribs, to have pierced his bowels; which the King
with his own hand, seeing the motion . . . with great courage and
force got the knife from him and therewith gave the Jacobin two
blows," killing him. Henri spoke to Lyly a short while later, telling
him: "I am sure the Queen your mistress will be sorry for this, but
I hope it shall be quickly healed and so I pray you write her from
me."[59] Having killed the assassin with his own weapon, Marlowe's
Henry proclaims:

> Agent for *England*, send thy mistres word,
> What this detested Jacobin hath done.
> Tell her for all this that I hope to live.
>
> (24. 1194–96)

It is possible that Marlowe knew someone who was acquainted
with Lyly or his report.[60] Is Lyly the mysterious English Agent? In
a sense he is, but the Agent is also a figure for Marlowe, or rather
for the playwright-spy who must warn Elizabeth and her subjects
of regicidal Catholic plotters, making public what he claims covertly to have witnessed.

As Oliver notes, it is likely that, in addition to the information
gathering among pamphlets and chronicles that eventually went
into *The Massacre at Paris*, "Marlowe may well have spoken with
men who saw, or even took part in, the actions he portrays in his
play."[61] He may have served, after all, as the messenger of the English representative to Henri of Navarre in the early 1590's. When
he was arrested in Flushing for coining in January 1592, Marlowe
claimed to be well known to the earl of Northumberland and Lord
Strange—a little unwisely, since both noblemen possessed Catholic associations and occult interests.[62] It was Strange's company,
however, who performed *The Massacre* in 1593. The play was most
probably composed in 1592, and Marlowe must have written it un-

der the shadow of Baines's first round of accusations.[63] If he was the "Marlin" of Rouen, he was in France on government service again in March. Marlin was sent back to London, and we know that Marlowe ran into trouble with the law there once more in May. He got into yet another fight in Canterbury during September of the same year—could the *Massacre* have been written in the intervening months, between brawls?[64] It is possible that Marlowe composed it in prison, although we have evidence that he was free later in the year.

If Marlowe intended to exorcise or excoriate an atheistic Catholicism through the Guise, he may have succeeded only in bringing more suspicion upon himself. When the Guise vaunts "My policy hath fram'd religion" (2. 122), he sounds a little like the Marlowe of the Baines report, who maintained "that the first beginning of Religioun was only to keep men in awe."[65] In any case, Marlowe had a reputation to live down and, perhaps, a job to perform, and in *The Massacre at Paris* he decries the Guisan atheism and papistry with which Baines was already linking his name.

The play is unique among Marlowe's works for the propagandistic stance it assumes toward the events it portrays. This is partly because it depicts current events, Henry's "news." It has come down to us in a "corrupt" form, but the contribution of voices other than Marlowe's, the voices perhaps of actors reconstructing from memory a text that must also have elicited a vigorous audience response, adds to the element of popular mythology that was already present in the original. And if Marlowe's public affected his plays, the plays reacted in turn upon their audience. According to Stephen Greenblatt, sixteenth-century drama "depended upon and fostered in its audience *observation*, the close reading of gesture and speech as manifestations of character and intention."[66] The representation of mutual observation at court in the theater of the period rendered it imitable, extending it outside the circle of court culture to the common spectator. Sidney's aristocratic romance depicts a shift in emphasis from the erotics of courtly display and scrutiny to an uneasy awareness of overarching surveillance. The works signed by Marlowe that I have discussed here register this movement from the viewpoint of a playwright and spy. Display becomes public spectacle and observation the grounds for a generalized paranoia. Yet in constructing both his self and his sovereigns through his sexuality, Marlowe's theater stages history from below in another way, engaging the paranoia of the heterosocial court and affective family through dramatic representations of the social bonds that preceded them.

CHAPTER 4

Lights of Base Stuff
Jonson's Roman Plays

I N an epigram entitled "Of Spies," Ben Jonson ridicules
intelligencers by contrasting the useful work they do
with their low origins and violent ends:

SP*ies*, you are lights in state, but of base stuffe,
Who, when you'have burnt your selves down to the snuffe,
Stinke, and are throwne away. End faire enough.[1]

These jeers recall similar condemnations of espionage that may be
found throughout Jonson's works, and particularly in his first two
plays set in ancient Rome, *Poetaster* and *Sejanus his Fall*. Yet in *Catiline his Conspiracy*, written a few years after *Sejanus* and something
of a "prequel" to it, political intelligence has become a necessary safeguard against treason—it is condemned by the villains,
not the heroes. "All is true, your spies haue told you," the conspirators taunt Cicero in this play, "See, they do not / Die in a
ditch, and stinke, now you ha' done with 'hem" (V. 523, 525–26).
Spying is rehabilitated in *Catiline* amid thunder, lightning, and
evocations of divine surveillance over human actions, an apotheosis of visual power that seemingly undoes the irony of the spy
epigram's "lights in state."

Catiline does not represent a change of heart about the morality
of spying. It would be a mistake to think of Jonson as a full-fledged
bourgeois subject, or as a modern author who articulated consistent opinions on political ways and means. Like Marlowe before
him, Jonson was a self-fashioning monarchical subject, although
his self-fashioning helped to create the very standards of agency
and authorship that tempt us, retrospectively and often inaccurately, to reconstruct his intentions.[2] Instead of articulating a stable

set of beliefs, Jonson's Roman plays embody an ambiguous attitude toward surveillance at court and the sort of knowledge it produces. They repeat many of the problematics of sovereignty and selfhood that Montaigne investigated in his *Essais*, developing them within the English context inherited from Elizabeth's reign and the anxieties over sovereignty and sexuality it produced. But these restatements of themes we have run across before occur under new conditions—the movement away from the representation of sovereign power by a single individual and toward the idea of the abstract state.

As the image of the personal sovereign receded in early modern times, that of the coherent authorial subject came slowly into view. Jonson's motto was *Tamquam explorator*, "like a scout"—or spy. This Senecan tag refers primarily to his strategy as a writer who infiltrates the texts of others and carries away what is most useful to his own, but Jonson may have had first-hand experience at a less metaphorical kind of reconnaissance as well. *Poetaster*, *Sejanus*, and *Catiline* enact the subject's progress from ambivalent client of the great under sovereignty to agent within a new notion of the abstract and surveilling state. The Roman setting allowed Jonson to experiment with republican and imperial theories of the state remote from political realities in England. Yet the actual workings of surveillance depicted in the Roman plays were partly inspired by the urban culture of petty intelligencing that Jonson captured in his minor poems, like the epigram on spies, and dramatized in *Volpone*.

Jonson's lyrics, and particularly his epigrams, sketch an underworld of opportunistic newsmongering on the outskirts of the Jacobean Court.[3] His Captain Hungry is sustained by "Your yong States-men, (that first make you drunke, / And then lye with you, closer, then a punque, / For newes)" ("To Captayne Hungry," lines 19–21). Here, the association of sex between men and spying within the patronage relationship is part of a wider discourse about the body. Hungry is given food at other men's tables in exchange for news of European courts, "What States yo' haue gull'd, and which yet keepes yo'in pay" (line 10). In "Inviting a Friend to Supper" the would-be host promises that "we will haue no *Pooly*', or *Parrot* by" to inform in turn on his dinner companions (line 36), and "An Epistle answering to one that asked to be Sealed of the

Tribe of BEN" likewise excludes from his table those who would
defame others and spread rumors in return for hospitality (lines
16–28). The upstart statesmen of Ben Jonson's "The New Crie"
claim to know "what each prince doth for intelligence owe, / And
vnto whom," and who "carry in their pockets TACITVS, / And
the *GAZETTI*, or GALLO-BELGICVS" (lines 12–13, 15–16).
Tacitus, whose *Annals*, translated in 1598, provide an incisive description of life under a regime of informers, makes an odd companion to the newssheets; Jonson promises the friend whom he invites to supper that a servant will read from Virgil, Livy, and Tacitus while they eat (lines 21–22).

Volpone's Sir Politic Would-Be is Jonson's most famous commentary on the trend toward Tacitean skulduggery in later Elizabethan and Jacobean city gossip. The self-conscious theatricality of
Sir Pol's characterization was a large part of its satirical success.
"O, this Knight / (Were he well knowne) would be a precious
thing / To fit our *English* stage" (II. 1. 56–58). Both Sir Politic and
the appropriately named Peregrine are comic heirs of the Elizabethan gentlemen whose travels on the Continent were in part intelligence gathering missions for their country's good and their
own advantage. Jonson's knight-errant exposes to public view the
paranoia that reached its crest with the Gunpowder Plot of November 1605, which probably occurred shortly after *Volpone* was
written, perhaps right around the time it was acted.[4] News of the
plot, however, is missing from Peregrine's account of recent events
in London. Instead, his report culminates in the announcement that
Stone the fool has died, and Sir Politic's know-it-all response that
the jester was really one of the most dangerous agents at court. He
received weekly messages from the Low Countries in cabbages,
and relayed his intelligence to foreign ambassadors by means of
other foodstuffs (II. 1. 67–83).

It is significant that a performer like Stone the fool is singled out
as a spy by Sir Pol, for espionage and theater are juxtaposed elsewhere in the comedy. When *Volpone* enters disguised as the mountebank Scoto in the next scene, Sir Politic insists that his profession
is composed of

> the onely-knowing men of *Europe*!
> Great generall schollers, excellent phisicians,

> Most admir'd states-men, profest fauorites,
> And cabinet-counsellors, to the greatest princes!
>
> (II. 2. 9–13)

Later in the play, Peregrine tricks the knight into believing that a spy has accused him of treason. Sir Pol, who already fears that his correspondence has been spied upon (II. 3. 12–13), is driven to burn his papers, even though "I haue none, but notes, / Drawne out of play-bookes." Peregrine's reply—"All the better, sir" (V. 4. 41–42)—is pointed. The exchange recalls Jonson's arrest some years earlier for his hand in *The Isle of Dogs*, a supposedly seditious play in which he also performed. He had been turned in along with two other actors by a professional informer named Topcliffe. In recounting the incident to Drummond, Jonson complained of "two damn'd villains" who were set upon him in prison "to catch advantage of him." Drummond attributes the epigram on spies to this affair.[5]

Jonson's modern editors conjecture that the two villains of his imprisonment were the Pooly or Parrot of "Inviting a Friend to Supper," but this seems principally to be a reference to the household spying practiced by those who hung about the tables of the great and near great.[6] It is possible that the two spies were the same men as the pair of fellow actors who we know were imprisoned with Jonson in the Marshalsea for their roles in the play, Robert Shaa, or Shaw, and Gabriel Spencer.[7] Spencer was killed by the playwright the following year in a duel, the occasion of which remains unknown. Whatever the story behind these events may be, Jonson's opinions about both acting and spying remained tinged by the chaotic beginnings of his writing career, and they became more complex as it developed.

Poetaster (1601) inaugurates the treatment of political intelligence in a classical setting that *Sejanus* and *Catiline* develop in a tragic, or at any rate more serious, manner. The early comedy blends acting and informing in a satirical fantasia upon its author's recent experiences with *The Isle of Dogs* and the accusations and counteraccusations of the "war of the theaters."[8] The issues at stake in its plot—censorship, the professional writer's desire to be free from charges of political allegoresis, and the dangers of the prince's reliance upon spies—were critical for Jonson's ongoing construction of an authorial identity.

Poetaster is often taken today, as it was in its own day, as an out-right attack upon the players, but Jonson's stance toward this group was ambivalent, even neutral at times, as indeed he claims in the "apologeticall Dialogue" appended to the play ("To the Reader," lines 141–52). He had recently been an actor himself, albeit an un-successful and provincial one, and he pays the profession a com-pliment by having two of his principal villains attack it in an effort to dissuade young Ovid from writing for the theater. Lupus and Captain Tucca upbraid the players for their satirical ability to reveal the hidden vices of those in authority (I. 2. 36–53). Such rendering visible of the invisible must have been precisely what lent them value as instruments of the Jonsonian author.

This tribute, however, already contains the terms for an attack on acting, for performers could be unwieldy tools. Its indirect and ironic cast is characteristic of Jonson's strategy in general and of this subtle and underrated play in particular. *Poetaster* begins by pit-ting the lax, would-be dramatist Ovid against the pure poet Hor-ace, who starts out on the same side as Lupus and the other servants of the prince. Ovid is banished from the court, but Lupus, Tucca, and the poetaster Crispinus are soon revealed to be the real enemies of Caesar and of legitimate writing when they deliberately mis-construe an emblem Horace has created and charge him with trea-son. Caesar sees through their ruse, and Virgil concludes that it is not the satirist who threatens the state,

> But the sinister application
> Of the malicious, ignorant, and base
> Interpreter: who will distort, and straine
> The generall scope and purpose of an author,
> To his particular, and private spleene.
>
> (V. 3. 140–44)

All the same, Ovid remains in exile, a victim perhaps of his own poor judgment as well as of the sinister application of base inter-preters.[9]

Ovid was also the victim of an actor, who informed Lupus that his masque-like play, a saturnalian burlesque of the gods, required such politically charged properties as a crown and scepter. Tucca earmarks Horace for similar treatment even before Ovid is appre-hended: "I'le bee your intelligencer, we'll all ioyne, and hang vpon him like so many horse-leaches, the plaiers and all" (IV. 3. 126–28). *Poetaster* is introduced by the figure of Envy, who openly accuses the actors of betraying their author "With wrestings, comments, applications / Spie-like suggestions, priuie whisperings" (Induction, lines 24–25). They not only distort the text, they are liable to "Traduce, corrupt, apply, enforme, suggest" (Induction, line 54), like the players in the story they are about to perform.

E. K. Chambers conjectured that Jonson's informing players may be a reminiscence of the occasion when one of the Chamberlain's Men told the chief justice that a play on the deposing of Richard II was acted at the request of some followers of Essex the day before his rebellion.[10] The episode clearly recalls the *Isle of Dogs* incident as well. The offstage activities of actors, as Jonas Barish points out, were topical, a frequent object for attack by the enemies of the theater, who identified them with the lechers, criminals, and parasites they often portrayed.[11] We have already met with a player-spy in Sidney's Clinias, who uses his talents to feign and persuade,[12] and Marlowe himself may have worked for a time as a professional player.[13] In *Poetaster*, the behind-the-scenes role of actors in Lupus's intelligencing is a perversion of their public function as exposers of hidden vices to all: "Speake lower," he hisses at the first informer, "you are not now i' your *theatre*, Stager" (IV. 4. 8–9). Jonson feared that his actors, like the players in *Poetaster*, would betray the playwright to the authorities in private rather than interpret his plays to the audience of the public theater.

The paranoid construction of Jonsonian authorship sought to control audiences and readers as well as performers through the authority of the text. Barish has noticed how Jonson "aims precisely to de-theatricalize the theater, to strip it of just those attributes which, in the eyes of most of its devotees, made it theater in the first place." He continues: "The end result . . . is to make the printed script rather than the live performance the final authority; the play moves finally into the domain of literature."[14] This movement into the domain of literature in fact helped to create that domain, a separate territory with vaguely drawn borders that comprises a certain type of writing, a corresponding type of professional writing practice, and the construction of a particular kind of subject, the author.[15] "Hee is an errant learn'd man," one of the gossips remarks of him in *The Staple of News*, "and can write, they

say, and I am foully deceiv'd, but hee can read too" (First inter-
mean, lines 44–46).

Jonson's recourse to some of the privileges of what would come
to be regarded as literary writing is of a piece with his scornful re-
jection of political allegoresis. His writing practice feeds into the
formalist critical practice of later generations, in which the claim
that certain kinds of writing are essentially literary was used to dis-
courage political readings of them.[16] One of the clauses in the pre-
performance contract between the author and the *"Spectators or
Hearers"* that introduces *Bartholomew Fair* (1614) stipulates that
they "neyther in themselues conceale, nor suffer by them to be concealed any *State-decipherer*, or politique *Picklocke* of the *Scene*" who
might profess to reveal which worthies his costardmonger or pig-
woman represented. This mocking of one-to-one correspondences does not preclude an awareness in Jonson that his writings
were significant in other ways that we would call "political." But
it does indicate a discomfort with the close examination of his text
for topical allusions that is associated in *Poetaster* with spying, and
with acting as well.

As Francis Barker writes of *Hamlet*: "Elsinore is a place of spies
and actors, actual and metaphorical, where scenes are played out to
acknowledged and unacknowledged audiences, and where sight
transfixes or is stolen, but is never doubted as the dominant mode
of a (sometimes fraudulent) access."[17] The domination of sight in
the theater permits audience members to identify with characters
who observe other characters on stage. There are many such characters in Jacobean drama, and many scenes in which the spectators
are placed in the situation of eavesdroppers. Jonson, however,
feared an audience of spies and state-decipherers, and the initial unpopularity of his two plays of intrigue, *Sejanus his Fall* and *Catiline
his Conspiracy*, indicates their wordy failure to exploit the visual
character of theatrical identification.

Sejanus (1603) was Jonson's next play after *Poetaster*. Here the
epigrams' chaotic world of gossipy clientage becomes a centralized
intelligence system under Sejanus, although the real, if largely absent, center of surveillance is the emperor Tiberius. In *Sejanus* the
overt preoccupation with the theater takes second place in a story
about what spying and dissimulation can do to the state and its citizens. Something of *Poetaster*'s Lupus remains in Sejanus's entrap-

ment through espionage of the historian Cordus, "a writing fellow" who is accused of treason for allegorizing past events in present terms. Yet when Lupus turns into Sejanus, the object of the game becomes setting up one's political opponents rather than incriminating court poets.

Timber: or Discoveries contains a number of observations on the prince's relationship to such courtly competition. Of tyrants Jonson writes: "their fortune is often-times to draw a *Seianus*, to be neere about 'hem, who will at last affect to get above 'hem, and put them in a worthy fear" (8. 601). On the previous page we are told that the just ruler "needs no Emissaries, Spies, Intelligencers, to entrap true Subjects" (8. 600).[18] A little later he repeats these reflections on the domestic level in treating of household spies and detractors: "*These* are call'd instruments of grace, and power, with great persons; but they are indeed the Organs of their impotencie, and markes of weakness. For sufficient Lords are able to make these Discoveries themselves" (8. 613). Yet Jonson's own Tiberius is an example of a tyrant who remains strong despite, or because of, the devices of espionage and entrapment that his servants employ.

The visibility of the subject remains a principle of government in *Timber*—sufficient lords will make their own discoveries, and the people of the just prince "speake, what they thinke; and talke openly, what they doe in secret. They have nothing in their brests, that they need a Cipher for" (8. 600). Jonson is anticipating the opportunity for complete surveillance that is the other side of an idealized "freedom of speech." *Sejanus* is a more accurate picture of the way power operates, as its author was reminded soon after its completion—he was summoned before the Privy Council by Lord Henry Howard, soon to become the earl of Northampton, on vague charges of sedition and popery that may have been connected with the play.[19] Detraction and informing remained important organs of royal power, whatever weaknesses they concealed: Sejanus aspires to take Tiberius's place and urges his master to leave Rome, but Tiberius catches him out, and he uses another instrument to do so. He appoints Macro as "our eye, and eare" during his absence from the city: "we assigne thee both to spie, / Informe, and chastise; think, and vse they meanes, / Thy ministers, what, where, on whom thou wilt" (III. 681, 701–30). For his part, Macro makes love to his commission. "It is the bliss / Of courts," he says, "to be imploy'd, no matter how" (III. 715–16). The withdrawal of the sovereign leaves behind a network of intelligence and intrigue presided over by Sejanus, although Caesar maintains a distant oversight through the agency of Macro, his new servant.

Social exchanges in *Sejanus*'s Rome parody the movement from the court to the city, or from courtesy to civility, among elites in contemporary European history charted by Norbert Elias. "In order to be really 'courteous' by the standards of *civilité*," Elias remarks of the new regime, "one is to some extent obliged to observe, to look about oneself and pay attention to people and their motives."[20] But in *Sejanus* observation is clearly out of control— or rather, it has itself become a form of control in a manner that bespeaks both courtly and urban anxieties under new forms of interdependence and constraint. The conversation between Silius and Sabinus in the opening scene is famous for its description of a state under surveillance. The two friends agree that they are both ill-suited to life at court: "We haue no shift of faces, no cleft tongues, / No soft, and glutinous bodies, that can sticke, / Like snailes, on painted walls" (I. 7–9). Tiberius's lusts have subjected all of Rome, and now "euery ministring spie / That will accuse, and sweare, is lord of you, / Of me, of all, our fortunes, and our liues" (I. 64–68). This reversal of hierarchy disturbs every other institution in society. Germanicus's widow Agrippina is told that "euery second ghest your tables take, / Is a fee'd spie, t'obserue who goes, who comes, / What conference you haue, with whom, where, when" (II. 444–46). Here, as in "Inviting a Friend to Supper," the threat to social relationships posed by espionage is figured by the abuse of hospitality. The ties of household patronage are dissolving, and the perpetuation of this process beyond Sejanus's fall is shown by the unseemly haste of his own former allies to attend the Senate meeting convened to censure him, "for feare / Their bond-men should informe against their slacknesse" (V. 783–84).

As in Montaigne's *Essais*, friendship is a casualty of rule by intelligence. The self-exiled and debauched Tiberius is almost the archetype for the friendless monarch described by la Boétie.[21] Silius warns Agrippina that his wife, Sosia, is a dangerous companion precisely because of her free-spoken loyalty (II. 431–42). And in the well-known eavesdropping scene, it is Sabinus's cousin and friend Latiaris who draws him out on the subject of Tiberius's imperfections. Sabinus, however, seems more shocked that the eavesdroppers should be senators: "Spies of this head! so white! so full of years!" (IV. 221). This recalls his words in the first scene of the play, in which he deplores the base flattery of Tiberius practiced by even the most reverend statesmen (I. 41–55).

The eavesdropping episode is an exception to the judgment that Jonson failed in *Sejanus* to draw his audience into the various forms of spectatorship, among them spying, practiced by its ancient Romans.[22] The scene required careful staging. Following his principal source for the play in Tacitus's *Annals* closely, Jonson evidently placed the two spies above the main action, either in the chamber over the platform stage, or (if the action took place in the chamber itself) in the music gallery above that. This hiding place represented the space between roof and ceiling described by Tacitus, and when the senators "Shift to our holes" (IV. 1143) upon the entry of Sabinus and his betrayer they must have crouched down with their ears to the chamber or gallery floor. Here "the spies would be visible even to the groundlings near the stage."[23]

There are other, more figurative, eavesdropping scenes in the play. As it opens, Sejanus's clients Natta and Satrius hover about the Germanicans (I. 74–85, 258–60), and by the end of the fourth act the Germanicans themselves resort to eavesdropping when some wavering friends of Sejanus wander by them (IV. 410–45). The language of the play presents spying in ways that make it almost as tangible as the action of the eavesdropping scene. Christopher Ricks, writing about the isolation of various parts of the body within the dismemberment complex that he finds throughout *Sejanus*, noticed the extremely physical nature of its "world of spies" some time ago.[24] Eyes are everywhere. Macro, who warns his agents that "night hath many eyes, / Whereof, though most do sleepe, yet some are spies" (V. 169–70), becomes Tiberius's eye. Arruntius wonders whether "our night-ey'd TIBERIVS doth not see / His minions drifts" (IV. 363–64). Sabinus complains that he and his friends are made "The prey to greedie vultures, and vile spies, / That first, transfixe vs with their murdering eyes" (IV. 140–41). Agrippina is warned to be careful, "For your state is wayted on by enuies, as by eyes" (II. 442–43). She resolves nevertheless to remain steadfast,

Were all TIBERIVS body stuck with eyes,
And eu'ry wall, and hanging in my house
Transparent, as this lawne I weare, or ayre;
Yea, had SEIANVS both his eares as long
As to my in-most closet.   (II. 450–54)

Sexually charged and suggestive of violent bodily distortion, these grotesquely physical hyperboles are the most memorable emblems of rule by espionage in the play.[25]

Sejanus justifies his extensive intelligence operation against Agrippina's household by telling Tiberius that she is a "male-spirited dame" (II. 210) who is at the center of a conspiracy to replace him with one of her sons. The only way out of her predicament, she later declares, would be to become "Lewd SEIANVS strumpet. Or the baud / To CAESARS lusts" (IV. 16–17; punctuation modified). The Romans have lost their republican liberty and become "the slaues to one mans lusts; / And now to many: euery ministring spy" (I. 63–64). Tiberius withdraws to his pleasures, an unseen "private life" from which he rules by invading the inmost closets of others with his agents. The lowborn Sejanus, we are told, began his career in high places as a catamite (I. 12–16). Surveillance is associated with male pleasure elsewhere in the play. Sejanus seduces Livia, the wife of Tiberius's son, and enlists her in the murder of her husband. He first gains access to her through the doctor Eudemus, for "Yo'are a subtill nation, you Physitians! / And growne the onely cabinets, in court, / To ladies priuacies." He then asks Eudemus which of his patients "Is the most pleasant lady, in her physick?" (I. 299–300, 302). His invasion of women's secrets corresponds to the Renaissance tendency to conceive of power as the surveillance and subjection of the female body.

When told she should have patience under this regime of sexualized surveillance, Agrippina replies: "I must haue vengeance, first" (IV. 2). Agrippina's call for vengeance displaces Sejanus's political erotics and echoes the truculence of the younger members of her household, who advise the shortest way with the informers who frequent her home. " 'Twere best rip forth their tongues, seare out their eies, / When next they come," says her son Nero; "A fit reward for spies," her friend Sosia adds (II. 477–78). When the followers of Germanicus suspect that Sejanus has designs on their late leader's children, Arruntius boasts:

> If I could gesse he had but such a thought,
> My sword should cleave him downe from head to heart,
> But I would finde it out: and with my hand
> I'ld hurle his panting braine about the ayre,
> In mites, as small as *atomi*.   (I. 253–57)

Arruntius is an aristocrat under a surveilling mode of power that renders him helpless; he turns to a fantasy of open physical force, producing another violent image for the revelation of secret intentions. Ironically, two of Sejanus's agents listen even as he speaks these words.

"Nothing," as Arruntius observes, "hath priuiledge 'gainst the violent eare" (IV. 311). Violence in *Sejanus*, however, is not so much a modality of surveillance, like sexual subjection, as a product of it in those it subjects, who would turn to more traditional and open expressions of power to combat the hidden forces that monitor them. Arruntius's fantasy about cleaving Sejanus to the heart to find out his secrets foreshadows the dismemberment of Sejanus at the end of the play, a case of overkill ("What cannot oft be done, is now ore-done," V. 827) that extends itself to the rape and murder of Sejanus's children. "You pash yourselues in pieces, nere to rise," Arruntius apostrophizes ambitious politicians, "And he that lends you pitty, is not wise" (V. 896–97). Sejanus's victims among the Germanicans have become more perverse in their hatred than "my monster, / The multitude" (V. 879–80). His spectacular punishment takes place as part of the monopoly of violence that Tiberius's wider field of surveillance contains.[26]

Unlike Tiberius, Sejanus is obsessed with defining his identity through the magnification of his power. He sees usurpation as a matter of taking over knowledge, even self-knowledge ("his owne most deare affaires") from the nominal ruler, of drawing all dispatches through his own hands (III. 614–15). As Sejanus climbs higher, he does what his master, who is already at the top, never has to do—he brags and bullies in public, threatening the gods themselves.[27] When he temporarily realizes that he is out of favor, however, Sejanus reverts to Tiberius's model and begins to fawn on the clients he had hectored before: "I wish I could diuide my selfe vnto you" (V. 282). It is fitting that his drive toward absolute self-presence should end in the total division of his mind and body through dismemberment. *Sejanus* does not reflect absolutist sovereignty; it reveals its impossibility in a state where power has become disembodied, "spectralized," or "disincorporated."[28] Sejanus is a would-be absolutist who is torn apart the moment he enters a center of power that turns out to be a centrifuge.

Sejanus's failure to replace his master is due most immediately to Tiberius's canny decision to employ Macro against him. Yet we would be wrong to ascribe it entirely to Tiberius's presence of mind, for there is a sense in which his greatest advantage over Sejanus is his virtual absence, in mind and body, from much of the action. Sejanus cannot gain access to a position of power that in its lack of fixity seems hardly to exist at all.

It is in the closet scenes—when Sejanus asks the emperor for Livia's hand in marriage and Tiberius determines to replace him with Macro—that Jonson's Caesar is made to appear most tangible, and most like a Renaissance prince keeping watch over his servants and determining the necessary rivalry among them. For a moment it seems to the audience that the empire is within Sejanus's grasp; when we finally see Tiberius alone on stage, it appears that his superior ruthlessness is all that will keep Sejanus from power. But even in soliloquy Tiberius remains strangely impersonal—his musings are a series of *sententiae* about the necessary caution of those who wield power through favorites, similar to the ones recorded by Jonson in *Timber* (III. 633–60). Before and after these scenes he is even more remote, disappearing from the stage altogether after his talk with Macro.

The rulers of the early Roman Empire held sway without being monarchs in the usual sense. Often they did not occupy any public office or possess any title; they claimed merely to be the "first citizen" or *princeps*, whose *auctoritas* was respected by a Senate that relied voluntarily upon their counsels. Jonson shows himself to be aware of this history in *Sejanus*. Gerhard Oestreich demonstrates that during the later Renaissance, "the real facts of Roman life—administration and the structure of the financial and fiscal apparatus, as well as the ethical and spiritual foundations of the Roman state—were objects of intensive study and provided an important starting point for the shaping of the early modern state."[29] Oestreich's work was concerned in part with the influence of Lipsius's neo-Stoic version of Tacitus upon this movement; this is the edition and commentary that Jonson refers to in his marginal notes to *Sejanus*.[30]

Jonson's *princeps* is capable of referring to himself as a "prince" in the Renaissance sense, but most of the time Tiberius is associated with a self-denigrating rhetoric that avoids imperative speech except when it is used to forbid flattery or homage. (See I. 379–95.) "If this man / Had but a minde allied vnto his words," Silius observes, "How blest a fate were it to vs, and *ROME*?" (I. 400–403). Again, after Tiberius elevates Germanicus's sons, Arruntius marvels: "If this were true now! but the space, the space / Between the brest, and lips—TIBERIVS heart / Lyes a thought farder, then another mans" (III. 96–98). Tiberius is like a Renaissance ruler in possessing an elusive selfhood that is hard to pin down, but he extends this indeterminacy to his very relationship with the power he claims not to exercise.

It is important to recognize that Tiberius is something of a political and (as we would now say) psychological impossibility, a controlling personality without a personality, a prince before the age of princes who exercises power through perpetual abdication. Jonathan Goldberg, citing some asides of the Germanicans upon Tiberius's first appearance ("Rarely dissembled" and "Prince-like, to the life," I. 395), points out that Caesar is the play's most conspicuous actor: "Being prince*like*, Tiberius re-presents himself, doubles himself. . . . The prince plays the prince."[31] In refusing flattery and even official recognition of his rule, Tiberius is indeed playing the prince in the paradoxical sense that a false humility is characteristic of the all-powerful. Yet Tiberius does not represent or intensify himself so much as he attempts to erase himself. Actors, as Stephen Gosson complained and Jean-Christophe Agnew has recently reminded us, do not after all play themselves. They play people other than themselves, and it is in Tiberius's lack of a fixed identity that he most resembles an actor.[32] It is here that he most resembles the *moi* of Montaigne's *Essais* as well, which patterns itself on royal individuality in part because the sovereign best exemplifies the instability it finds in itself. As a figure for one version of this sovereignty, Tiberius is an impossible combination of absolute power and nearly absolute self-effacement.

His political theatricality assimilates republican forms and institutions, particularly the Senate. The Germanicans repeatedly call Tiberius an actor in an effort to define or contain this theatricality, but, as Arthur F. Marotti observes, "He stands behind the play's final two acts like the playwright hidden behind his creation, and more and more the characters on stage look like his creatures."[33] If Tiberius is the ultimate actor-spy, his characterization also reveals the dramatist's complicity in the mechanisms of surveillance that victimize writers in *Poetaster*. Sejanus is as much a creature of Tiberius as the Germanicans. Tiberius has his favorite's statue erected in the rebuilt Theater of Pompey, which had been destroyed by a fire that Sejanus's "vigilance" kept from spreading (I. 521). When the statue is discovered belching smoke before Sejanus's fall, the multitude "runne, in routs, to POMPEY'S theatre" to view the spectacle (IV. 28–29). The dismemberment of his statue there precedes his own, and this time the people are specifically compared to an audience: they rush to the place "with that speed, and heate of appetite, / With which they greedily devoure the way / To some great sports, or new theatre" (V. 763–65). In his dedication of *Sejanus* to Lord Aubigny, Jonson paralleled Sejanus's fate with the "violent" treatment of his play by its first audiences.

Tiberius has more control over the Roman audience than Jonson had over his English one; the dismemberment of his Sejanus was part of the script. The Senate is revealed to be the aristocratic counterpart of Pompey's Theater. This is implicit in all the Senate scenes, in which the backbenchers make comments on the action like Shakespeare's Athenian courtiers. In Act III Arruntius says that he does not know why the Senate has been summoned, for "We / That are the good-dull-noble lookers on, / Are only call'd to keepe the marble warme" (III. 15–17). The reduction of the Senate to a playhouse is fully accomplished in the final scene, during which Tiberius's "long doubtfull letter" ("The Argument," line 36) is read out to the assembly like the recitation of a poem or the performance of a dramatic text.

The masterstroke of the open letter was set up by a series of contradictory messages that sowed doubt in the minds of Sejanus's followers while seeming to exalt their patron still higher (V. 410–37). "These crosse points / Of varying letters, and opposing *Consuls*," Lepidus remarks, "Mingling his honours, and his punishments . . . cannot be / Emptie of practice: 'tis TIBERIVS arte" (V. 447–

49, 452–53). The art of government is largely an art of writing, the distribution of rewards "by speciall writ" and of punishments "By more speciall writ" (V. 417, 418), and Tiberius, of course, is one who is able to *proscribere* as well as *scribere*.[34]

Tiberius begins his final letter with a reference to his bodily absence: "The care of the common-wealth, howsoeuer we are remoou'd in person, cannot be absent to our thought; although oftentimes, euen to princes most present, the truth of their owne affaires is hid: then which, nothing fals out more miserable to a state, or makes the art of gouerning more difficult" (V. 548–52; italics removed here and throughout). But, he goes on, the industry of "so vigilant a Senate" (V. 554) has made his retirement to a life of pleasure excusable. Caesar continues to employ the self-negating rhetoric he has used throughout the play, and he adroitly manages to condemn Sejanus outright without departing from it. In the midst of a series of contradictions, Tiberius first lists the charges against Sejanus and then claims that even though he finds them "most malicious" he must succumb to "those needfull iealousies of state" and recommend the suspension of his favorite's offices. Were it left to him, he would absolve Sejanus—but he does not have the power to limit the Senate's authority (V. 598–601, 612, 631–36).

The ultimate display of power is couched in the ultimate self-denying ordinance. The condemnation of Sejanus by letter is the revenge of writing for the prosecution of the "writing fellow" Cordus, or rather, it demonstrates that writing can serve despotic as well as republican ends.[35] The emperor wields the rhetorical power Jonson would ascribe to authorship, but unlike the emerging figure of the author Tiberius remains an impersonal force behind the rhetoric. Sabinus regrets that "our writings are . . . made to speake / What they will haue, to fit their tyrannous wreacke" (IV. 132, 134–35), but if writing can be twisted by the tyrant's servants, then it can also twist them. Once the standards of interpretation are revealed as unfixed and rendered politically opportunistic or blankly prudential, we have reached the end of the cycle begun by Lupus in *Poetaster*, where Virgil says that it is not the satirist who wounds the body of the state but the base interpreter whose applications turn another's public writings to private ends.

Sejanus, who would take on the body of the state that Tiberius

has virtually put off, is disembodied by the people amid the tumult
that Tiberius's opaque letter has created. The mob dismember Sejanus linguistically through their shouted questions before they
tear him apart in deed ("What beard he had? what nose? what
lips?": V. 786–89). Much earlier in the play, Sejanus reveals the
masochism that underlies his megalomania while contemplating
his plan to murder Tiberius's son:

> If this be not reuenge, when I haue done
> And made it perfect, let *A Egyptian* slaues,
> *Parthians*, and bare-foot *Hebrewes* brand my face,
> And print my body full of iniuries.   (II. 139–42)

The play's "Argument" makes clear what is only implied in its language and action—Sejanus is dismembered by writing, as Tiberius, "with a long doubtful letter, in one day, hath him suspected,
accused, condemned, and torne in pieces" (lines 36–38; italics removed). Yet the "printing" or inscription of his person is accomplished at one or two removes from the absent emperor; the mob
that produced the lowborn Sejanus absorbs and dissolves his body
back into itself. Throughout *Sejanus*, writing represents the operation of a discourse that manufactures consent and agency, rather
than the presence of a personal monarch ruling with his pen. Sejanus's death is the result of the obscurity and misinformation that
characterize the deployment of this power throughout the play,
rather than the open display of royal force that Foucault describes
in his account of public executions.[36] The invisible distribution of
punishments and rewards is one mark of a regime of surveillance
somewhere beyond absolutism, a regime into which the political
world of *Sejanus* gradually fades.

Tiberius does not stand for the absolutist sovereign that James I
aspired to be after he came to the throne in 1603, the year *Sejanus*
was staged. Jonson's Caesar is not a Renaissance potentate; he is a
learned Renaissance playwright's idea of what an early Roman emperor would be like. Jonson's attempt to reconstruct antiquity does
not rob *Sejanus* of political relevance to his own times; on the con-
trary, his historical consciousness is at the very heart of the play's
contemporaneity.[37] There are points at which the family resem-
blances between *princeps* and prince are unavoidable, and Jonson
does not hesitate to make use of them (see, for example, I. 536–

40). It is also significant that Jonson chose to dramatize events in Rome during Tiberius's reign rather than during some other period. Yet he did not do so to exploit at length the sort of correspondences that the unfortunate historian Cordus is charged with. The correspondences with James's rule had not in any case had time to emerge. Sejanus's rise and fall glances at Essex's, but Tiberius is certainly no Elizabeth, however similar he may be to James in his later years.[38]

Jonson chose the Rome of the treason trials because this setting allowed him to imitate the ironic austerity of Tacitus while playing out his own political ideas. He told Drummond that Tacitus was one of the three best Latin stylists, and that he "wrott the secrets of the Councill and Senate, as Suetonius did those of the Cabinet and Courte" (1. 136). A number of Tacitus's readers in the Renaissance, most notably Guicciardini and Montaigne, treated the *Annals* as a manual on how to survive under a tyranny.[39] The element of survival is strong in *Sejanus*: Jonson had already felt, and was to feel again, the heavy hand of authority, and his interest in how a ruler's servants could abuse their delegated power was personal as well as scholarly. Nevertheless, he does not seem to have believed that he was living under a tyranny. Jonson's political outlook followed another trend in Renaissance Tacitism. His politics were close to the Tacitean royalism described by J. G. A. Pocock, which

accepted the prince's authority as natural, or at least established, rather than innovative, and was thus enabled to share in the general denunciation of Machiavelli . . . but it focused upon the relations of courtiers, senators, and other aristocrats with a jealous and suspicious prince and was thus able to draw upon Machiavellian modes of depicting a restless and dangerous political world which, however, was part of the universal structure of authority.[40]

This Tacitism is indeed most evident in the subtle characterization of the Roman aristocrats in the play.

Jonson indicated his debt to Tacitus and other sources through the cross-references that fill the margins of the quarto *Sejanus*. Yet his pride in an almost archaeological "truth of argument" was accompanied by what Katharine Maus describes as "the crucial assumption upon which his classicism depends—the conviction that thorough immersion in a lost culture is a prerequisite for compre-

hension of, and contribution to, one's own culture."[41] *Sejanus* and
Catiline fictionally enact in a Roman setting some of the developments that were actually taking place in the wider political sphere
of their times. In emphasizing the instances of espionage and informing in Tacitus's account, Jonson is probably ringing changes
upon the role of intelligence in the politics of the preceding decade,
particularly the involvement of Essex in it. But he is also trying to
construct the sort of state that espionage produces; furthermore,
he is following some elements in the politics of his time through
to their potential in order to show what they could become on the
basis of what they had become in the distant past. "[H]e which can
faine a *Common-wealth* (which is the *Poet*) can governe it with *Counsels*, strengthen it with *Laws*, correct it with *Iudgements*" (*Timber*,
8. 595), and this goes for the worst possible state as well as the best.

In Roman history, Tiberius represented a definite stage in the
passage from the abstract sovereignty the republic embodied to the
individual sovereign of the empire and, eventually, the kingdoms
and principalities of the Middle Ages and Renaissance. In delving
back into the past, Jonson is in effect contemplating the potential
reversal of this process in contemporary Europe, the movement
from the sovereign toward abstract sovereignty. In *Sejanus*, Tiberius's intangibility already suggests a vague personification of such
sovereignty rather than the strong personal monarch of absolutism, which was a transitional stage in the process I am sketching.
Geoffrey Hill remarks that Jonson's Sabinus, who begins as a
"Tudor apologist," ends up sounding like a "post-Restoration
Whig."[42] Yet Jonson was foretelling neither the vagaries of James's
reign nor the rise of the European nation-state. He was experi-
menting with the politics of ancient Rome, where the concept of
a republican sovereignty was thinkable, in light of the present and
with an eye to the future. The result in both his Roman tragedies
is a mixture of Tacitean royalism with a general statism that is tangential to James's attempts at absolutism rather than accurately prophetic of them.[43]

Surveillance might seem to be an attribute of individual sovereignty in this scheme, were it not for Tiberius's disappearing act in
Sejanus, and the even greater role played by intelligence in *Catiline
his Conspiracy* (1611), a play about republican Rome that Jonson
wrote some years later. Surveillance retains much of its problem-

atic nature in *Catiline*. As John J. Enck points out, the presence of the Allobroges in *Catiline* is a signal that the empire is at stake in this play about the republic; only the fate of Rome itself seemed important during the claustrophobic action of *Sejanus*.[44] *Catiline* is more pertinent to a later stage of imperial statism than its predecessor, even though it is set in the republic and *Sejanus* in the empire.

Following *Sejanus*, *Catiline* attempts to redeem and idealize surveilling state power in a Roman republican context by turning to the theological category of divine vision and its justice. The withdrawn Tiberius has been replaced by "The kingdome of the *Senate*" (I. 225), and it is Cicero who legitimately practices on its behalf the vigilance that Jonson had earlier criticized. If the plays are read in the order in which the events they describe occurred, however, we see Rome declining into a Caesarism supported by *arrivistes* and the urban middle class. Cicero's "bourgeois virtue," as Geoffrey Hill calls it, temporarily saves the state, yet, as Hill notes, Sejanus was a "new man" as well.[45] The victims of espionage in both plays are the same—a group of disenfranchised aristocrats. It is not certain whether the state declines because of the intelligence methods that would later be used against republican liberty or in spite of them.

Catiline is not a symmetrical mirror image of *Sejanus*, in which the earlier play's evil characters have all become virtuous, but neither is it an ironic repetition of *Sejanus* that slyly reveals Cicero and Cato to be the real ancestors of Sejanus and Tiberius. It reverses *Sejanus*, but more in the manner of a glove that has been turned only partially inside out, with a few of its fingers sticking in their original positions. Pockets are created in the story by Jonson's efforts to save surveillance for just, if prudential, statecraft; "significant and potentially compromising similarities" among Cicero, Catiline, and Sejanus remain.[46]

To some extent, Cicero is "another version" of Catiline, the true successor to (or rather, precursor of) Sejanus.[47] Robert Ornstein has emphasized Cicero's Machiavellianism. Ornstein principally means that he is a "political realist" who "willingly accepts the disparity between moral ends and political means," although a failure in the character's "moral vision" seems also to be implied.[48] Pocock's treatment of English Machiavellianism before the Civil War provides a fuller and more satisfactory explanation for Cicero's readiness to compromise, or rather, for Jonson's decision to write about a compromising Cicero after *Sejanus*. There were "elements of Machiavellism in Jacobean thought: elements, that is, of a 'machiavellian' account of the English polity, depicting it as a one, few and many held together by arms, statecraft, and moral ambiguity. From such an account it might not be too long a step to recommending its reconstitution on the higher (if still not unambiguous) moral level of the republic." But, Pocock stresses, such a development was held back "by minds clinging to the vocabularies of monarchy and common law." These minds, which eventually contributed to the revolution of 1642, operated "under the guidance of theologically based concepts, of casuistry and apocalyptic" as well.[49] This helps to explain the return to theological categories in *Catiline*, yet here we are still haunted by the suspicion that Cicero is indebted to the Machiavelli who commended earlier Roman leaders for their use of religion to manipulate the populace.[50]

The divine justice that Cicero claims to administer is figured through thunder and lightning, both actual and metaphorical. *Catiline* thus represents something of a rehabilitation of theatrical display in Jonson's dramaturgy as well as espionage. Divine pyrotechnics are the vehicle for the introduction of spectacle into Jonson's theater, and they also literalize the sudden illuminations and revelations produced by Cicero's intelligence system. When the conspirators meet for the first time, "A darknesse comes over the place," followed by a burst of fiery light after "A grone of many people is heard under ground" (stage direction at I. 313 and following, italics removed). One of the plotters discerns "A bloudy arme . . . that holds a pine / Lighted, aboue the *Capitoll*" (I. 320–21). An optimistic Catiline interprets these marvels as omens favorable to their enterprise. William A. Armstrong, arguing that Jonson customarily avoided elaborate stagecraft because it interfered with the verbal nature of his art, calls all this "a cluster of special stage effects which is unique in Jonson's plays." He also notes that the scene at the end of Act IV in which a lightning flash discovers the assassins at Cicero's gate is the only time Jonson called for thunder in the stage directions to his plays.[51] Cicero, who would replace punishment with the threat of surveillance, has just told his hidden assailants that "The common-wealth hath eyes, that wake as sharpely / Over her life, as yours doe for her ruine" (III. 818–19), and Cato upbraids him after the thunderbolt with the words, "Heare: The gods / Grow angrie with your patience" (III. 836–37).

It is ironic that in the wordiest and (at its first staging) least popular of his works Jonson should also have compromised the most with spectacle and theatricality. In his epistle "To the reader in ordinarie" he implies that the doses of sensationalism early in *Catiline* went down well enough—it was Cicero's long oration in Act IV, a virtual translation of *In Catilinam* I, that enraged the contemporary audience. Allusions to divine police powers shift at this point in the play from special effects to Cicero's thundering eloquence. Addressing Catiline before the Senate, he says:

> I haue those eyes, and eares, shall still keepe guard,
> And spiall on thee, as they haue euer done. . . .
> Thou canst endeauour nothing, nay not thinke,
> But I both see, and heare it; and am with thee,
> By, and before, about, and in thee, too.
> (IV. 232–33, 260–62)

This last line is Jonson's expansion of the historical Cicero's simple *planeque sentiam.*[52] Jonson's character tells Catiline that "thy selfe [is] clos'd in / Within my strengths" (IV. 250–51). Like the introspective essayist in Montaigne, he defines an identity by means of his knowledge, only here the identity is that of an enemy, and thus knowledge is more clearly the exercise of power. The speech is framed by comparisons between its ambitions and the thunderstorm that has preceded it, sent by the gods to admonish the lax Senate. Cicero begins (and this passage is original with Jonson) by saying that the thunder has already spoken for him, and loud enough to warn the senators even if their danger was still hidden in the dark breasts of the conspirators, "so, that no / Beame of the light could pierce 'hem" (IV. 464–65).

Unlike Tiberius, who uses the indirection made possible by writing and absence to trap Sejanus, Cicero is trying to make Catiline's guilt immediately obvious and absolutely present to the senators through the power of direct speech, and he aligns himself with the authority of Jupiter in doing so. (See IV. 450–56.) Yet Cicero's theologizing of political speech failed with the Jacobean audience despite its success with the Senate. Catiline himself provides a figure for the play's unsuccessful theatricality when he describes the political position his followers find themselves in: "We, all this while, like calme, benum'd Spectators, / Sit, till our seates doe cracke, and doe not heare / The thundring ruines" (I. 404–6). For all its thunder, the spectators are alienated from the scene they witness, frozen in a posture of impotence. This may be one reason why Jonson's early audience, like the malcontents on stage, eventually rebelled.

Cicero's rhetoric begins to ring a little hollow in Act IV because his discourse of divine vision and omniscience fails to conceal that he came by his information about the conspiracy through espionage. Yet earlier in the action he realized that all his talk of divine discipline was underlain by more sordid channels of information. In Act III he chides Rome for having fallen so low that the gods should choose a prostitute like the informer Fulvia to be the means of the city's salvation: "They could haue wrought by nobler wayes: haue strooke / Thy foes with forked lightning; or ramm'd thunder" (III. 447–48). A few pages later Catiline voices similar regrets about his instruments:

> What ministers men must, for practice, vse!
> The rash, th'ambitious, needy, desperate,
> Foolish, and wretched, eu'n the dregs of mankind,
> To whores, and women!   (III. 714–17)

The resemblance between the methods of Cicero and Catiline, not to mention Cicero and Sejanus, becomes increasingly apparent after this point in the play.

Cicero's Fulvia is matched on the Catilinarian side with Sempronia, whose ambitions exceed mere instrumentality:

>   I do wonder much,
> That states, and common-wealths employ not women,
> To be ambassadors, sometimes! we should
> Doe as good publicke seruice, and could make
> As honorable spies.   (IV. 714–18)

Sempronia's remark, like her presence in the play itself, provides the audience with an opportunity to practice interpretive resistance against the pretensions of Cicero and Catiline alike, yet its satire comes from a new stress on the supposed unlikelihood of women being "employed" in "public service" in any capacity. Although Fulvia and Sempronia flesh out the specter of female conspiracy identified with Agrippina in *Sejanus*, the political role assigned to women in the later Roman drama is much less important.[53] They represent the belittlement of the association between surveilling power and women in the aftermath of Elizabeth's reign.

Jonson, in leaving the Elizabethan model behind, nevertheless expresses his remaining ambivalence toward espionage in misogynist terms, allowing his protagonist only inadequate cover for his tracks through the stews of a declining Rome. Questions about the source of Cicero's knowledge soon give way to doubts about its extent, or the extent of his ability to act upon it. Although *Catiline* is a play about information gathering, it withholds information from its audience at crucial moments, replacing intelligence with spectacle and grandiloquence. An opacity, akin to the uncertainty that espionage creates in political events, obscures our judgment of Cicero's motives in the play, despite the Chorus's attempt to dispel it:

> Now, do our eares, before our eyes
>> Like men in mists,
> Discover, who'ld the state surprise,
>> And who resists.

If we call the watchfulness of those who guard the state "but lying in wait," the Chorus concludes, we will begin "To loue the disease: and broke the cures / Worse than the crimes" (IV. 843–46, 893–94).

Yet the issue becomes how effective Cicero's selective cure of the commonwealth will be. In the last act, he rejects the information of his own agents when it implicates Crassus and Caesar in the conspiracy (V. 337–66). This is not simple naiveté, for all Cicero's protestations that these honorable men are above suspicion. In the previous act, he concedes to Cato that he, too, is suspicious of this pair, but

> CAESAR, and CRASSUS, if they be ill men,
> Are mightie ones . . .
> They shall be watch'd, and look'd too. Till they doe
> Declare themselues, I will not put 'hem out.
>> (IV. 530–31, 534–35)

Later, Cicero says that he cannot move against Caesar without positive proof, and that he will not make his consulship the means of satisfying private grudges (V. 86–93). "But," asks Richard Dut-

ton, "how are we to judge the political expediency of a man of virtue who judges some of his enemies to be simply too powerful and
refuses to move against them at all?"[54]

There are two gaps in knowledge here. Cicero either doesn't
know, or refuses to know, whether or not Caesar and Crassus are
guilty; he says he will watch them, but this is one intelligence operation whose outcome we do not see. It is possible that Cicero
does know of their involvement with Catiline—but here we come
to another gap in knowledge. The defects in Cicero's knowledge
of the plot cannot be understood apart from what the audience
knows or does not know about him. If the audience assumes that
he does know, then it still does not know whether his inaction proceeds from fear, cynicism, or some remote code of honor. Jonson's
play fails to idealize espionage through the figure of Cicero, and it
leaves us with serious doubts about the scope and effectiveness of
divine justice.

Jonson, who decried "sinister application" in *Poetaster*, and who
would go on to strike a contract with the spectators against state
deciphering in *Bartholomew Fair*, was forced to leave the burden of
interpretation to the hostile audience of *Catiline* in order to preserve his own aloof ambiguity. Contemporary political events
spurred the apparent alteration in Jonson's opinion of espionage,
and they may also account for why this ambiguous stance toward
it was indispensable for him. Jonson had been involved in circumstances touching on the Gunpowder Plot of 1605. He had converted to Roman Catholicism while in Newgate prison for killing
Gabriel Spencer in 1598, and he subsequently had developed many
contacts in the English Catholic community. Shortly before the
plot, or putative plot, was uncovered, a spy's report lists him
among the guests at a supper party given by Robert Catesby along
with several prominent Catholics; three or four of the other participants were later said to have been involved in some way with
the conspiracy.[55] Then, a few days after its discovery, Jonson was
employed by Robert Cecil, now Lord Salisbury, to conduct a priest
to the House of Lords so that he could tell what he knew about the
recent events. A letter from Jonson to Salisbury survives in which
he claims to have enlisted the aid of the Venetian ambassador's
chaplain in his attempt to find the priest, or perhaps some other
informer, who had disappeared. The letter also reveals that Jonson

was engaged in reconnaissance of a more general sort, for he writes of discovering information "by second Meanes" that supposedly implicated some five hundred Catholic gentlemen.[56]

Barbara N. De Luna tentatively concludes from this evidence that Jonson was not really a Catholic during this phase of his life, but rather a crypto-Protestant spy whom Salisbury had set among the discontented Catholic circles of London. He may himself have been a Pooly or Parrot at someone else's table. Even the cautious Dutton feels that "the possibility that he was all along Salisbury's agent . . . cannot easily be dismissed."[57] David Riggs calculates that Jonson and his wife began attending Anglican services again shortly after the discovery of the Gunpowder Plot; they were admonished for refusing Communion in 1606 but let off easily, and Jonson officially reconverted to the English Church in 1608.[58] Riggs maintains that Jonson was sincere throughout his religious transformations; this may be true, but in the seventeenth century sincerity and prudence in matters of faith were not necessarily incompatible. I think it likely that Jonson was allied to both sides at once in 1605; as De Luna notes, his protestations of faithfulness to Salisbury at the beginning of the letter suggest that his employer did not completely trust him.[59] Even as late as 1611 his attitude toward spying was still marked by the ambivalence of the double agent.

Although Jonson's involvement with espionage in 1605 on behalf of the authorities is the most immediate explanation for his idealization of it in *Catiline*, historical allegoresis provides false genealogies for his Roman plays if it is pushed too far.[60] His "double agency" is circumscribed by the way he meditates on the state and its fate through the imitation of Roman history.[61] Joseph A. Bryant maintains that the knowledge of subsequent events in Roman history that Jonson expected of his audience places the limited victory of Cicero and his methods in perspective: the Caesar whom Jonson clearly incriminates and Cicero mysteriously spares went on to destroy the republic.[62] The idealization of intelligence in *Catiline* contains the seeds of its own undoing, for the methods that let slip one Caesar lend themselves to the tyranny of another. It would take Francis Bacon to fathom the abstract sovereignty that Montaigne glimpsed and render the base stuff of espionage a light in state.

CHAPTER 5

Surveillance and Enlightenment
Toward Bacon's 'New Atlantis'

Max Horkheimer and Theodor Adorno open the first chapter of *Dialectic of Enlightenment* with a lengthy quotation from Francis Bacon's "In Praise of Knowledge." It reads in part: "The sovereignty of man lieth hid in knowledge: wherein many things are reserved, which kings with their treasure cannot buy, nor with their force command; their spials and intelligencers can give no news of them, their seamen and discoverers cannot sail where they grow."[1] The rationalization and quantification of the world that Bacon helped initiate means that "knowledge, which is power, knows no obstacles; neither in the enslavement of men nor in compliance with the world's rulers." "Enlightenment," they later assert, "is totalitarian."[2] Their equation of enlightenment with domination complements both Elias's notion of a specifically courtly rationality based upon political observation, and Foucault's wider-ranging category of surveillance.[3]

"In Praise of Knowledge" was probably composed for a royal entertainment commissioned by Robert Devereux, earl of Essex, one of the would-be spymasters at Elizabeth's court in the early 1590's. With the help of his brother Anthony, Bacon became Essex's principal strategist and decoder in the earl's competition with Robert Cecil for the queen's attention and gratitude.[4] The political context of "In Praise of Knowledge" is thrown into relief by its companion piece, "Mr. Bacon's Discourse in Praise of his Sovereign," performed on the same occasion. In this speech, sovereign power is represented in terms of the knowledge and vision of a perspicacious woman ruler. Bacon compliments Elizabeth for her famous wisdom and learning. He praises not only "her inventing wit in contriving plots and overturns," but more especially the queen's "not prejudicing herself by looking to her estate through too few windows; her exquisite judgment in choosing and finding good servants," and "her penetrating sight in discovering every man's ends and drifts" (8. 139).[5]

These speeches, delivered at an entertainment staged before the sovereign, present two different political epistemologies in confrontation with one another. The queen's reputation for political intelligence, placed on display and elaborately praised, is also shown to have been superseded. Scientific knowledge is greater even than the penetration of the queen and her servants, for in it "the sovereignty of man lieth hid" (8. 125). A public display for, and also of, the queen became an opportunity for the relocation of power and knowledge away from the problematic person of the female monarch to the hidden sovereignty of "man."

The sort of knowledge that spies and intelligencers retrieve is contrasted with a deeper and unspecified wisdom, yet the diligent secrecy of espionage parallels the search for such wisdom as well. Bacon's *Essays* similarly evoke courtly observation and information gathering in claiming to offer the reader universal knowledge of men and manners. *The History of the Reign of Henry VII* depicts the first Tudor as a spy monarch obsessed with the details of the intelligence system upon which he bases his regime, yet his command of knowledge ultimately makes Henry a figure for abstract statism like Jonson's Tiberius. Surveillance and enlightenment come together again in the *New Atlantis*, where the themes of the speech in praise of knowledge, written nearly thirty years earlier, reach utopian fruition. Bacon's final work foretells the development of the European state and its program of enlightened government, or government by the enlightened, by those with access to knowledge about the natural world and its human subjects.[6] If the sovereign's seamen and discoverers cannot sail to the source of this knowledge in the early speech, Bacon's voyagers do attain its embodiment in Bensalem and Salomon's House. Yet the Bensalemites are not without seamen, discoverers, and spials of their own: scientific knowledge and moral wisdom maintain a covert tie with the world of political intelligence in the *New Atlantis*. The abstract state it imagines masters and contains the memory of Elizabeth and the paranoia fostered by a court society founded on surveillance and display.

Bacon helped Essex to create another royal display that alluded to intelligence on the queen's Accession Day in 1595. Rowland Whyte recounted the spectacle in a letter to Robert Sidney. Essex was met with gentlemen portraying a Hermit, a Soldier, and a Secretary of State when he came in to joust in the queen's presence. The first performer gave him a "Booke of Meditations," the second offered political discourses, the third, military orations. Whyte describes the sequel: "Comes into the Tilt Yard vnthought upon, thordinary Post Boy of *London*, a ragged Villain all bemired, vpon a poore leane Jade, gallaping and blowing for Liff, and deliuered the Secretary a Packet of Lettres, which he presently offred my Lord of *Essex*; and with this dumb Shew our Eyes were fed for that Time.'" After falling into Elizabeth's displeasure over a book on the succession question that had been dedicated to him, Essex had just regained his position as favorite. The dumb show portrays him receiving and answering letters sent to the queen from abroad on her behalf (8. 374). The faint line between theater and statecraft dissolves altogether when "thordinary Post Boy of London" bursts upon the scene; political intelligence shoves wise counsel aside, yet Essex's reception of the queen's letters is really part of the show Bacon was staging. It betokens Essex's hold, shaky though it may have been, on the position of spymaster or head of intelligence, although such formulations can be misleading because as we have seen, spying was part of a complex system of patronage rather than a professional "secret service."

Bacon was indispensable to his patron Essex in the gathering and interpretation of political intelligence, as well as in creating public displays of his political status.[8] In exchange for support, recognition, and some access to the queen, Bacon helped Essex build a foreign espionage network in the 1590's. Yet Bacon in turn would not have been able to accomplish this without the aid of his brother Anthony, who played a submerged role in both Essex's covert operations and the publication of the first edition of the *Essays* in 1597.[9]

In Bacon's Accession Day entertainment, the three books that Essex is given are finally rejected, but a year later, in 1597, another book would be presented to Essex by Francis Bacon, or rather by his brother Anthony, a book of meditations that also contained political and strategic advice. Bacon's first collection of essays was contained in a slim volume that included the *Meditationes Sacrae* (their theological counterparts) and *Of the Colours of Good and Evil*. The book was preceded by a letter of dedication, not to the queen or one of her powerful servants, but to the author's own brother. Though older than Francis, the unhealthy and impoverished Anthony was ultimately the less successful of the two Bacons. In the 1570's and 1580's he had lived the life of a spy among the Catholic exiles on the Continent, returning in the early 1590's to help Francis manage Essex's espionage network. Anthony himself wrote another, typically invisible and unpublished dedicatory letter, which he seems to have sent to Essex along with a presentation copy of his brother's book. Here he secretly transferred his symbolic ownership of the volume and its observations to the true patron, in return for Essex's continued protection.

In order to understand the patronage relationships behind the dedication of the *Essays*, it is necessary to compare the differing careers of the Bacon brothers. The story of their partnership is also the story of how many crucial intelligence operations came to be conducted by Essex in the decade following Walsingham's death in 1590. Anthony Bacon was an experienced intelligencer with links to the networks of both Walsingham and Lord Burghley (10. 7–8). While in France, he consorted with the spy Nicholas Faunt, one of Walsingham's secretaries and a man of strong Protestant sympathies, and he remained in constant correspondence with his brother Francis (8. 9 note; 16). Nevertheless, their mother, Lady Ann Bacon, suspected him of being a secret convert to Catholicism (8. 31–32, 110). The queen, as we read in a letter to Anthony from Walsingham himself, had greater faith in his allegiance. She trusted his reports from France, for "you have had better intelligence in that corner than hath been received from any others in those parts" (10. 8). Anthony kept up a correspondence with spies in various places on the Continent after his return to England in 1592, and two years later Francis wrote to ask him "whether it were not a good time to set in strongly with the Queen to draw her to honour your travels. For in the course I am like to take, it will be a great and a necessary stay to me, besides the natural comfort I shall receive" (8. 349). Francis offered to raise the matter of Anthony's "travels" with his patron Essex.

Essex and Francis Bacon were both sojourners in the world of court society, where the art of observing people shaded into an intense competition for information about immediate rivals and foreign affairs. Such knowledge meant political power, and during the early 1590's Essex strove with Burghley and his son Robert Cecil for access to it. Immediately upon Walsingham's death the principal conduct of intelligence fell temporarily into the hands of Sir Thomas Heneage.[10] Thomas Phelippes, or Philips, a cipher expert under Walsingham, simultaneously went freelance, setting up his own espionage service with a few of his old master's agents in the field. He approached Burghley for employment, but was rebuffed: the Cecils wanted to build their own network of trusted reporters.[11] Anthony Bacon seems to have remained one of their correspondents (8. 118, 252 note).

Francis, in the meantime, had become an affectionate client of Essex (8. 104–6), and by his own account in his later "Apology" over his part in the Essex affair he soon enlisted his brother in the earl's rival service (10. 143).[12] Bacon finally drew the available Phelippes into Essex's enterprise as well, giving the cipher expert his first mission with the words: "in this beginning of intelligence I pray spare no care to conduct the matter to sort to good effect" (8. 252). Another letter, dated September 1592, indicates that Phelippes was sent to Europe; the "matter" he was to look into may have concerned the new fears over seminary priests and Spanish invasion plans that the Privy Council, to which Essex was anxious to be admitted, was currently addressing (8. 118). The efforts of the Bacon brothers and Phelippes probably helped bring about the earl's appointment to the Council in the summer of 1593.

It may have been during this period that Elizabeth, as Bacon once claimed to James I, called him "her watch-candle, because it pleased her to say I did continually burn (and yet she suffered me to waste almost to nothing)" (11. 280). But Bacon was really Essex's watch candle. In his exhaustive documentary biography, James Spedding argued convincingly that Bacon's labors on Essex's behalf were probably even more extensive than the ample but accidentally preserved information we have indicates (8. 119). By the time of his appointment to the Council, the earl patronized a number of intelligencers in France and Spain; Francis handled the correspondence while Anthony acted as chief decoder. Both brothers gave advice concerning the conduct of operations in the process. By the end of 1593 one of Anthony's contacts described in a letter to him how the earl had set aside several chambers in Essex House for conferences with "friends," "for I see all matters of intelligence are wholly in his hands, wherein the queen receiveth great liking."[13] "The Queen," Essex wrote to Bacon, "did require of me a draft of an Instruction for matter of intelligence, seeming willing now she hath sworn me one of her Council to use my service in that way. . . . I pray you, as your leisure will serve, send me your conceipt as soon as you can; for I know not how soon I shall be called on. I will draw some notes of mine own which I will reform and enlarge by yours" (8. 251). Francis Bacon remained an important part, perhaps the most important part, in Essex's newfound prominence "in that way," largely by virtue of his talent as a writer and strategist.

We have one example of this from 1594. Early in that year, some of the followers of Don Antonio, the pretender to the throne of Portugal whom Elizabeth had received in London to discountenance Philip of Spain, were discovered to be spying in England on Philip's behalf. A conspiracy to murder the queen was detected or invented from the evidence, the most important piece of which was a letter to Roderigo Lopez, a client of Don Antonio and Elizabeth's personal physician.[14] The Lopez affair inspired Bacon to draft a document for Essex that he entitled "The first fragments of a discourse touching intelligence and the safety of the Queen's person" (8. 305). Very little of the discourse survives. "The first remedy in my poor opinion," it begins, "is the reputation of good intelligence. I say not only good intelligence, but the reputation and fame thereof." Observing that thieves will not risk stealing near booths set to watch them, even when they suspect the booths to be unoccupied, he writes: "So likewise if there be sown an opinion abroad that her Majesty hath much secret intelligence, and that all is full of spies and false brethren," mutual suspicion and fear of surveillance will prevent Jesuit priests and other malefactors from successfully conspiring together (8. 305–6).

This public program was to some extent the plan of action that Bacon followed in his own career as well. He sought to parlay his reputation for all kinds of intelligence into favor at court. He found an opportunity to do so by writing a few theatrical pieces during the 1590's; the speeches in praise of knowledge and the queen and the tiltyard "dumb show" are examples. Bacon also made his brother part of his program of personal advancement by drafting him into Essex's service. Anthony had fallen ill after his long period of service abroad, but he turned his expertise to the advantage of Francis and their patron. Two years after promising to bring his work to the attention of the queen, Francis wrote to him recounting how his most recent "advertisements," as intelligence reports were called, had been given to Elizabeth and had again earned her thanks: "The advertisements her Majesty made estimation of as concurring with other advertisements and belike concurring also with her opinion" (9. 37). Nothing else was said of Anthony, but "The Queen saluted me today," and "I do find in the speech of some ladies and the very face of this Court some addition of reputation, as methinks, to us both" (9. 36–37). A gesture from the queen, the compliments of her ladies—these were the signs of a mysterious and unpredictable authority that the courtier deciphered at second hand for his brother.

Bacon's career at court as Essex's client and as Elizabeth's intelligence expert was the setting for the *Essays*'s appearance in 1597. As we have seen, one tribute that Anthony did receive from his brother was Francis's dedication of the first edition to him. In the "Epistle Dedicatorie," Francis compares his writings to unripe fruit that has been gathered to prevent stealing, claiming that he published them because they had been intercepted by others, as if, I would add, they were dispatches or spies' reports. Fearing the unauthorized publication of uncorrected versions, he claims to "haue played my selfe the Inquisitor" in their revision. And "since they would not stay with their Master, but would needes trauaile abroad, I haue preferred them to you that are next myself," Anthony the unfortunate traveler.

Anthony may have become acquainted with Michel de Montaigne while spying in France; if he told his brother about the peculiar writings of his continental friend there is the intriguing possibility that the essay form was translated to England within the context of political intelligence, which, as we saw, had in fact provided one model for Montaigne's discourse of introspection and putative neutrality.[15] Francis sounds very like Montaigne when he tells Anthony in the dedicatory epistle that "I sometimes wish your infirmities translated uppon myselfe, that her Maiestie mought haue the seruice of so actiue and able a mind, & I mought be with excuse confined to those contemplations & studies for which I am fittest" (6. 523–24).

The essay, like the memoir or the collection of aphorisms, was typical of the sort of writing that Elias traces to the habit of courtly observation; more clearly in Bacon's essays than in Montaigne's, we already find the claim to "certain forms of knowledge the possession of which could give the courtier a special reputation in society and so an expectation of a court or diplomatic office."[16] Francis's dedication exemplifies his policy of gaining credit in the face of the court through the reputation of intelligence, an intelligence that, in the guise of wisdom, transcended the political services of his ailing brother while alluding to them as the source of a mysterious but practical power.

In the dedicatory letter, Anthony served as a stalking-horse for Essex, to whose patronage the essays were really intended. The rash earl had become a dangerous patron, and Francis avoided an open dedication of his first publication to him.[17] In his edition of the 1597 *Essays*, Spedding includes the rough draft of a letter from Anthony to Essex that was evidently sent to the earl along with a manuscript or printed copy of the volume. This letter, with its opening image of immature fruit picked to prevent stealing, parallels the published epistle, resolving the question of theft or interception into the legitimate, if covert, transfer of property. Since Francis "hath bestowed by dedication the property of them upon myself," Anthony writes, "so your Lordship, to whose disposition and commandment I have entirely and inviolably vowed my poor self, and whatever appertaineth unto me . . . will vouchsafe first to give me leave to transfer my interest unto your Lordship, and humbly to crave your honourable acceptance and most worthy protection." Although Essex had returned a hero from the Cadiz expedition in the autumn of 1596, Francis felt, as he told Essex in a letter, that his popularity would antagonize the queen (9. 41). He used Anthony to preserve a secret link with Essex, while hinting at his brother's services to the crown in a vague way through the official dedicatory epistle.

Anthony's complex role in the way the *Essays* were presented was consistent with his position between Francis and Essex in the intelligence triangle they formed. What the *Essays* themselves have to say likewise reveals their implication in the world of spying and close observation at court. There can be little friendship between equals, Bacon concludes in his essay "Of Followers and Friends," for they have nothing to offer each other. He maintains that clients should expect no more than "countenance, recommendation and protection from wrong" (here one is reminded of Anthony's letter). But it is honorable to take the advice of friends, "For lookers on many times see more then gamesters," a proverb that accurately describes the Bacon brothers' crucial position in the shadows of Essex's intelligence venture.[18] The *Essays*, which in later editions Bacon would call *Essays or Counsells*, are indirect pieces of advice themselves. Bacon assures his reader that a following of retainers who share one's occupation, "as of Souldiers to him that hath beene imployed in the warres, and the like hath euer beene a thing ciuile, and well taken euen in Monarchies, so it bee without too much pompe or popularitie" (6. 528). One wonders if Essex recalled this sentence a few years later when he was arrested by Elizabeth after returning from Ireland at the head of an armed band.

Bacon, of course, was to advise against the Irish expedition, and in 1597 he warns his reader about factious followers, "which follow not vpon affection to him with whome they raunge themselues, but vpon discontentment conceiued against some other, wherupon commonly ensueth that ill intelligence that wee many times see between great personages" (6. 528). Clients are the intermediaries who both link patrons together and keep them apart, and "ill intelligence"—animosity, but also a breakdown in this communications network—is a threat that gives followers a certain power in the patronage relationship. In "Of Faction," Bacon begins by denouncing the "newe wisedome" that holds princes and patrons should operate through factions, but goes on to recommend ordering things so that "men of severall Factions doe neuerthelesse agree," while "dealing with correspondence to particular persons one by one" (6. 532). True wisdom lies in the manipulation of parties and the maintenance of correspondence or intelligence through clients. "I say not," Bacon admits, "that the consideration of Factions is to be neglected." There is a similar sly contradiction in "Of

Honour and Reputation," where Bacon asserts that to win honor is but to reveal the virtue one already possesses, and then suggests cynical ways of seizing it by tempering one's actions to content every faction (6. 531).

"Of Discourse," the second essay in the 1597 collection, sets the pattern for later essays in which supposedly natural attributes like honor are revealed to be artificial acquisitions. Truth and the ability to discern it are the ends here, although Bacon admits that discourse is sometimes abused by wits who will argue for any position without regard to its truth (6. 526). By "discourse" he means primarily conversation in a courtly setting, where "The honourablest part of talke is to guide the occassion," and narration should alternate with interpretation, questions with opinions. "He that questioneth much shall learn much, and content much," Bacon recommends, "specially if hee applie his questions to the skill of the person of whome he asketh, for he shal giue them occasion to please themselues in speaking, and himselfe shall continually gather knowledge." Courtly truth is among other things accurate or plausible intelligence, and "Of Discourse" turns out to be a list of practical ways that one can obtain it.

More is involved than simply gathering intelligence, however; one must also cultivate a reputation for already possessing this kind of learning. Bacon includes a devious formulation of his personal program for doing so in "Of Discourse": "If you dissemble sometimes your knowledge of that you are thought to knowe, you shall bee thought another time to know that you knowe not." It is hard fully to unpack this sentence: does it mean that we should pretend to know rather more than we do about something familiar, or that an element of fakery should be added to the style of our expertise so that our ignorance can't be told apart from it? "Of Studies," the first essay in the book, similarly cautions that studies "teach not their owne vse, but that is a wisdome without them: and aboue them wonne by observation" (6. 525). The *Essays* are clearly a conduct manual for lowly practitioners of courtly observation as well as for the great.

Bacon's final essay in the 1597 series, "Of Negociating," deals with openly political discourse or conversation. "It is generally better," we read here, "to deale by speech then by letter, and by the mediation of a thirde then by a mans selfe. Letters are good . . .

when it may serue for a mans iustification afterwards to produce his owne letter" (6. 533). The double dedication of the 1597 volume is an example of how both letters and the mediation of a third party could be employed in a complex negotiation with a patron under the eyes of the court. The series of letters that mark the end of the Bacon brothers' relationship with Essex provide another illustration of these principles. Bacon served as a secret mediator between Essex and the queen after the earl's first imprisonment. Once more his pen was of service: he drafted letters to the queen for Essex to copy or modify, and—to give her a view of the earl's feelings for her untainted by any suspicion of flattery—he also wrote a letter to Essex in Anthony's name, drew up Essex's reply to it, and showed both letters to Elizabeth (9. 193–201).

It was not long, however, before Essex's attempt at rebellion ruined any effect this interlude may have had, and Bacon of course took a leading part in his former patron's prosecution (9. 213, 225–27). Anthony's death a year later in 1601 is not mentioned in his brother's surviving correspondence, although upon James I's succession in 1603 Francis used the old intelligence contacts of his brother and Essex once more, this time to ingratiate himself with the new regime. Essex had been negotiating with the Scottish king for some time, and Anthony Bacon was one of his principal agents. "In choyce of instruments," the essay on negotiating advises, "it is better to choose men of a plainer sorte . . . then those that are cunning to contriue out of other mens businesse somewhat to grace themselues" (6. 533). On trial, this is precisely what Essex accused Bacon of perpetrating with the "artificially framed" letters (9. 226). He may, understandably, have been too harsh on the client who had become his chief accuser, but it can't be denied that Francis Bacon contrived his early career out of the business of both Essex and Anthony Bacon, and that he continued to do so even after their deaths.

Bacon's *Essays* should be read as part of this contrivance. Although still sometimes thought of as an introspective and private form of writing, the essay was introduced to England within the political context I have sketched above. Bacon's ten essays of 1597 are indeed private, but they are also shot through with the anxieties and preoccupations of a would-be public person.[19] When the staged delivery of the queen's letters superseded the speeches of Bacon's

Statesman, Soldier, and Hermit during the Accession Day device in 1595, it may have seemed as if a new order of practical political knowledge was rendering the old order of wise counsel obsolete. Yet Bacon combined the two orders in his first *Essays*, which, starting with the dedication to Anthony, refer repeatedly if indirectly to the world of secret observation and intelligence gathering that helped constitute the field of patronage.

Later editions of the *Essays*, which develop the early version's concern with the relationship between the courtier and sovereign power, register Bacon's own rise within the *cursus honorum* during James I's reign, from treason investigator to attorney general to lord chancellor, as well as his subsequent fall. In the essay "Wisdom for a mans Selfe," which first appeared in 1612, Bacon writes: "The referring of all to a mans selfe, is more tolerable in a soueraigne Prince; because themselues are not themselues; but their good and euill is at the perill of the publicke fortune. But it is a desperate euil in a seruant to a *Prince*, or a Citizen in a *Republicke*" (6. 562). Only rulers, whose "selves" are bound up with the good of others, have some excuse for self-reference. Bacon similarly advised James's favorite, George Villiers, to substitute political information for self-knowledge and self-love. "You are as a continual sentinel," he told the future duke of Buckingham in 1616, "always to stand upon your watch, to give him true intelligence. If you flatter him, you betray him" (13. 15). "Of Love," another essay from 1612, is cut from the same cloth: "the *Arch-flatterer* with whome al the petty-flatters haue intelligence, is a Mans selfe" (6. 557). The self, like the king's favorite, is the arch-flatterer at the center of a network of petty gossips and intelligencers. But as "Wisdom for a mans Selfe" reminds us, "It is a poore centre of a mans actions, *himselfe*" (6. 561). Bacon, an essayist like Montaigne, is developing his own version of a self defined by public service and royal servitude and, in its deflection from the general or sovereign good, by the consequent vices of public life—flattery, ambition, and the misuse of political intelligence.

In "Of Followers and Friends," Bacon blames "ill intelligence" among the great on factious followers. In the 1625 edition of the essay he adds: "There is a kind of followers likewise which are dangerous, being indeed espials; which inquire the secrets of the house, and bear tales of them to others. Yet such men, many times, are in great favour, for they are officious, and commonly exchange tales" (6. 494). This observation may reflect his disillusionment with high office. Bacon had fallen from power in 1621 after a number of disappointed suitors came forward and charged him with accepting bribes—their own bribes—while their suits were pending (7. 212–15). In the 1612 edition of the essay "Of Great Place," he advises the king's servant to avoid temptation: "do not only bind thine own hands, or thy seruants hands that they may take; but bind the hands of them that should offer" (6. 551). In the 1625 version, the last clause becomes: "but bind the hands of suitors also from offering" (6. 400). Later on the same page, we read that "a servant or favourite, if he be inward, and no other apparent cause of esteem, is commonly thought but a by-way to close corruption." The words "to close corruption" do not appear in 1612 (6. 551). Earlier in the version of that year the royal servant is admonished to "Imbrace and inuite helpes, and intelligence touching the execution of thy place; and doe not driue away such as bring thee information, as meddlers, but accept of them in good part" (6. 551). In 1625, "intelligence" is changed to "advices" (6. 400). Whether these changes reflect Bacon's disgrace or not, they do indicate that by the 1620's intelligence had become for him something to be purified or redeemed from self-interest and confusion.

These vacillating views concerning espionage and the king's servants were tentatively resolved in the ambiguous figure of the first Tudor monarch in *The History of the Reign of King Henry VII*. This work, which Bacon wrote sometime after his fall in 1621, was influenced by Tacitus's portraits of the early Roman emperors. Pocock identifies Bacon's Henry with the type of the Tacitean prince, who "did well to be suspicious," but who had to keep his suspicions in check if his power was to function properly.[20] For Bacon, Henry, though a "dark prince, and infinitely suspicious" (6. 242), was nevertheless a great and good king. But his reign was marred by "the dazzling of his suspicions," for "his thoughts were so many, as they could not well always stand together" (6. 244, 243). Bacon often figures this defect in visual terms, writing that Henry was mentally nearsighted, that he was sometimes blinded by policy (6. 244, 238). Like the strong light that surrounds the sovereign in

Montaigne's "De l'incommodité de la grandeur," Henry's dazzling suspicion was the source of a contradictory and occasionally self-defeating power.

Henry's suspicious nature is explained as the mark left on him by the exile he suffered before attaining the throne, which "had quickened in him all seeds of observation and industry" (6. 244). Although he made his first entry into London amid a great crowd of nobles and attendants, he did not display his own person. "He rode not in any open chair or throne, but in a close chariot," we read, "as one that having been sometimes an enemy to the whole state and a proscribed person, chose rather to keep state and strike a reverence into the people" (6. 32). In this passage, Bacon canonizes as historical fact the chronicler John Speed's misreading of an adverb in his source's description of Henry's entry. Speed took *laetenter* ("joyfully") to be *latenter* ("secretly"), and then conjectured that the king entered the city in a "close chariot," a conjecture that Bacon amplified.[21] Judith Anderson argues that "the 'close chariot' becomes for Bacon a perfectly plausible expression of the larger 'closeness' of Henry's character . . . [that] extends from secrecy, suspicion, strategy, and vision to avarice."[22] All this reminds us that Henry the spy king, or at any rate the version of him that we find in *Henry VII*, is largely Bacon's invention. *Henry VII* is Bacon's attempt to render techniques of governing that he associated with the superseded Tudor dynasty applicable to a new age that he felt was even better suited to the Tudors' exemplary closeness and secrecy. It was important for the success of Bacon's program that Henry's excesses and deficiencies be avoided. They are explained away as the unfortunate results of his exile, the event that lies in turn behind the close chariot and everything it represents.

Henry VII is built around two other events, the conspiracies associated with the royal impostors Lambert Simnell and Perkin Warbeck. Both of these "idols," as Bacon calls them (6. 194, 46), exiles in effect and proscribed persons indeed, employed, or were used by others who employed, intelligence practices similar to Henry's own. The anti-Lancastrians used rumor as a political weapon, and raised Simnell, a resurrected Edward Plantagenet, out of it. From their base in Ireland they sent "privy messengers" over to England to cause trouble for the legitimate king (6. 44, 52).

Yet how legitimate a king was Henry? Bacon makes it clear that his claim to the throne was hardly better than Simnell's or Perkin Warbeck's, the "false" or "feigned" persons (6. 45, 165) who sought to become the "fictitious person" that the sovereign was often said to be in constitutional theory.[23] Henry attained the throne by promising to marry Elizabeth of York, in whose right he would rule. Marry her he did, but according to Bacon he treated her coldly, and the popular belief that he slighted her and her claim was responsible for much of the unrest during his reign (6. 29–30, 41–42, 60, 140). The Wars of the Roses, like the civil wars in Montaigne's France, had rendered hereditary rights to the crown inadequate and absurd as a basis for government. Bacon's *Henry VII* monumentalizes another type of legitimacy, a sovereignty grounded in intelligence.

Henry ruled, and continued to rule, because he was a better conspirator than his enemies, according to Bacon's account. If he was not an "idol" himself, it was largely because he managed his own schemes, and was not a tool in anyone else's. He possessed wisdom for a man's self, and this was justified because he was the king, and thus in a sense not himself. His self-spying took the form of spying upon his subjects, seemingly without any intervening introspection. "For never Prince was more wholly given to his affairs," Bacon informs us, "nor in them more of himself" (6. 244).

The Lambert Simnell crisis offers our first real sight of this man, or monster, in action. The Irish plotters send their privy messengers to John, earl of Lincoln, but Henry, aware that Richard III had intended to disinherit his brother's children so that the earl might succeed him, already "had an eye secretly upon him" (6. 52). Bacon stresses the way in which, during the ensuing military campaign, the rebels are pursued by knowledge as well as by arms. Chasing them into York, Henry had his scouts "intercept some stragglers of the enemies, by whom he might the better understand the particulars of their progress and purposes . . . though the King otherways was not without intelligence from espials in the camp" (6. 56). The king is pursued himself, however, by the shadows cast by his own intelligence methods, for his "continual vigilance did suck in sometimes causeless suspicions which few else knew" (6. 57).

When Simnell himself is captured, Henry spares his life out of policy as well as magnanimity, making him an admonitory "spectacle" by taking him "into service in his court to a base office in his

kitchen; so that . . . he turned a broach who had worn a crown."
This singular solution pleased Bacon; unlike Marx, he professed to
believe that "fortune commonly doth not bring in a comedy or
farce after a tragedy" (6. 59).[24] Perkin Warbeck's end is quite different from Simnell's, and in this instance Bacon's view of Fortune's usual ways prevailed. Fortune, however, was not principally
responsible for Warbeck's fall; in Bacon's account it was brought
about by Henry's use of a complicated counterintelligence apparatus.

Henry employs a network of "divers nimble scouts and spies":
some pretend to go over to the upstart, others infiltrate his supporters in Flanders, others still gather whatever intelligence they
can (6. 143–44). The commission of these agents was almost me-
chanically self-perpetuating, "giving them also in charge, to ad-
vertise continually what they found, and nevertheless still to go on.
And ever as one advertisement and discovery called up another, he
employed other new men" (6. 143). Yet Bacon stresses that Henry
himself kept strict control of what was revealed and what was not.

Bacon was struck by the way in which this apparatus, which he
supposed had been erected more than a century before he wrote,
continued to interfere with his own information gathering as a historian. The Warbeck case deserves to be chronicled in full, he
wrote, but "the King's manner of shewing things by pieces, and
dark-lights, hath so muffled it, that it hath left it almost as a mystery
to this day" (6. 132). There are indications in *Henry VII* that the
king's "dark-lights" hampered him as well as Bacon, but on its surface the narrative suggests that Henry's knowledge of the Warbeck
affair was almost total, and is now almost totally lost. However,
Anderson demonstrates that Bacon's errors in his account of Warbeck, though partly due to genuine confusion in the face of his
sources, were often intended to make the adventurer's rise seem
more plausible and, I would add, more politically threatening to
Bacon's Stuart readers. She remarks "the method of the Baconian
historian, who, like a wise counselor, attends not only to other
men's facts but also to their perceptions and interpretations of
them."[25] The relationship between spying and the figure (and style)
of the wise counselor in Montaigne's *Essais* is another case in point
here. The discretionary historian, a politician in the eyes of both

Montaigne and Bacon (6. 305), must deal with the opacity left behind by the discretion of earlier politicians.

Bacon associates Henry's political intelligence of the conspiracies against him with the voluminous records the king is supposed to have kept. Henry instructs his spies to find out all the particulars of Warbeck's past and present, and "to have a journal (as it were) of his life and doings" (6. 143). Bacon uses the same expression later on when describing Henry's intelligence practices in general: "He was a Prince, sad, serious, and full of thoughts and secret observations; and full of notes and memorials of his own hand, especially touching persons . . . keeping (as it were) a journal of his thought" (6. 243). An English ambassador tells the archduke of Flanders that Henry's "good friends abroad" have provided him with intelligence of Warbeck from the cradle on, joking: "if you have any good poet here, he can help him with his notes to write his life, and to parallel him with Lambert Symnell" (6. 146). Henry's writings have disappeared, and Bacon is the one who is left to write parallel lives of the two pretenders.

Henry finds a still more ephemeral way to spread his intelligence of the Warbeck affair, "not by proclamation . . . but by court-fames, which commonly print better than printed proclamations" (6. 144), and it is not long before the rebels counter with their own rumors, "the gusts of liberty of speech restrained, and the females of sedition" (6. 153). Margaret of Burgundy turns out to be behind the conspiracies. A flesh-and-blood female of sedition, Margaret represents the return of the repressed. For Bacon, the Tudor dynasty that he glorifies was marked at its origins by women's rule. Margaret is a reminder that Henry held the throne through the claim of his neglected wife, Elizabeth of York, Margaret's niece. Like Sidney's Cecropia or Marlowe's Catherine de Médicis, she also brings to mind the half-feared, half-nostalgically desired figure of Queen Elizabeth, Henry's granddaughter and Bacon's former sovereign.

According to Bacon, Margaret was the one who discovered Perkin Warbeck through her agents in Europe. She spread the rumor that the young duke of York was still alive and "had some secret espials, (like to the Turks commissioners for children of tribute,) to look abroad for handsome and graceful youths, to make Plantagenets and Dukes of York" (6. 132). Bacon justifies Henry's own use of "secret espials" by claiming that "the fame and suspicion of them kept (no doubt) many conspiracies from being attempted" (6. 241–42). This did not prevent Margaret's bold attempt, but she failed to exploit the people's fear of their king's reputation for governing by means of intrigue and surveillance. Under such a regime, paranoia becomes the general, abstract condition of politics, not just a characteristic of the court. When Warbeck is captured and put on display in London like Simnell, and his confession is extracted and widely published, the people begin to suspect that the affair has been stage-managed throughout by their secretive king. And when Warbeck breaks free of his prison, it is widely assumed that Henry has contrived his escape in order to kill him. Instead, Warbeck is recaptured and imprisoned anew, this time with another claimant to the throne, the duke of Warwick, "and in this again the opinion of the King's great wisdom did surcharge him with a sinister fame, that Perkin was but his bait to entrap the Earl" (6. 202). Warbeck is finally executed at Tyburn shortly afterward. "This was the end of this little cockatrice of a King," Bacon concludes, "that was able to destroy those that did not espy him first" (6. 203). The cockatrice kills with looks. Bacon represents Warbeck's challenge to the throne—or rather, the challenge to the throne mounted by Margaret through her own intelligence apparatus—as a deadly contest of vision from which Henry emerges as the quicker cockatrice-king. He succeeds because he is the one more adept at using not just the power of surveillance, but the reputation of using it, in order to rule.

But *Henry VII* demonstrates that what Bacon had once called "the reputation of good intelligence" has disadvantages as well as advantages for the sovereign as an individual. The political legitimacy and epistemological foundations of personal monarchy become unstable and ambiguous when its authority is seen to be based upon the control of information and the fabrication of truth. Bacon associates Warbeck's remarkable powers of deception with his having been "such a wanderer, or (as the King called it) such a land-loper," for no one was able "to say or detect well what he was; he did so flit from place to place" (6. 133). But the impostor's European wanderings and the aptitude for secrecy and deception they foster in him call to mind Henry's own background and abilities.

In creating the duke of York out of Perkin Warbeck, Margaret of Burgundy is shown challenging Henry's sovereign authority by manufacturing and disseminating false intelligence and representing it as new knowledge, knowledge that we, like Bacon before us, would call an outright lie. But Bacon indicates that Henry's claims to the throne—conquest, his marriage, and the "long disputed title . . . of the house of Lancaster" (6. 29)—were, respectively, almost as repugnant, hypocritical, and implausible as Warbeck's. Although Henry wins by his adeptness at the game of political intelligence, the legitimacy of his claim to sovereignty is clouded by the very skills that bring this success.

The personal monarch—suspicious, dazzled, beset by rumor— is almost unable to bear the full weight of sovereign power and the reputation of intelligence that goes with it. The advantages of government by surveillance, however, remained when the personal monarch was dispensed with as the active embodiment of political power. Bacon envisioned the dissolution of the sovereign self into the collective agency of the abstract modern state. The *New Atlantis*, written, like *Henry VII*, during the last years of Bacon's life, supplements his effort to redeem the culture of surveillance, this time not by reconstructing the lost history of a past intelligence system, but by writing an explicitly feigned history that looks to the future. The *New Atlantis* is meant to represent the genuine possibility of new knowledge allied with a new form of power, a political power untrammeled by the constraints imposed by the culture of courtly surveillance under the personal monarch's paranoia-inducing gaze.

In the *Essays*, Bacon had been largely concerned with the constitution of what he calls "a man's self"; in the *New Atlantis*, the production of a new self by means of a reconceptualization of the relationship between knowledge and power is part of Bacon's narrative method. Timothy Reiss has pointed out "the use throughout the fiction of the first person, both singular and plural" by which "the new scientist *imposes* the discursive *I* upon the world outside him."[26] Bacon's European explorers, however, are in a more complex relation to the land they stumble upon than this statement might suggest. As John C. Briggs observes, "the sailors who find it are also utterly lost, with no idea of what they have found until they land."[27] They come across a civilization "beyond both the old world and the new" (3. 147), one that has already explored, and in an intellectual sense colonized, their own.

The colonialism that accompanied and sustained the development of the European nation-state generated many narratives of imposition and appropriation, but Bacon's story presents us with colonialism's mirror image. The dominant first person of this narrative is best represented by the relentless "we have" of the Father of Salomon's House in his catalogue of Bensalemite discoveries in natural science. It is this "we," the first-person pronoun of the other, that Bacon holds out to his readers, who are invited to find (or lose) themselves in the new machine for the production of knowledge that he describes: "if there be a mirror in the world worthy to hold men's eyes, it is that country" (3. 147).

The New Atlantis suggests a world of specialized knowledge that is always just beyond the reader's grasp. "From its opening page," as Briggs remarks, "the narrative is a highly coherent play of light and shadow that intimates the paradoxical power of the new universal science and its wisdom of persuasion." The narrator claims plainly to discern an island that is shrouded in darkness; its inhabitants open themselves to their visitors yet maintain a closed society; and as we shall see, they seek to reveal the secrets of nature by spying on the discoveries of others.[28] The illusion of this chiaroscuro reality, I would add, is created by the seemingly random accretion of fictitious detail. Bacon creates information by describing familiar substances while varying accidental attributes such as color. The reader shares the mariners' astonishment "to hear so strange things so probably told" (3. 147). The Bensalemites ward off infection with a fruit "like an orange but of colour between orange-tawney and scarlet" (3. 132), their parchment is shiny and flexible (3. 130), and their building materials are "of somewhat a bluer colour than our brick" (3. 133). Bacon's fiction proceeds through the accumulation of putative fact: it opens with a set of fictitious directions and breaks off with the equally fictitious (but supposedly more feasible) scientific achievements of Salomon's House.

Bacon masterfully creates an impression of strangeness while reproducing the conventional symbols of authority. The supposedly alien sign system that the Europeans confront when they sail into the harbor of Bensalem is really quite familiar to them, and to the reader. Among all the gestures and "signs," we have "a tipstaff of a yellow cane, tipped at both ends with blue," a robe with wide sleeves, and the supreme sign of the Cross (3. 130, 131). The scroll the voyagers are handed by the islanders may be made out of an unfamiliar material, but it is written upon in the languages of the Mediterranean world. By varying the accidentals in this way, Bacon creates fictitious knowledge about a fictitious power in a manner that imitates the powers and knowledges of Europe.

This mimesis also consists in a partial revelation of the potential of Europe's developing structures of authority. When the sailors offer money to one of the members of the welcoming party, "he smiling said, he must not be twice paid for one labour, meaning (as I take it) that he had salary sufficient to the state for his service" (3. 132). Bensalem possesses an adequately paid bureaucracy, something with which the strangers, accustomed to giving gratuities to the servants of monarchs, are practically unfamiliar. Bacon himself, of course, had been caught in the ambiguities of this system, which led to his downfall in 1621 and the enforced leisure during which he wrote the *New Atlantis* shortly afterward.

The regular and sufficient payment of government officials was to become an important part of the growth of the modern state, a development that was also accompanied by proposals for the creation of a medical bureaucracy. Charles Webster, in his book *The Great Instauration*, has noted the "definite medical bias" of both the *New Atlantis* and *Sylva Sylvarum*, the treatise with which it was published through eight editions between 1626 and 1658: "The general public were probably more familiar with these works than with any of Bacon's more philosophical writings." Medicalization was featured in a number of other utopian writings from England and the Continent before and during this period; state laboratories were envisioned and physicians "were characterized as devout public servants, or as 'ministers of nature.'" These humanitarian schemes were also programs for a new disposition of political power in its relations with its subjects.[29] Bacon's mariners are told by a representative of the governor: "My lord would have you know that it is not of pride or greatness that he cometh not aboard your ship; but for that in your answer you declare that you have many sick amongst you, he was warned by our Conservator of Health of the city that he should keep a distance" (3. 132). Here the

Europeans are introduced to a new form of political authority, one that holds aloof in the interests of public health rather than greatness of place.

If the *New Atlantis* mirrors the transition to new forms of power, the old forms are nevertheless not completely cast off. The Europeans must swear that they are not pirates, "whereupon one . . . being (as it seemed) a notary, made an entry of this act" (3. 131). Foucault writes that the surveillance of individuals entails their placement in a network of writing, "a whole mass of documents that capture and fix them."[30] The strangers in Bacon's fiction are subjected to the beginnings of such "small techniques of notation, of registration, of constituting files." But the narrator is unsure what to make of them, and hesitantly applies the old name of "notary" to their agent. This official also possesses the medical function of fumigating the European vessel with the orange-like fruit. He is the one who refuses to be "twice paid" because his government salary is sufficient (3. 132).

The depiction of those public functionaries in Bensalem who possess a more exalted rank reveals the remnants of Europe's established power structures in Bacon's fiction more clearly. In the *New Atlantis*, power often makes itself spectacularly visible in addition to rendering its subjects visible. Bacon's delight in the costumes of various great men, for instance, culminates in the detailed set piece devoted to the accoutrements of the Father of Salomon's House, certainly the most visible figure of authority in Bensalem—when he chooses, that is, to make a public appearance. Stephen Greenblatt has pointed out the Tudor fascination with "detail, in knowing precisely what kinds of cloth were used, what color, what cut" in the conventional description of the entry or pageant. There is none of this, he remarks, in *Utopia*.[31] More's work, written more than a century before Bacon's, is more accurately prophetic of the abstract program of power sketched by Foucault. In Utopia everyone is watched by everyone else; those in authority may dress the same as other citizens, but during meals they keep watch over their charges from the highest table in the dining hall.[32] On the other hand, Bacon's fable is closer to the transitional state of historical reality in his own time. More foresaw the ideal program of power described retrospectively by Foucault, but Bacon's Bensalem captures something of the imperfect fulfillment of this schematic program in the nation-state during the Enlightenment and its aftermath. No state has ever thrown the trappings of power completely aside.

Two institutions stand at the threshold of Bacon's Bensalem, the Strangers' House and Salomon's House. The first is a benign combination of prison and hospital. It is spacious and well-appointed, and the Europeans marvel at the "parent-like usage" they receive there (3. 135). They do not resist the paternalism of their new way of life, even though they are required to remain within the house for three days, and may not go beyond a mile and a half outside the city's walls without leave after this period (3. 133, 135). The narrator, indeed, enjoins his fellows:

let us look up to God, and every man reform his own ways. . . . For they have by commandment (though in form of courtesy) cloistered us within these walls for three days: who knoweth whether it be not to take some taste of our manners and conditions? and if they find them bad, to banish us straightways; if good, to give us further time. For these men they have given us for attendance may withal have an eye upon us. (3. 135)

It is clear that it does not matter whether the six attendants are filing reports on the newcomers or not, for the sailors have already begun to internalize the generalized surveillance to which they are being subjected.[33]

If the gaze of surveillance is inward-turning in the Strangers' House, it is directed toward the outside world by means of Salomon's House, "the very eye of this kingdom" (3. 137). In the first account of this foundation, we discover that there are six Brethren (compare the six servants) "whose errand was only to give us knowledge of the affairs and state of those countries to which they were designed, and especially of the sciences, arts, manufactures, and inventions of all the world; and withal to bring unto us books, instruments, and patterns in every kind" (3. 146). Later we are told that there are twelve "Merchants of Light" with this function, "that sail into foreign countries, under the names of other nations (for our own we conceal)" (3. 164). Although the Bensalemites are "especially" interested in science and technology, their intellectual imperialism is accompanied, and to some extent preceded, by political information gathering on "affairs and state."[34]

The Fathers' mastery of global knowledge has given Salomon's

House control over the affairs and state of Bensalem; without the account of "the best state or mould of a commonwealth" that Bacon's secretary William Rawley claimed his master intended to append to the *New Atlantis*, we are driven to assume that it is the de facto government of the island.[35] It secretly inquires into the affairs of other nations, and at home its members, the Fathers, travel about in pomp, using their expertise to warn people about plagues and natural disasters, and distributing "great largesses where they come upon all occasions" (3. 166). They also freely decide "which of the inventions and experiences which we have discovered shall be published, and which not . . . though some of these we do reveal sometimes to the state, and some not" (3. 165). The sovereign has withdrawn into the background in the ancient figure of King Salomona, and the sovereignty he has left behind is divided between the discipline of fathers over their households and the knowledge of the Fathers of Salomon's House.[36]

The remoteness of earthly sovereigns, even in their manifest glory, is a frequent complaint of Montaigne and other writers. The doctrine of state secrets and *arcana imperii*, as Jonathan Goldberg has shown, was a traditional way in which power and knowledge were coupled in the reign of James I.[37] In "Of Empire," Bacon observes: "This is one reason also of that effect which the Scripture speaketh of, *That the king's heart is inscrutable.* . . . Hence it comes likewise, that princes many times make themselves desires, and set their hearts upon toys; sometimes upon a building; sometimes upon erecting of an order" (6. 419). The King Salomona who built the order of Salomon's House, however, "had a *large heart*, inscrutable for good" (3. 144; Bacon's emphasis). In the same fashion, the passage from "In Praise of Knowledge" about the inability of the spials and seamen of monarchs to gain access to the sovereignty of knowledge is revised by the fictional success of Salomona's Merchants of Light in their voyages of discovery. Goldberg notices the explicit association of James with the biblical Solomon in Stuart propaganda, and suggests that the Banqueting House of 1619 was echoed in Bacon's Salomon's House.[38] Nevertheless, the personal sovereign plays a severely limited role in the *New Atlantis* (we never catch a glimpse of him in the portion that Bacon completed), and his sovereignty is subsumed in the sovereignty of knowledge that his explorers provide.[39] The reigning monarch is important chiefly as a sponsor of the patriarchal authority celebrated in a social ritual called the Feast of the Family (3. 149). The almost mythical Salomona is the principal figure of the sovereign, and his greatest act was to found the institution that has taken over most of the functions and privileges of royal power. For this reason, I would argue that in the *New Atlantis* Bacon was moving away from the glorification of James's absolutism, or putative absolutism, and toward an idealization of the disembodied sovereignty of the remote state.[40]

The Europeans marvel at the disembodied, indeed almost divine, operation of Bensalem's sovereign power in response to the governor's mention of his island's "laws of secrecy," and his assertion that "we know well most part of the habitable world, and are ourselves unknown" (3. 136): "That they should have knowledge of the languages, books, affairs of those that lie such a distance from them, it was a thing we could not tell what to make of, for that it seemed to us a condition and propriety of divine powers and beings to be hidden and unseen to others and yet to have others open and as in a light to them" (3. 140). When the governor objects that this "imported as if we thought this a land of magicians, that sent forth spirits of the air into all parts, to bring them news and intelligence of other countries," the mariners reply that they think of his island "rather as angelical than magical" (3. 140). Here the novel power of the disciplinary state is inscribed within older ideas about the angelic intelligence of the remote sovereign and the all-seeing eye of a hidden God.[41] The frankly political version of this principle is found in Bacon's *Henry VII*, where we learn that "they may observe best who are themselves observed least" (6. 227). In the *New Atlantis*, however, power's self-concealment remains almost divine, despite the governor's misgivings about magic. Salomon's House is also called the College of Six Days' Works in memory of the biblical creation narrative, and the governor feels that it was probably named after the King of the Hebrews rather than its founder, King Salomona. "It is dedicated," he says, "to the study of the Works and Creatures of God" (6. 146, 145).

The voyage to Bensalem, and its inhabitants' own circulation throughout the world, are part of a wider political theology of knowledge and power in Bacon's works. The *New Atlantis* brings to a head the apocalyptic rhetoric that Bacon often used when urging the importance of science. The principal formulation of the Baconian maxim "knowledge itself is power" occurs in his essay on heresy in *Meditationes Sacrae* (7. 253), where it is God's power and God's knowledge that are said to be the same. In *Valerius Terminus* (1603), the earliest version of what became the *Instauratio Magna*, he cites Daniel 12:4, "where speaking of the latter times it is said, *Many shall pass to and fro, and science shall be increased*; as if the opening of the world by navigation and commerce and the further discovery of knowledge should meet in one time or age" (3. 221). Bacon gives this prophecy the same interpretation in *Redargutio Philosopharum*, another early tract, and in *Novum Organon* (1621), written a few years before the *New Atlantis* (3. 584; 1. 200). A version of the biblical phrase also appears on the frontispiece to the *Instauratio*, accompanied by the famous illustration of a ship passing through the pillars of Hercules.

All the same, knowledge gathering cannot be reduced to a symptom of millenarianism in Bacon's work any more than his science can. The millenarian attitude made available to Bacon a predictive mode of writing that enabled him to forecast some of the elements associated with the development of the modern state. This is particularly true of the *New Atlantis*, where social organization and social surveillance are inseparable from the achievements of science. Bacon's sailors witness marvels in both realms. He had always insisted that pure or "luciferous" science should precede applied or "fructiferous" technology (1. 128–29), but in his utopia he allows his readers to catch a glimpse of the great instauration's projected fruits. In the social sphere, these fruits take the form of well-run patriarchal families whose success in producing offspring is represented by the artificial bunches of grapes carried in procession during the Feast of the Family. These grapes bring another biblical passage to mind: the thirteenth chapter of Numbers, in which the spies that Moses has sent into Canaan to report on its fruitfulness return with a magnificent cluster. The Europeans in Bensalem are themselves spies of a sort, the first explorers of a new Promised Land. Yet they are also the willing victims of Bensalemite surveillance. Bensalem has concealed itself from the world by absorbing strangers; like the Canaan described by Moses's spies, it is "a land that eateth up the inhabitants thereof" (Numbers 13:32).

The New Atlantis has retained a hierarchical social organization, and it still glories in the manifestation of power through pageantry and costume. The viewers of its pageantry, however, are expected to comport themselves with the discipline of an army, and large gatherings seem on the way to becoming opportunities for surveillance by power as well as occasions for its display (3. 155). The Feast of the Family is the crowning example of this trend. The male head of a sufficiently large clan holds court upon the dais or "half-pace" that occupies one end of a big room. "Against the wall, in the middle of the half-pace, is a chair placed for him, with a table and carpet before it" (3. 148). His descendants stand about him, ranked "in order of their years without difference of sex" (3. 149). At this point in the ceremony seniority overrides the gender hierarchy. Both the family members and their guests are neatly arranged, "the room being always full of company, but well kept and without disorder" (3. 149). A few days before this public ritual the Father has examined the state of his family in private, settling disagreements among its members and censuring the wicked. "So likewise direction is given touching marriages and the courses of life which any of them should take, with diverse other the like orders and advices" (3. 148). The public gathering is the ceremonial counterpart of this *in camera* examination.

From the start of the account we are repeatedly reminded of the participation of women in the examination and its ceremony (3. 148). The Father enters the room at the head of a procession, "with all his generation or lineage, the males before him, and the females following him" (3. 148), but when the room is full and the children are ranked according to age, the gender hierarchy appears to subside somewhat, so that the Father and the spectators alike can be presented with the seemingly neutral spectacle of a living, visible genealogy. Yet it is the Father who is credited by the state with the power of procreation and the production of new citizens, "for they say the king is debtor to no man, but for propagation of his subjects" (3. 149). If women predominate in a particular family, the ritual's ornamental cluster of grapes is green rather than purple, and is topped by a crescent moon rather than a sun. During the meal, the Father is served by his sons, "and the women only stand about him, leaning against the wall" (3. 150). Most important, it is the Father who is placed on display as the visible manifestation of power. He sits on the dais beneath an embroidered canopy that "is ever of the work of some of the daughters of the family" (3. 148).[42]

The Feast of the Family, in which the fructiferous powers of nature are ultimately attributed to the patriarch, mirrors Salomon's House and its patriarchal domination of the natural world. Yet the new program of power that informs so much else in the *New Atlantis* makes its appearance in an unexpected form here. We are told in passing that "if there be a mother from whose body the whole lineage is descended, there is a traverse placed in a loft above on the right hand of the chair, with a privy door, and a carved window of glass, leaded with gold and blue; where she sitteth, but is not seen" (3. 148–49). The mother is carefully included in the ritual of power upon the dais, but her concealment means that she is excluded from any direct share in it according to the old scheme of things. Yet she is placed above the Father, a reversal of the spatially conceived hierarchy that also gives her a better vantage point from which to survey the entire ceremony. She is not part of the procession, and she enters her compartment invisibly through her "privy door." She sits in front of a window, not in order that she may be seen, but so that she may view the proceedings while remaining concealed. The window is "leaded with gold and blue," and yellow and blue, the colors of the tipstaff at the beginning of the *New Atlantis*, evidently signify authority in Bensalem. Is it not "a condition and propriety of divine powers and beings, to be hidden and unseen to others and yet to have others open and as in a light to them" (3. 140)? The mother, though excluded from the open display of power, is in the same position in relation to her family that Bensalem is to the rest of the world.

The *New Atlantis* embodies a conflict in the historical relationship between knowledge and power: Bacon was caught up in a contradiction between the historical conditions that made his program possible and those it was intended to create. He continued to associate women with surveillance even as he sought to exclude them from the "masculine birth of time" that is its correlate in scientific methodology.[43] Bacon's mother, Anne, had been a strong and vigilant presence in his life, and there is surely something here of what Coppélia Kahn calls the "maternal subtext" in Renaissance writing by men, "the imprint of mothering on the male psyche."[44] By extension, the hidden mother may also represent the fructiferous power that Bacon envied in a nature traditionally personified as a woman—the quotation from "In Praise of Knowledge" that opens *Dialectic of Enlightenment* proposes "the happy match between the mind of man and the nature of things."[45] But another, more remote woman may have served as the principal model for the mother in the Feast of the Family. We must recall Alice Jardine's feminist revision of critical theory's account of the origins and consequences of modernity. Her definition of male paranoia as a response to the watching mother, "a woman who *knows*," locates the initial moment of this response "in the European transition from the Middle Ages to the Renaissance."[46] Psychological explanations of the presence of the mother in the Feast of the Family reinforce a political one, for her position in the background, seeing but unseen, is also like the repressed memory of the feminized image of sixteenth-century English sovereignty.

Queen Elizabeth had wisely avoided "looking to her estate through too few windows" (8. 139). When she attended cathedral services among the people who composed the church of which she was the head, the queen was often accommodated in a manner that Bacon could well have been recalling a few decades later when he wrote the *New Atlantis*. "The Queene's Majestie to come to the body of the churche, and soe to enter in at the weste dore of the quier, and so uppe to her travase by the communion table," we read in a description of her reception at Westminster in 1597. At St. Paul's in 1588, "shee was, under a rich canopie, brought through the long west isle to her travers in the quire, the clergie singing the Letanie: which being ended, she was brought to a closet of purpose made out of the north wall of the church."[47] Despite her dependence upon the regime of pomp and display that is also evident in these passages, there were already strong elements of surveilling power in Elizabeth's rule. These elements helped make possible Bacon's creation of both Salomon's House and the hidden mother in the traverse.[48]

A final example of Bacon's involvement in Elizabethan surveillance will cast light on the origins of the scientific method that the *New Atlantis* was intended to promote. During the summer of 1594 Bacon served as inquisitor in an intense series of examinations in the Tower of London. The subjects were various men accused of a plot to assassinate the queen, and the method used in questioning them was called "examination upon interrogatories." Suspects who had implicated each other in earlier testimony were rigorously re-questioned, until—in James Spedding's words—"at last by successive siftings the several witnesses (each being carefully kept in the dark as to the others' tale) find themselves involved in irreconcilable contradictions" (8. 317). The *Novum Organon* (1620) advocates the extraction of hidden knowledge about nature from the senses in a similar manner. Bacon describes a form of inductive reasoning that analyzes experience by "submitting to examination those things which the common logic takes on trust." "The information of the senses itself I sift and examine in many ways," he continues, "For certain it is that the senses deceive; but then at the same time they supply the means of discovering their own errors" (4. 25–26; Latin 1. 137–38). The senses are like prisoners examined upon interrogatories or the foreign inventors covertly monitored by Bensalem's Merchants of Light. Bacon's induction, which was an active—indeed, in some ways a deductive—operation rather than a passive openness to facts, owes much to his intelligence background and juridical experience in the nascent Elizabethan state.[49]

"On the threshold of the classical age," Foucault remarked, "Bacon, lawyer and statesman, tried to develop a methodology of investigation for the empirical sciences. What Great Observer will produce the methodology of examination for the human sciences?" He goes on, however, to ask if such a methodology is even possible, for "the great investigation that gave rise to the sciences of nature has become detached from its politico-juridical model; the examination, on the other hand, is still caught up in disciplinary technology."[50] We must read Francis Bacon through Horkheimer and Adorno as well as Foucault and Elias if we wish to complete the critique of the movement Bacon helped inaugurate. A new regime of state power was at stake along with the disciplinary power of surveillance, as Horkheimer and Adorno remind us:

Bacon dreamed of the many things "which kings with their treasure cannot buy, nor with their force command," of which "their spials and intelligencers can give no news." As he wished, they fell to the burghers, the enlightened heirs of those kings. . . . Today, when Bacon's utopian vision that we should "command nature by action"—that is, in practice—has

been realized on a tellurian scale, the nature of the thralldom that he ascribed to unsubjected nature is clear. It was domination itself.[51]

Thus, in the *New Atlantis* the representation of the sciences of nature implies the unwritten methodology of the sciences of human
control within the modern state. Yet in Bacon's final work we see
the operation of the dialectic of enlightenment as well, whereby
"the capacity of representation is the vehicle of progress and
regression at one and the same time"—regression not so much to
the repressed maternal realm of nature and myth as to the Elizabethan image of sovereignty contained in Bacon's influential program for an impersonal, technocratic, and surveilling state.[52]

Reference Matter

Notes

Introduction

1. Francis Bacon, *New Atlantis*, in *The Complete Works of Francis Bacon*, ed. James Spedding et al. (London: Longman, Green, 1857–74), 3: 146.

2. John Milton, *Areopagitica*, in *Complete Poems and Major Prose*, ed. Merritt Y. Hughes (Indianapolis: Odyssey, 1957), p. 732.

3. Michel Foucault, *Discipline and Punish: The Birth of the Prison*, trans. Alan Sheridan (New York: Vintage, 1979), p. 27.

4. J. G. A. Pocock, *The Machiavellian Moment: Florentine Political Thought and the Atlantic Republican Tradition* (Princeton: Princeton University Press, 1975), pp. 21–22; Pocock acknowledges C. H. McIlwain, *Constitutionalism Ancient and Modern* (Ithaca, N.Y.: Cornell University Press, 1958) here.

5. For the term *character angelicus*, see Ernst H. Kantorowicz, *The King's Two Bodies: A Study in Mediaeval Political Theology* (Princeton: Princeton University Press, 1957), p. 495.

6. Ibid., pp. 8, 144 n. 168; Claude Lefort, *The Political Forms of Modern Society: Bureaucracy, Democracy, Totalitarianism*, ed. John B. Thompson (Cambridge, Mass.: The MIT Press, 1986), p. 303.

7. Kantorowicz, p. 272.

8. Pocock, pp. 334–35, 353.

9. Ibid., p. 354.

10. On the court, see Geoffrey Elton, "Tudor Government: The Points of Contact III: The Court," *Transactions of the Royal Historical Society* 26 (1976), 211–28; Wallace T. MacCaffrey, "Place and Patronage in Elizabethan Politics," in *Elizabethan Government and Society*, ed. S. T. Bindoff et al. (London: Athlone Press, 1961), esp. p. 106; Lawrence Stone, *The Crisis of the Aristocracy, 1558–1641*, abridged ed. (London: Oxford University Press, 1967), pp. 183–232; idem, *The Causes of the English Revolution* (London: Routledge & Kegan Paul, 1972), pp. 85–86; Perez Zagorin, *The Court and the Country* (New York: Atheneum, 1969); and R. Malcolm Smuts, *Court Culture and the Origins of a Royalist Tradition in Early Stuart England* (Philadelphia: University of Pennsylvania Press, 1987), pp. 3–4, 16–18, 66. My view of the court and patronage is especially indebted to Smuts, who sharpens the picture of the court in Zagorin and corrects Stone's depiction of court and country as necessarily antagonistic.

11. Cesare Ripa, *Iconologia*, in 3 parts (Padua: Donato Pasquardi, 1630), 3: 90, 91.

12. See Roy Strong, *Gloriana: The Portraits of Queen Elizabeth I* (London: Thames and Hudson, 1987), p. 159.

13. Geoffrey Elton, *Policy and Police: The Enforcement of the Reformation in the Age of Thomas Cromwell* (Cambridge, Eng.: Cambridge University Press, 1972), pp. 327–82; Arnold Oskar Meyer, *England and the Catholic Church Under Queen Elizabeth*, trans. J. R. McKee (London, 1916; reprint, New York: Barnes & Noble, 1967); Conyers Read, *Mr. Secretary Walsingham and the Policy of Queen Elizabeth*, 3 vols. (Cambridge, Mass.: Harvard University Press, 1925), 2: 281–83, 318.

14. J. R. Alban and C. T. Allmand, "Spies and Spying in the Fourteenth Century," in C. T. Allmand, ed. *War, Literature, and Politics in the Late Middle Ages* (Liverpool: Liverpool University Press, 1976), pp. 73–101. See also Garrett Mattingly, *Renaissance Diplomacy* (New York: Russell and Russell, 1970).

15. Michel Foucault, *Power/Knowledge: Selected Interviews and Other Writings*, ed. Colin Gordon (New York: Pantheon, 1980), p. 121.

16. Ibid., p. 104.

17. Foucault, *Discipline and Punish*, pp. 187–88.

18. Ibid., pp. 200–209, and *Power/Knowledge*, pp. 156–60.

19. Foucault, *Power/Knowledge*, p. 105.

20. Foucault, *Power/Knowledge*, p. 90.

21. Foucault, "War in the Filigree of Peace: Course Summary," trans. Ian Mcleod, *The Oxford Literary Review* 4 (1980), 15–19.

22. Foucault, *The History of Sexuality*, vol. 1, *An Introduction*, trans. Robert Hurley (New York: Vintage, 1980), p. 135.

23. For the relationship between medieval reconnaissance and diplomacy, see again Alban and Allmand, pp. 74–85.

24. For a recent introduction to Elias's work, see Stephen Mennell, *Norbert Elias: Civilization and the Human Self-Image* (Oxford: Basil Blackwell, 1989). Discussions of his background and influence may be found in *Human Figurations: Essays for Norbert Elias* [no editor] (Amsterdam: Amsterdam Sociologisch Tijdschrift, 1977).

25. Norbert Elias, *The Civilizing Process*, vol. 2, *Power and Civility*, trans. Edmund Jephcott (New York: Pantheon, 1982), p. 331.

26. Ibid., p. 171.

27. Ibid., pp. 238–39.

28. Ibid., p. 271.

29. Foucault, *Discipline and Punish*, p. 192.

30. Elias, *Power and Civility*, pp. 197–98.

31. Ibid., p. 259.

32. Elias, *Court Society*, trans. Edmund Jephcott (New York: Pantheon, 1983), pp. 63–64; 136.

33. Elias, *Power and Civility*, p. 274.

34. Ibid., pp. 282, 285–86.

35. Elias's court society furnishes a historical setting for the theory of

identification as rivalry or mimetic desire advanced in the work of René Girard and, more recently, Mikkel Borch-Jacobsen. See particularly Girard, *Violence and the Sacred*, trans. Patrick Gregory (Baltimore: The Johns Hopkins University Press, 1979), chapter 7, which draws upon Freud's "Group Psychology and the Analysis of the Ego" in a critique of the Oedipus complex and the familial determination of traditional psychoanalysis. Mimetic desire, as Borch-Jacobsen emphasizes in extending this critique, is different from, and even precludes, libido, because it is without an object: *The Freudian Subject*, trans. Catherine Porter (Stanford: Stanford University Press, 1988), pp. 10–29. Elias uses the term "libido" in an almost biological way, yet it only makes sense within his argument if it is recognized as socially constructed, perhaps on the basis of the psychic mechanism of a primary identification conducive to later socialization as described by Borch-Jacobsen (pp. 180–81). See also Borch-Jacobsen's lengthy discussion of Freud's "Group Psychology" piece (pp. 127–239).

36. Lacan, *The Four Fundamental Concepts of Psycho-Analysis*, trans. Alan Sheridan (New York: Norton, 1978), p. 88. On *The Ambassadors*, see Michael Levey, *The German School* (London: National Gallery, 1959), pp. 46–54; and Jurgis Baltrušaitis, *Anamorphic Art*, trans. W. J. Strachan (Cambridge, Eng.: Chadwyck-Healey, 1977), pp. 91–114.

37. Lacan, *Four Fundamental Concepts*, p. 86.

38. Stephen Greenblatt's thorough discussion of Holbein's painting likewise relates the skull to "self-cancellation": *Renaissance Self-Fashioning: From More to Shakespeare* (Chicago: University of Chicago Press, 1980), p. 18. The skull is effaced insofar as one can see the ambassadors clearly, and one must efface the ambassadors to see the skull. Thus it "expresses the death that the viewer has, in effect, himself brought about by changing his perspective" (p. 20). Yet for Greenblatt these changes are effected by the mobile viewpoint of the independent beholder, rather than a viewpoint that is always outside, or other than, the beholder. Holbein's anamorphism is closer to the perspectivism of the influential late medieval philosopher Nicholas of Cusa as described by Ronald Levao. Nicholas cites the example of a portrait whose eyes seem to follow several differently placed beholders simultaneously to show, in Levao's words, "that one's status as an observer is itself illusory; it is the observer who is observed": *Renaissance Minds and Their Fictions* (Berkeley: University of California Press, 1985), p. 78. See also Levao's comments on the disorienting effects of Shakespeare's language in his theatrical presentation of court culture in *Richard II* (pp. 306–33).

39. Lacan, *Four Fundamental Concepts*, p. 92.

40. The lute that occupies the center of the picture has a single broken string, and this barely perceptible detail, like the skull, may allude to the collapse of the League of Cognac in 1533, which brought discord once more into the relations between France and England: Ernest B. Gilman, *The Curious Perspective: Literary and Pictorial Wit in the Seventeenth Century* (New Haven: Yale University Press, 1978), p. 102.

41. Lacan, *Four Fundamental Concepts*, p. 87.

42. Ibid., p. 72.

43. Lacan, "Aggressivity in Psychoanalysis," in *Ecrits: A Selection*, trans. Alan Sheridan (New York: Norton, 1977), p. 17. See also "The Mirror Stage as Formative of the Function of the I" in the same volume, pp. 1–7.

44. Max Horkheimer and Theodor W. Adorno, *Dialectic of Enlightenment*, trans. John Cumming (New York: Continuum, 1982), pp. 188–89.

45. Ibid., p. 195.

46. Ibid., p. 197.

47. Ibid., pp. 204, 34–35. On the Frankfurt School's adaptation of psychoanalysis, see Martin Jay, *The Dialectical Imagination: A History of the Frankfurt School and the Institute of Social Research, 1923–1950* (Boston: Little, Brown, 1973), especially chapter 3. He discusses paranoia in *Dialectic of Enlightenment* on p. 231. Although Jessica Benjamin neglects the role of paranoia, she provides a fine overview of Adorno's and Horkheimer's encounter with Freud and its problems in "The End of Internalization: Adorno's Social Psychology," *Telos* 32 (1977), 42–64.

48. Horkheimer and Adorno, p. 191.

49. Ibid., p. 226. Elias also invokes Leibnitz's monadology, but in positive terms, casting it as an early attempt at a social psychology of interdependent beings rather than isolated egos: *The Civilizing Process*, vol. 1, *The History of Manners*, trans. Edmund Jephcott (New York: Pantheon, 1978), p. 251.

50. Foucault might well have been influenced by Horkheimer and Adorno, who already realized that "the bourgeois republics have attacked man's soul, whereas the monarchies attacked his body. . . . The new martyrs do not die a slow death in the torture chamber but instead waste away spiritually as invisible victims in the great prison buildings which differ in little but name from madhouses," p. 228. See also Otto Kirchheimer and Georg Rusche, *Punishment and Social Structure* (New York: Columbia University Press, 1939), an Institute for Social Research publication cited by Foucault in *Discipline and Punish*, p. 24. There is, however, a substantial difference between Foucault's concept of power and the role of domination in the Frankfurt School's theory of penality: see David Couzens Hoy, "Power, Repression, Progress: Foucault, Lukes, and the Frankfurt School," in David Couzens Hoy, ed. *Foucault: A Critical Reader* (Oxford: Basil Blackwell, 1986), pp. 129–37.

51. Elias, *Power and Civility*, pp. 71, 281.

52. Ibid., p. 6.

Chapter 1

1. Foucault, *Discipline and Punish*, pp. 187–88.

2. Elias, *Court Society*, p. 129; on classes, see p. 168.

3. Ibid., pp. 104–5.

4. Maurice Merleau-Ponty, "Reading Montaigne," in *Signs*, trans. Richard C. McCleary (Evanston, Ill.: Northwestern University Press, 1964), p. 204.

5. Elias, *Court Society*, pp. 105–6.

6. On Montaigne's politics, see Donald Frame, *Montaigne's Discovery of Man* (New York: Columbia University Press, 1955), who views him as a democrat in spirit; and Frieda S. Brown, *Religious and Political Conservatism in the Essais of Montaigne* (Geneva: Droz, 1963), whose title is self-explanatory. Richard A. Sayce tries to steer a middle course, but lists toward the liberal side: *The Essays of Montaigne: A Critical Exploration* (London: Weidenfeld and Nicolson, 1972), chapter 10. Recently, an unabashed effort has been made to claim Montaigne for free-market capitalism and its political science: David Lewis Schaefer, *The Political Philosophy of Montaigne* (Ithaca, N.Y.: Cornell University Press, 1990), pp. 392–93 and throughout. John O'Neill sensibly reaffirms Sayce's view of a Montaigne who is both conservative and revolutionary: *Essaying Montaigne: A Study of the Renaissance Institution of Writing and Reading* (London: Routledge & Kegan Paul, 1982). Yet such large categories can be deceptive; the mixture of motives in the *Essais* is due in part to the doubleness of Montaigne's position—as a servant of both Henri III and Navarre, as an aristocrat of bourgeois origins, as a pragmatist whose anxiety over continuity was prompted by an extreme of skeptical relativism.

7. Michel de Montaigne, *Essais* 3: 13, in *Les Essais de Michel de Montaigne*, ed. Pierre Villey (Paris: Presses Universitaires de France, 1965), p. 1080. The English translation is from *The Complete Essays of Montaigne*, trans. Donald M. Frame (Stanford: Stanford University Press, 1965), p. 827. Subsequent citations of the *Essais* have been made with reference to these editions. Quotations from the translation are cited by book and essay number, followed by the page number of the Frame edition; when the French edition is also cited, its page number is given after the editor's name, Villey. Indirect quotations are made with reference to Frame, while brief quotations in French only are followed by references to Villey.

8. Victoria Kahn, "The Sense of Taste in Montaigne's *Essais*," *Modern Language Notes* 95 (1980), 1269. Kahn's paper has been reprinted in revised form in her book *Rhetoric, Prudence, and Skepticism in the Renaissance* (Ithaca, N.Y.: Cornell University Press, 1985); for the passage quoted here in its new context, see p. 131. On the origins of *essai* in *exagium*, its denotation of tasting, and other components of its "semantic field" in sixteenth-century French, see also Hugo Friedrich, *Montaigne*, trans. Robert Rovini (Paris: Gallimard, 1968), pp. 254–56.

9. The letters a, b, and c are conventionally used to designate the three main strata in the composition of the *Essais*. The (a)-text consists of material published before 1588, the (b)-text, material published for the first time in the fifth edition of 1588, and the (c)-text, material published after that date. A single essay might consist of all three layers of text.

10. Translated in Donald Frame, *Montaigne: A Biography* (New York: Harcourt, Brace & World, 1965), p. 235. Original text from Montaigne, *Oeuvres complètes*, ed. A. Thibaudet and M. Rat (Paris: Gallimard-Pléiade, 1962), p. 1409.

11. Frame, *Montaigne: A Biography*, p. 271.

12. Ibid., p. 272.

13. James Cleugh, *Chant Royal: The Life of Louis XI* (Garden City, N.Y.: Doubleday, 1970), pp. 172–74, 231–35, and passim, and Philippe de Commynes, *Memoirs*, ed. Samuel Kinser, trans. Isabelle Cazeaux (Columbia, S.C.: University of South Carolina Press, 1969), pp. 226–28 and passim.

14. Frame, *Montaigne: A Biography*, pp. 285–86.

15. See Friedrich's pioneering fifth chapter in *Montaigne*. Among more recent discussions of the self in Montaigne, see Frederick Rider, *The Dialectic of Selfhood in Montaigne* (Stanford: Stanford University Press, 1973), Richard L. Regosin, *The Matter of My Book: Montaigne's Essais as the Book of the Self* (Berkeley: University of California Press, 1977), and Michel Beaujour, *Memoirs d'encre: Rhétorique de l'autoportrait* (Paris: Editions de Seuil, 1980).

16. I am influenced here by Jacob Burckhardt, *The Civilization of the Renaissance in Italy*, 2 vols., trans. S. G. C. Middlemore (New York: Albert and Charles Boni, 1935); and Stephen Greenblatt, *Renaissance Self-Fashioning*.

17. Timothy Reiss, "Montaigne and the Subject of Polity," in *Literary Theory/Renaissance Texts*, ed. Patricia Parker and David Quint (Baltimore: The Johns Hopkins University Press, 1986), pp. 115–49.

18. Kantorowicz, pp. 219–21.

19. Reiss, "Montaigne," p. 118.

20. Sayce (p. 73) quotes this passage among others in describing how "the observer himself is under observation" in the *Essais*. In the sixteenth century *espier* denoted first of all the act of looking: see Edmond Huguet, *Dictionaire de la Langue Français de la Seizième Siècle* (Paris: Didier, 1946). But covert observation is often implied, as Huguet's examples for such cognates as *espieur* and *espiat* (which both mean "secret observer" or "intelligence agent") clearly indicate—*espier* appears as a verb in his quotation for the latter word. See also the historical section in Littré, s.v. *épier*.

21. Horace, *Odes* I. 26, 3: "quis sub Arcto / Rex gelidae metuatur orae, / Quid Tyridatem terreat, unice / Securus" (Quite without care / What king, in frigid lands beneath the Bear, / Is feared, or what makes Tiridates quake). Trans. in Frame, *Essays*, p. 425.

22. "The magistrate who fled the servitude of Parlement and sought repose 'in the bosom of the learned Muses' found instead endless movement": Jean Starobinski, *Montaigne in Motion*, trans. Arthur Goldhammer (Chicago: University of Chicago Press, 1985), p. 244. I am indebted to Starobinski, as all recent writers on Montaigne must be, throughout this chapter on a number of levels, although a few disagreements will also be apparent. Thomas M. Greene attributes Montaigne's early fascination with negotiation during sieges to his fear that both his self and his text were being infiltrated by foreign authorities: "Dangerous Parleys—Montaigne's *Essais* 1:5 and 6," in *The Vulnerable Text: Essays on Renaissance Literature* (New York: Columbia University Press, 1986), p. 127.

23. Samuel Kinser, "Introduction," *Memoirs of Philippe de Commynes*, p. 71.

24. Compare Craig B. Brush, "Montaigne Tries Out Self-Study," *L'Esprit Créateur* 20 (1980), 23–35. Brush points out (p. 33) that Montaigne uses the verb "essayer" seven times in the essay from which this passage comes, "De l'exercitation."

25. These passages may owe something to the description of the Persian Great King and his intelligence system in the pseudo-Aristotelian work *De mundo*, which was translated into Latin during the Middle Ages twice and which was also included in the Aldine edition of Aristotle's works. For the *De mundo*, see Kantorowicz, p. 263. And recall Montaigne's reference to the King of Persia in his remarks on the *Roytelets* (1. 42, Villey 265).

26. Michael Burn, *The Debatable Land: A Study of the Motives of Spies in Two Ages* (London: Hamish Hamilton, 1970), p. 40.

27. Montaigne, *Oeuvres complètes*, p. 1388.

28. Max Horkheimer, "Montaigne et la fonction du scepticisme," in *Théorie critique: Essais*, ed. Luc Ferry and Alain Renault (Paris: Payot, 1978), p. 267.

29. Frame, *Montaigne: A Biography*, p. 140; Alphonse Grün, *La vie publique de Montaigne* (Paris: Librairie d'Amyot, 1855), pp. 302–3, 311–14.

30. Baldesar Castiglione, *The Book of the Courtier*, trans. Charles Singleton (Garden City, N.Y.: Doubleday, 1959), pp. 327–28. Ottaviano sidesteps the paradox with the analogy of the whetstone that sharpens iron while cutting nothing itself (p. 330).

31. Francesco Guicciardini, *Maxims and Reflections (Ricordi)*, trans. Mario Domandi (Philadelphia: University of Pennsylvania Press, 1972), p. 40.

32. See Burn, p. 122.

33. On prudence and adaptability, see Victoria Kahn, *Rhetoric*, especially pp. 56, 67–75.

34. This passage bears a marked similarity to Thomas Nashe's ironic praise of spies and their use of drink in *The Unfortunate Traveller*, *Works*, vol. 2, ed. Ronald McKerrow (London: A. H. Bullen, 1904), p. 220.

35. Elias, *Court Society*, pp. 108–9, 110. See also Greenblatt's reading of Thomas Wyatt's love lyrics in terms of diplomacy in *Renaissance Self-Fashioning*, pp. 139–45.

36. Etienne de la Boétie, *Discours de la servitude volontaire*, ed. Maurice Rat (Paris: Armand Colin, 1963), p. 56; translations are my own.

37. Aristotle, *Politics* 1313b, in *The Politics of Aristotle*, trans. Ernest Baker (Oxford: Clarendon, 1948), p. 245.

38. Guicciardini, p. 67.

39. La Boétie, pp. 90–91.

40. Aristotle, 1287b, p. 148.

41. Merleau-Ponty, p. 207. See also Anthony Wilden, "Par divers moyens on arrive à pareille fin: A Reading of Montaigne," *Modern Lan-*

guage Notes 83 (1968), 577–97, and François Rigolot, "Montaigne's Purloined Letters," *Yale French Studies* 64 (1983), 145–66.

42. Jacques Derrida, "The Politics of Friendship," *The Journal of Philosophy* 85 (1988), 642.

43. Kantorowicz, pp. 219, 220–21.

44. Foucault, *Discipline and Punish*, pp. 187–88; *Surveiller et punir: Naissance de la prison* (Paris: Gallimard, 1975), p. 189.

45. Horkheimer, "Montaigne," p. 291.

46. Foucault, *Power/Knowledge*, p. 155.

47. On spying in Europe before the mid-sixteenth century, see Donald E. Queller, *The Office of Ambassador in the Middle Ages* (Princeton: Princeton University Press, 1967), pp. 90–98; Alban and Allmand, pp. 73–101; and Burn, pp. 25–31, 39–43.

Chapter 2

1. Elizabeth I, *The Public Speaking of Queen Elizabeth*, ed. George P. Rice, Jr. (New York: Columbia University Press, 1951), p. 115. This speech was read to the House of Commons on the queen's behalf by one of its members.

2. See Louis Adrian Montrose, "The Elizabethan Subject and the Spenserian Text," in *Literary Theory / Renaissance Texts*, ed. Patricia Parker and David Quint (Baltimore: The Johns Hopkins University Press, 1986), p. 310, and Leonard Tennenhouse, *Power on Display: The Politics of Shakespeare's Genres* (New York: Methuen, 1986), p. 25.

3. Read, *Walsingham*, 1: 103; 3: 430; 2: 370–71.

4. See Wallace T. MacCaffrey, *Queen Elizabeth and the Making of Policy* (Princeton: Princeton University Press, 1981), pp. 189–90, 252–54. MacCaffrey provides the best overview of the Alençon negotiations, pp. 243–79. On English spying upon the duke's interests and diplomatic speculation about the marriage negotiations in London, see Read, *Walsingham*, 1: 281–82, 2: 34, 90–99.

5. Read, *Walsingham*, 2: 7n.

6. MacCaffrey, *Elizabeth*, p. 252.

7. Lacan, *Four Fundamental Concepts*, p. 72.

8. Tennenhouse, pp. 26–29.

9. Philip Sidney, *The Countess of Pembrokes Arcadia*, in *The Prose Works*, 4 vols., ed. Albert Feuillerat (Cambridge, Eng.: Cambridge University Press, 1962), 1: 12. Henceforth cited within the text as the *New Arcadia*, contractions removed. Sidney started work on the first version of the *Arcadia* in 1577, but did not complete it until about 1580; his friend Fulke Greville referred to it as the "old arcadia" as early as 1586 in a letter to Walsingham. Sidney began the second version in 1581–82 and had probably completed most of what we now have of it by 1584. The *Old Arcadia* circulated in manuscript among a courtly readership for decades; the *New Arcadia*, with which I am mostly concerned here, was published in its unfinished form in 1590. A conflated edition was printed in 1593. See *The*

Countess of Pembroke's Arcadia (The Old Arcadia), ed. Jean Robertson (Oxford: Clarendon, 1973), pp. xv–xix; and *The Countess of Pembroke's Arcadia (The New Arcadia)*, ed. Victor Skretkowicz (Oxford: Clarendon, 1987), pp. xiv–xvii.

10. Smuts convincingly argues this point, pp. 53–54, 17–18.

11. Edwin A. Greenlaw contended long ago that Basilius's withdrawal from power reflects Sidney's fear during his Wilton retreat that Elizabeth was neglecting her role as a defender of Protestantism on the Continent by wasting her time in amorous dallying with Alençon. See his "Sidney's *Arcadia* and the Example of Elizabethan Allegory," in *Anniversary Papers by Colleagues and Pupils of George Lyman Kittredge* (Boston: Ginn and Company, 1913), p. 337. Dorothy Connell prefers the notion of inexact "analogy" to Greenlaw's allegory, but Annabel Patterson finds her too cautious and argues for a frank acknowledgment of Sidney's intention to persuade his reader against Elizabeth's courtly pacifism. See Dorothy Connell, *Sir Philip Sidney: The Maker's Mind* (Oxford: Clarendon, 1977), p. 109; Patterson, p. 33. Tennenhouse helpfully shifts the emphasis from strict allegory, reading the *Arcadia* almost as a phantasia on the theme of female succession (pp. 18–25). It is true that allegory was a recognized writing and reading practice during the period. But full-fledged political allegories such as those in Books 5 and 6 of the *Faerie Queene* tend to signal their readers through devices like characters' names and episodes that closely resemble historical situations, and I am not convinced that either *Arcadia* bears such generic marks.

12. See Connell, pp. 104–111.

13. On erotic desire as a sublimation of political ambition in pastoral poetry, see Louis Adrian Montrose, "Of Gentlemen and Shepherds: The Politics of Elizabethan Pastoral Form," *ELH* 50 (1983), 440–42. Sidney remarks that pastoral poetry, "under the pretty tales of wolves and sheep, can include the whole considerations of wrong-doing and patience": *A Defence of Poetry*, ed. Jan Van Dorsten (Oxford: Oxford University Press, 1973), p. 43.

14. Tennenhouse, pp. 18–25.

15. "How many courtiers, think you, I have heard under our field in bushes make their woeful complaints, some of the greatness of their mistress' estate, which dazzled their eyes and yet burned their hearts. . . . So that with long lost labour, finding their thoughts bare no other wool but despair, of young courtiers they grew old shepherds": *The Lady of May*, in *Miscellaneous Prose of Sir Philip Sidney*, ed. Katherine Duncan-Jones and Jan Van Dorsten (Oxford: Clarendon, 1973), p. 28. These lines are from a pastoral entertainment mounted for the queen at Leicester's country estate, in which Sidney presented her with a choice between idle shepherd and aggressive forester; although the masque is biased toward the latter model of royal servitude, Elizabeth pointedly chose the pastoral one when she was asked to decide. *The Lady of May* dates from the spring of 1578, or more probably 1579, when the Alençon affair was at its height; it is one of Sidney's first compositions, contemporary with the early stages of the *Old*

Arcadia, and perhaps the first specifically pastoral piece directed at the queen. See Robert Kimbrough and Philip Murphy, "The Helmingham Hall Manuscript of Sidney's *The Lady of May*," *Renaissance Drama* n.s. 1 (1968), 103–19, and Louis Adrian Montrose, "Celebration and Insinuation: Sir Philip Sidney and the Motives of Elizabethan Courtship," *Renaissance Drama* n.s. 8 (1977), 3–35. Spenser's *Shepheardes Calander*, dedicated to Sidney at the end of 1579, takes up the pastoral program; Colin's song in the "Aprill" eclogue presents the classic contrast between unrequited shepherd's boy and exalted "*Elisa*, Queene of shepheardes all" who is symbolically married to her kingdom. See *The Shorter Poems of Edmund Spenser*, ed. William A. Oram et al. (New Haven: Yale University Press, 1989), p. 72, and editors' commentary, pp. 67–69. Colin's elegy for Dido in "November" may reflect fears about the kingdom's impending loss of Elizabeth (186); E. K. informs us that it is based upon a lament of Clement Marot, and in the gloss to "Januarye" we are told straight off that "the word Colin is Frenche, and used of the Frenche Poete Marot" (33). The pastoral tradition developed in France before it did in England, and its importation during the loveplay of the marriage crisis may not be a coincidence. The classic studies of French pastoral's influence on Spenser are by Merritt Y. Hughes: "Spenser and the Greek Pastoral Triad," *Studies in Philology* 20 (1923), 184–215, and *Virgil and Spenser* (Folcroft, Pa.: Folcroft Press, 1928), chapter 1.

16. MacCaffrey, *Elizabeth*, pp. 250, 278. Read, *Walsingham*, p. 251, mentions Maisonfleur's poems.

17. On Thomas Walsingham, see John Bakeless, *The Tragical History of Christopher Marlowe*, 2 vols. (Cambridge, Mass.: Harvard University Press, 1942), 1: 161–68. For Watson, see Mark Eccles, *Christopher Marlowe in London* (Cambridge, Mass.: Harvard University Press, 1934), pp. 128–58.

18. Edmund Spenser, *The Faerie Queene* 6. 9, in *The Poems of Edmund Spenser*, ed. J. C. Smith and E. de Selincourt (London: Oxford University Press, 1912); on Meliboe and Walsingham, see p. liii, note.

19. On patronage, see Smuts, pp. 16–18; and MacCaffrey, "Place and Patronage," pp. 108–9. Smuts claims that patronage was "decentralized" under Elizabeth after its consolidation in the reign of Henry VIII. This choice of terminology unfortunately oversimplifies the early Tudor situation and obscures the symbolic centrality of the person of Elizabeth: see MacCaffrey, pp. 97, 102. The queen may have delegated her prestige and moved about her domains, but she nevertheless remained the realm's cynosure. Smuts's treatment of patronage and the court builds upon the work of Stephen Orgel and Roy Strong, particularly in this context Strong's *Splendour at Court: Renaissance Spectacle and Illusion* (Boston: Houghton Mifflin, 1973) and *The Cult of Elizabeth* (London: Thames and Hudson, 1977), and Orgel's *The Illusion of Power* (Berkeley: University of California Press, 1975). See also the essays collected in Guy Lytle and Stephen Orgel, eds., *Patronage in the Renaissance* (Princeton: Princeton Uni-

versity Press, 1981). I am indebted throughout to these scholars for my view of the Elizabethan court as well.

20. MacCaffrey, "Place and Patronage," pp. 95–126.

21. See Linda Levy Peck, " 'For a King not to be bountiful were a fault': Perspectives on Court Patronage in Early Stuart England," *Journal of British Studies* 25 (1986), 31–61. Peck discusses patronage as both exchange and performance.

22. Smuts, p. 78. On Bungey, see John Harington, *The Letters and Epigrams*, ed. N. E. McClure (Philadelphia: University of Pennsylvania Press, 1930), pp. 132–33.

23. Read, *Walsingham*, 2: 343, 168–70, 222, 206; on the use of bribes and pensions, see 2: 124–26, 135–37, and chapter 9.

24. Elias, *Court Society*, p. 73.

25. A list of the many places from which Walsingham received intelligence during the 1580's is described by Read, *Walsingham* 2: 369–71, where the increase in the intelligence allowance is also discussed. The list is printed in Lawrence Stone, *An Elizabethan: Sir Horatio Palavicino* (Oxford: Clarendon, 1956), pp. 323–24.

26. Read, *Walsingham*, 2: 287.

27. Louis Adrian Montrose provides the best account of aristocratic pastoralism in England after the 1570's, associating it with the involvement of landed aristocrats in the wool trade. Montrose sees the pastoral fictionalization of country life through courtly forms as an attempt to resolve the contradiction between ideals of fixed hierarchy and the social mobility made possible by patronage: see "Of Gentlemen and Shepherds," pp. 415–59, esp. p. 432. I would add that intelligence gathering was part of the patronage system, and that the pastoralism of Walsingham and the spy-turned-country-gentleman Horatio Palavicino (mentioned by Montrose on p. 423) is part of the pattern of legitimation that Montrose traces. See Stone, *An Elizabethan*.

28. Dudley Digges, ed., *The Compleat Ambassador* (London: Thomas Newcombe, 1655), p. [iv]; italics removed.

29. On spies in France, see Read, *Walsingham*, 1: 120, 257; *The Compleat Ambassador*, p. [iii]; italics removed.

30. Read reproduces the tract: *Walsingham*, 1: 69.

31. Ibid., 1: 207. Walsingham expressed reservations about "the contentment of the eye" again in 1573 (1: 256).

32. Ibid., 1: 206–7; Elizabeth had sent him on a similar mission in 1571 when she was courting Alençon's brother the king, then duke of Anjou (1: 110).

33. Elizabeth managed to keep Spain occupied with Alençon in the Low Countries for a few years during the early 1580's without having to marry him or pledge herself to a foreign war. Unfortunately, she did not foresee the duke's considerable incompetence as a military commander. Even this turned out for the best, however: in 1583, Alençon suddenly tried to take Antwerp for himself—and was defeated by the very burghers

he was supposed to be defending. The debacle at Antwerp came as a total surprise to Walsingham, who typically explained it by a conspiracy theory, assuming collusion between the French court and Spain against England (Read, *Walsingham*, 2: 107–8).

34. On the dynastic and affective models of family relationship, see Catherine Belsey, "Disrupting Sexual Difference," in *Alternative Shakespeares*, ed. John Drakakis (London: Methuen, 1985), p. 175.

35. Read, *Walsingham*, 2: 19–20, 14; 1: 415, 220–99; Roger Howell, *Sir Philip Sidney* (London: Hutchinson, 1968), pp. 68–73, 33–42.

36. Fulke Greville, *Life of Sir Philip Sidney* (1652), ed. Nowell Smith (Oxford: Clarendon, 1907), p. 62; typography modernized.

37. Greville, pp. 63–66. For Sidney's charge against his father's secretary, see Howell, p. 57; the threatening letter to the secretary is reproduced in Sidney, *Prose Works*, 3: 124. Sidney mentions his argument with Oxford in a letter to Sir Christopher Hatton in *Prose Works*, 3: 128. The Privy Council seems to have intervened to prevent a proper duel between Sidney and Oxford, and the queen herself reminded Sidney of the significant difference in rank between them (Greville, pp. 68–69).

38. On domestic architecture, see Elias, *Court Society*, pp. 41–53. Maureen Quilligan has recently discussed the tennis court encounter in terms of Pierre Bourdieu's model of the improvisatory nature of honor in traditional societies: "Sidney and His Queen," in *The Historical Renaissance: New Essays on Tudor and Stuart Literature and Culture*, ed. Heather Dubrow and Richard Strier (Chicago: University of Chicago Press, 1988), pp. 171–73. See also Bourdieu, *Outline of a Theory of Practice*, trans. Richard Nice (Cambridge, Eng.: Cambridge University Press, 1977), pp. 10–22.

39. Henry Goldwell, ed., *A briefe declaration of the shows, deuices, speeches, and inuentions* (London: Robert Waldegrave, 1581), A3v–A5r.

40. Philip Sidney, *Astrophel and Stella*, in *The Poems of Sir Philip Sidney*, ed. William A. Ringler (Oxford: Clarendon, 1962), p. 185.

41. Howell, pp. 85–88. See also Montrose, "Celebration and Insinuation," pp. 24–30, and more recently, Richard C. McCoy, *The Rites of Knighthood: The Literature and Politics of Elizabethan Chivalry* (Berkeley: University of California Press, 1989), pp. 59–62.

42. On Sidney's letter and Walsingham, see Read, *Walsingham*, 2: 20; Howell, p. 71.

43. "A discourse of Syr Ph. S. to the Queenes Majesty," in Sidney, *Prose Works* 3: 60. See Connell, p. 106.

44. Elias, *Court Society*, pp. 62–64, 72–73.

45. One of the messenger's speeches on this occasion repeated the request for royal display in a more submissive mode: "I will daily pray that all men may see you, & then you shall not feare any arms of aduersaries": Goldwell, A5 recto.

46. Alan Sinfield, "Power and Ideology: An Outline Theory and Sidney's *Arcadia*," *ELH* 52 (1985), 270–71, 272.

47. See Quilligan's fine discussion of this issue, pp. 175–80.

48. Sidney, *Prose Works*, 3: 57.

49. William Camden, *Annales. The true and royal history of Elizabeth, Queen of England*, trans. A. Darcie (London: H. Lownes, 1625), books 1–2: 383.

50. Sidney, *Defense of Poetry*, pp. 40–41.

51. John J. O'Connor, *Amadis de Gaule and Its Influence on Elizabethan Literature* (New Brunswick, N. J.: Rutgers University Press, 1970), p. 187. O'Connor is the first to notice the Book 8 parallel; the similarities with Book 9 were familiar to earlier scholars: see Robertson, "General Introduction," *Old Arcadia*, pp. xxi–xxii. O'Connor does not connect Sidney's possible use of the *Amadis* with the French marriage negotiations. On other portraits, see O'Connor, pp. 45, 57, 194; on magic mirrors, pp. 94, 65, 166.

52. It is interesting to compare it with the family portraits discussed by Belsey, "Disrupting Sexual Difference," pp. 167–77; and Jonathan Goldberg, *James I and the Politics of Literature* (Baltimore: The Johns Hopkins University Press, 1983), pp. 88–104.

53. Jon S. Lawry, *Sidney's Two Arcadias: Pattern and Proceeding* (Ithaca, N.Y.: Cornell University Press, 1972), p. 173.

54. Robertson, *Old Arcadia*, p. 429; Skretkowicz, *New Arcadia*, p. 545.

55. Baldesar Castiglione, *The Book of the Courtier*, in *Three Renaissance Classics*, ed. Burton A. Milligan (New York: Charles Scribner's Sons, 1953), pp. 524–25. This explanation for erotic love, although subject to a Neoplatonic asceticism, as in Bembo's discourse in Book 4 of *The Courtier*, can be traced back through Andreas Capellanus's medieval seduction manual to the Latin elegiac poets.

56. See O'Connor, *Amadis de Gaule*, pp. 54, 272; the association of this passage with Miso's Cupid is my own.

57. Montrose, "Celebration and Insinuation," p. 11.

58. Compare Robertson's view in *The Old Arcadia*, p. xxxiv. On court and country, see Smuts, p. 54.

59. See Elias, *History of Manners*, pp. 150, 190. Compare Jonathan Dollimore, "Transgression and Surveillance in *Measure for Measure*," in *Political Shakespeare*, ed. Jonathan Dollimore and Alan Sinfield (Ithaca, N.Y.: Cornell University Press, 1985), p. 79.

60. Compare Richard C. McCoy, *Rebellion in Arcadia* (New Brunswick, N.J.: Rutgers University Press, 1979), p. 191: "Gynecia is the epitome of full-blown feminine sexuality. . . . In the *New Arcadia*, her villainy is surpassed by that of Cecropia, another evil mother."

61. Levao, *Renaissance Minds*, p. 236. I want to acknowledge here a debt to Levao that is apparent on every page of my analysis of Sidney.

62. Sigmund Freud, *Introductory Lectures on Psychoanalysis*, in *The Standard Edition of the Complete Psychological Works*, ed. James Strachey (London: The Hogarth Press, 1953–64), 15–16: 381, 182; this edition hereafter cited as *SE*.

63. On the increasing threat posed by shape-changing actors to the tra-

ditional social order during the period, see Jean-Christophe Agnew, *Worlds Apart: The Market and the Theater in Anglo-American Thought, 1550–1750* (Cambridge, Eng.: Cambridge University Press, 1986), esp. p. 118.

64. The shift from direct narration in the *Old Arcadia* to indirect reporting in the *New* was noticed by Kenneth Myrick, *Sir Philip Sidney as a Literary Craftsman* (Lincoln: University of Nebraska Press, 1965), pp. 134–41. He explains the change in terms of Minturno's demands for *in medias res* beginnings and exposition through characters in an epic, but these formal requirements do not account for all the examples. See also Lawry, who either idealizes (pp. 173–75) or ironizes (p. 188) indirect narration.

65. Connell notes that these fears were involved in the revision of the rebellion scene. In the *Old Arcadia*, the people are determined to rescue their prince from "foreign hands," while in the later version "danger of practises" is the menace. "By 1584," Connell remarks, "the prospect of the French marriage had failed, and a greater threat seemed to be from plots," p. 111n. For a discussion of espionage by and against Catholics in England during this period and its relation to the notion of conscience, see Lowell Gallagher, *Medusa's Gaze: Casuistry and Conscience in the Renaissance* (Stanford: Stanford University Press, 1991), pp. 94–120.

66. Sidney, *Prose Works*, 3: 52. Edwin Greenlaw argued, too absolutely, that Cecropia should be identified with the historical Catherine. Cecropia tries to marry her son into the Arcadian royal family just as Catherine pushed for a match between Alençon and Elizabeth. See "The Captivity Episode in Sidney's *Arcadia*," in *The Manly Studies in Language and Literature* (Chicago: University of Chicago Press, 1923), pp. 54–58. Myrick (p. 265) recognizes the similarity.

67. See Lawry, p. 250; and Montrose, "Celebration and Insinuation," pp. 10–20.

68. Lacan, *Four Fundamental Concepts*, p. 75.

69. On the power of women at court, see Elias, *Court Society*, p. 243.

70. Levao, p. 235.

71. James M. Osborne, *Young Philip Sidney, 1572–1577* (New Haven: Yale University Press, 1972), pp. 478–79, 491–97; Howell, pp. 42–47.

72. Osborne, pp. 509–10; Howell, pp. 93–96.

73. Camden, books 1–2: 391–92; McCaffrey, *Elizabeth*, pp. 261–62; Osborne, p. 503.

74. Sidney, *Prose Works*, 3: 147. Ironically, Mary Stuart's supporters placed a double-agent in Sidney's retinue about this time, to spy on his father-in-law Walsingham—none other than Robert Poley, who was later present at Marlowe's death: see Frederick Boas, *Christopher Marlowe: A Biographical and Critical Study* (Oxford: Clarendon, 1940), pp. 121–22. I owe this reference to David Riggs.

75. John Bruce, ed., *The Correspondence of Robert Dudley, Earl of Leycester . . . in the Years 1585 and 1586* (London: Camden Society, 1844), pp. 118, 192, 345.

76. Sidney, *Prose Works*, 3: 167.

77. Freud, *Introductory Lectures, SE* 16: 42. On Schreber, see "Psychoanalytic Notes upon an Autobiographical Account of a Case of Paranoia (Dementia Paranoides)," *SE* 12: 21–22, 55–56. Freud based his analysis upon Schreber's own account, originally published in 1903. See Daniel Paul Schreber, *Memoirs of My Mental Illness*, trans. Ida Macalpine and Richard A. Hunter (London: W. M. Dawson & Sons, 1955).

78. Lacan, "On a question preliminary to any possible treatment of psychosis," in *Ecrits*, pp. 190–92; Macalpine, "Discussion," in Schreber, *Memoirs*.

79. See Alan Bray, *Homosexuality in Renaissance England* (London: Gay Men's Press, 1982), chapter 3.

80. For a recent discussion of the term "homosocial," see Eve Kosofsky Sedgwick, *Between Men: English Literature and Male Homosocial Desire* (New York: Columbia University Press, 1985), pp. 1–5.

81. Francis Bacon, "In felicem memoriam Elizabethae," trans. in *Works*, 6: 317.

82. Alice Jardine, *Gynesis: Configurations of Woman and Modernity* (Ithaca, N.Y.: Cornell University Press, 1985), p. 11.

83. Ibid., pp. 98, 99.

Chapter 3

1. Thomas Nashe, *The Unfortunate Traveller*, pp. 271–73. Subsequent references will be included in the text.

2. On Nashe and Catholicism, see Charles Nicholl, *A Cup of News: The Life of Thomas Nashe* (London: Routledge & Kegan Paul, 1984), pp. 117–18 and passim. On p. 158 Nicholl points out that Surrey is a figure of Catholic knighthood himself—no doubt, but perhaps his slightly ridiculous portrayal in the tilting episode and elsewhere should caution us against taking Nashe's Catholic tendencies too seriously. Sidney anticipated Nashe's parody to some extent by having the coward and spy Clinias joust with the boorish Dametas toward the end of the *New Arcadia* (428).

3. Nashe, p. 220.

4. Ben Jonson, "To Captayne Hungry," lines 19–21, *Ben Jonson [Works]*, ed. C. H. Herford et al. (Oxford: Clarendon, 1947), 8: 69.

5. Francis Meres, *Palladis Tamia* (London, 1598; reprint, New York: Scholars' Facsimiles, 1938), pp. 286v–287r.

6. Jonathan Goldberg, "Sodomy and Society," *Southwest Review* 69 (1984), 373 (Goldberg's emphasis), 377. A similar path from Machiavellian manipulation through the recording of voices to theatrical subversion in Elizabethan England is traced by Stephen Greenblatt in "Invisible Bullets," the second chapter of *Shakespearean Negotiations: The Circulation of Social Energy in Renaissance England* (Berkeley: University of California Press, 1988), pp. 21–65, parts of which first appeared in *Glyph* 8 (1981), 40–61. Greenblatt also begins with a discussion of the Baines libel.

7. Read, *Walsingham*, 2. 327n. Despite his own extreme Protestantism, Walsingham created Queen Elizabeth's Men in March of 1583. See E. K.

Chambers, *The Elizabethan Stage*, 2 vols. (Oxford: Clarendon, 1923), 2. 104–5. In demonstrating that sixteenth-century "Puritans" were not necessarily antitheatrical, Margot Heinemann suggests that although Walsingham and other nobles patronized theater companies principally to please the queen, "they may also have had an eye to influencing public opinion"; see *Puritanism and Theatre: Thomas Middleton and Opposition Drama under the Early Stuarts* (Cambridge, Eng.: Cambridge University Press, 1980), p. 13. On one occasion Walsingham protected an allegorical "Play of the Cards" that satirized courtiers (Heinemann, p. 159n). In 1588, the comedian Richard Tarlton was on good enough terms with Walsingham to write him from his deathbed to ask for legal help: see Eccles, p. 125.

8. Eccles, p. 36.

9. Stone, *An Elizabethan*, pp. 234–35; Read, *Walsingham*, 2: 322–35. Spies in the service of Burghley and his son Robert Cecil after Walsingham's death followed more or less the same pattern: see P. M. Handover, *The Second Cecil* (London: Eyre & Spottiswoode, 1959), p. 103.

10. Read, *Walsingham*, 2: 329.

11. Bakeless, 1: 77; italics removed.

12. Bakeless 1: 84; Philip Henderson, "Marlowe as a Messenger," letter to the editor in *The Times Literary Supplement*, June 12, 1953, 381. Both these names are variant spellings of "Marlowe"—the dramatist seems to have preferred "Marley" himself: Bakeless 1: 96, x.

13. R. B. Wernham, "Christopher Marlowe at Flushing in 1592," *English Historical Review* 91 (1976), 344–45. For a summary of, and some useful additions to, scholarship on Baines, see Constance Brown Kuriyama, "Marlowe's Nemesis: The Identity of Richard Baines," in *"A Poet and a filthy Play-maker": New Essays on Christopher Marlowe*, ed. Kenneth Friedenreich, Roma Gill, and Constance Brown Kuriyama (New York: AMS Press, 1988), pp. 343–60.

14. Quoted in Clifford Leech, *Christopher Marlowe: Poet for the Stage*, ed. Anne Lancashire (New York: AMS Press, 1986), p. 9. Leech gives the original text of the Baines report in full. I have also found his concise summary of events in Marlowe's life on pp. 2–11 very helpful.

15. Eccles, p. 37.

16. Bakeless, 1: 104–5; William Urry, *Christopher Marlowe and Canterbury* (London: Faber and Faber, 1988), pp. 64–65. This meant that Marlowe would be fined a sum of money should he fail to keep the peace.

17. Kuriyama (p. 357) comes to a similar conclusion.

18. Kyd may have been the unlucky one. Verses threatening aliens in London were found tacked on the wall of the Dutch Church yard in May 1593; this "Dutch Church Libel" was glossed with the words *"per Tamburlaine,"* an apparent attribution that may have led the authorities to stumble across Kyd in the course of tracking down Marlowe. See Arthur Freeman, "Marlowe, Kyd, and the Dutch Church Libel," *ELR* 3 (1973), 44–52.

19. The letters are reproduced in A. D. Wraight, *In Search of Christopher Marlowe* (New York: Vanguard Press, 1965), pp. 314–16.

20. See Bakeless, 1: 142–84; and J. Leslie Hotson, *The Death of Christopher Marlowe* (Cambridge, Mass.: Harvard University Press, 1925). It is to Hotson that we owe the discovery of most of the documents relating to Marlowe's death and his Cambridge days. Urry, in *Christopher Marlowe* (pp. 97–98), discusses and disposes of most of the conspiracy theories: it used to be thought that Thomas Walsingham's wife, Audrey Shelton, was involved, for Frizer went on to become her business agent, but there is no evidence that the couple were married as early as 1593. Yet Urry also intimates that Marlowe's contacts with both espionage and court circles may have played some role in his murder; he shows, for instance, that Marlowe was killed in the house of a respectable widow who was mentioned in the will of one of the queen's gentlewomen (pp. 84–86).

21. On Frizer and Skeres, see Bakeless, 1: 163–71, 180–82. The best account of Poley is in Boas, *Marlowe*, pp. 263–68. Boas reveals that Poley was a double-agent who spied for Mary Stuart as a servant in Sidney's household at Walsingham's estate, Barn Elms. According to Urry, in May 1593 Poley had just returned from a mission to the Hague (p. 86). Urry (*Christopher Marlowe*, p. 68) has also turned up evidence that Poley must have passed through Canterbury twice bearing messages from the court to Dover and back again in September 1592, when Marlowe was also in Canterbury facing yet another assault charge.

22. Wraight, p. 316.

23. A letter survives from the spy Thomas Drury to Anthony Bacon, brother of Francis Bacon and chief intelligencer for Essex. Drury complains that he has not been awarded 100 crowns by the City of London for obtaining information about a mutinous libel; the City had offered such a reward in May 1593, during the investigation that led to Kyd's arrest. The libel he brought to light was also connected with a book and some articles of atheism, and his contact had been "one Mr. Bayns." If the book was *The Fall of the Late Arian*, and the libel the Dutch Church Libel or Baine's "libel" against Marlowe, then Marlowe's old enemy may have been involved in Kyd's, and thus his own, arrest. Furthermore, the possibility of a connection to the Essex faction through Anthony Bacon cannot be discounted. See S. E. Sprot, "Drury and Marlowe," *Times Literary Supplement*, August 2, 1974, p. 840, and Urry, *Christopher Marlowe*, pp. 78–79.

24. See Burn, pp. 29–30, 31, 34.

25. Christopher Marlowe, *The Tragical Historie of Doctor Faustus* (1604), 1. 81, 5. 610, in *Marlowe's Doctor Faustus, 1604–1616*, ed. W. W. Greg (Oxford: Clarendon, 1950). Subsequent references, by scene and line numbers, are from this edition. The original version of *Doctor Faustus* was probably written after the English translation of the German Faust book appeared in 1592. There are two texts of *Faustus*, stemming from the quarto of 1604 (the A-text), and that of 1616 (the B-text). It is usually as-

sumed that the lost original of these texts was written by Marlowe and another author, who is assigned the comic scenes. Marlowe and his "collaborator" may have planned the play together, or they may have been hired separately and contributed their scenes independently of one another. The B-text probably incorporates material added in 1601, long after Marlowe's death, but it is much in favor with modern editors because many of its readings seem closer to what Marlowe and his collaborator must actually have written than those of the A-text, which is the actors' memorial reconstruction. I am basing what follows upon the A-text because it gives a better idea of the plot of the play as Marlowe may have known it. I am also presuming that Marlowe had a greater hand in the comic scenes of this version than is generally supposed, and I am basing my assumption upon the issues of patronage, sexuality, and surveillance that the comic scenes raise, issues that my study attempts to uncover elsewhere in Marlowe's life and works. On these textual issues, Fredson Bowers, ed., *The Complete Works of Christopher Marlowe*, 2nd ed., 2 vols. (Cambridge, Eng.: Cambridge University Press, 1981), 2: 123–59, has generally superseded Greg, pp. 15–139.

26. Leech, p. 9.

27. Wraight, pp. 355, 354; see Urry, p. 74.

28. John W. Shirley, "Sir Walter Ralegh and Thomas Harriot," in *Thomas Harriot: Renaissance Scientist*, ed. John W. Shirley (Oxford: Clarendon, 1974), pp. 23–25. It is clear that sensational assumptions about a secret society of freethinkers should be abandoned: see Muriel Bradbrook, *The School of Night* (Cambridge, Eng.: Cambridge University Press, 1936); Wraight, pp. 134–74; and, for a corrective view, John W. Shirley, *Thomas Harriot: A Biography* (Oxford: Clarendon, 1983), pp. 359–60.

29. Wraight, pp. 315, 316.

30. Leech, pp. 8, 9. On Ralegh and tobacco, see Shirley, *Thomas Harriot*, p. 147 and note; for a fuller discussion, see Jeffrey Knapp, "Elizabethan Tobacco," *Representations* 21 (1988), 27–66.

31. Leech, p. 9.

32. Wraight, p. 316; contractions removed. Corydon's love for the young Alexis forms the subject of Virgil's second Eclogue.

33. Bray, *Homosexuality in Renaissance England*, pp. 48, 67, 77.

34. Ibid., pp. 70–76, 15–20.

35. In addition to Bray, see Arthur N. Gilbert, "Conceptions of Homosexuality and Sodomy in Western History," *Journal of Homosexuality* 6: 1–2 (1980–81), 57–68; David F. Greenberg, *The Construction of Homosexuality* (Chicago: University of Chicago Press, 1988), and Ed Cohen, "Legislating the Norm: From Sodomy to Gross Indecency," in *Displacing Homophobia*, ed. Ronald R. Butters, John H. Clum, and Michael Moon (Durham, N.C.: Duke University Press, 1989), pp. 169–205. See as well the articles by Stephen Orgell and Jonathan Goldberg in the same volume. On "constructivist" as opposed to "essentialist" approaches to homosexuality, see Martin Duberman, Martha Vicinus, and George Chauncey, Jr., eds., "Introduction," *Hidden from History: Reclaiming the Gay and Lesbian*

Past (New York: New American Library, 1989), p. 1–13; see also the essays by John Boswell, David Halperin, Robert Padgug, James Saslow, and Randolph Trumbach in this collection. Valerie Traub cautions us that the stress on urbanization and its subcultures may reflect a male perspective on early modern sexualities. I owe much to her broader reading of homoerotic desire in the period, "Desire and the Difference it Makes," in *The Matter of Difference: Materialist Feminist Criticism of Shakespeare*, ed. Valerie Wayne (Ithaca, N.Y.: Cornell University Press, 1991), pp. 81–114 (on urbanization, see p. 110, n. 24). I am also indebted to Gregory Bredbeck's important book *Sodomy and Interpretation: Marlowe to Milton* (Ithaca, N.Y.: Cornell University Press, 1991), which provides a nuanced reading of antiessentialist arguments about the construction of male homosexual identity in the period; see particularly his first and fourth chapters. Jonathan Dollimore likewise advocates a strategic use of essentialist presuppositions when considering homosexuality in early modern Europe. See *Sexual Dissidence: Augustine to Wilde, Freud to Foucault* (Oxford: Clarendon, 1991). On the notion of subculture in general, see Dick Hebdige, *Subculture: The Meaning of Style* (London: Methuen, 1979).

36. Jonathan Goldberg, "Colin to Hobbinol: Spenser's Familiar Letters," in *Displacing Homophobia*, pp. 121–22. Spenser left Harvey's university patronage for service as the Bishop of Rochester's secretary; his duties as secretary are uncertain, but it is interesting to note that he was probably employed by his next patron, Leicester, as a confidential messenger—that is, a spy. See Smith and de Selincourt, "Introduction," *The Poetical Works of Edmund Spenser*, p. xii.

37. Alan Bray's recent work has also concerned patronage among men, male homosexual practice, and ideas of "manliness." See "Homosexuality and the Signs of Male Friendship in Elizabethan England," *History Workshop Journal* 26 (1990), 1–15.

38. *Edward II* was written either in the winter months of 1592–93, or sometime in 1591. See Marlowe, *Complete Works*, 2nd ed., 2:12. Ralegh and his wife were imprisoned by Elizabeth in August 1592 after he tried to depart for the West Indies without her permission; the queen had discovered that Elizabeth Throckmorton was pregnant as early as February. The secret marriage may date from 1588. See Shirley, *Thomas Harriot*, pp. 177–78.

39. Christopher Marlowe, *Edward II*, I. 1. 10–11, in *Complete Works*, 2nd ed., vol. 2. Further references to Marlowe's works will be from this edition and will be placed in parentheses. The probable pun was a familiar one: for instance, "Elizium" is the name of Eliza's, or Queen Elizabeth's, realm in George Peele's entertainment *The Araygnement of Paris* (ca. 1582).

40. Richard C. McCoy briefly compares Edward's tournament in Marlowe's play with Elizabeth's more successful containment of her nobles' aggression in the Fortress of Perfect Beauty tilt. See *The Rites of Knighthood*, p. 62. On the failure of Elizabeth's "chivalric compromise" later in her reign, see his chapter on the Earl of Essex.

41. See Simon Shepherd, *Marlowe and the Politics of Elizabethan Theater*

(Brighton: Harvester, 1986), p. 115. I would like to acknowledge a general debt to Shepherd's reading of Marlowe, and particularly of *Edward II*, throughout what follows.

42. See Leonard Barkan, "Diana and Actaeon: The Myth as Synthesis," *English Literary Renaissance* 10 (1980), 317–59.

43. Compare Bray, *Homosexuality in Renaissance England*, pp. 62–67.

44. On Ganymede and male homosexuality during the Middle Ages and Renaissance, see John Boswell, *Christianity, Social Tolerance, and Homosexuality* (University of Chicago Press, 1980), chapter 9; James M. Saslow, *Ganymede in the Renaissance: Homosexuality in Art and Society* (New Haven: Yale University Press, 1986), and Leonard Barkan, *Transuming Passion: Ganymede and the Erotics of Humanism* (Stanford: Stanford University Press, 1991). In discussing two poems in which Ganymede debates Helen and Hebe on the merits of same-sex love, Boswell links this figure to the short-lived emergence of a homosexual identity in twelfth-century Europe, and Saslow (p. 117) relates the medieval context to Marlowe's *Dido, Queen of Carthage*. Barkan's book is a general meditation on Ganymede in humanist thought and the visual arts.

45. Marlowe reverses the order of Juno's grievances in *Aeneid* I here, placing her jealousy of Ganymede first where Virgil has her mention it last.

46. On the relationship between the opening scene of *Dido* and the rest of the play, see Eugene M. Waith, "Marlowe and the Jades of Asia," *Studies in English Literature* 5 (1965), 233–34, Shepherd, pp. 200ff., and Bruce R. Smith, *Homosexual Desire in Shakespeare's England: A Cultural Poetics* (Chicago: University of Chicago Press, 1991), pp. 205–8.

47. On "the polymorphous potential of desire" in early modern texts, particularly Shakespeare's, see Traub, p. 101 and throughout.

48. My reading of the Ganymede pattern in *Dido* and *Edward II* is corroborated by two rather different discussions. Saslow, *Ganymede* (chapter 5), demonstrates that in northern European art of the seventeenth century, Ganymede was appropriated for the celebration of the dynastic link between father and son and thus ceased to be a cipher for sexual love between men; he traces this development back to Vasari's designs for Cosimo de' Medici's rooms in the Palazzo Vecchio in Florence during the 1550's (pp. 168–70). Eve Kosofsky Sedgwick shows how the dynastic order itself finally breaks down in the "paranoid" Gothic novel of early nineteenth-century England, where "the hero intrusively and in effect violently carves a *small, male, intimate* family for himself out of what had in each case originally been an untidy, non-nuclear group of cohabitants" (pp. 116–17; her emphasis). *Dido* registers the first of these transitions, while the proto-Gothic *Edward II* projects the second through the hero-villain Mortimer.

49. Foucault, *Discipline and Punish*, p. 29. I have tacitly corrected a spelling error, and modified the translation with reference to *Surveiller et punir*, p. 34.

50. Kantorowicz, p. 30.

51. Bredbeck, p. 76. On Edward's murder and Holinshed's *Chronicle*, see also Smith, pp. 220–21.

52. Compare, for instance, Shakespeare's *Twelfth Night*, II. 5. 67.

53. See Smith, pp. 219–20.

54. Sidney, *New Arcadia*, p. 78.

55. P. H. Kocher, "Contemporary Pamphlet Backgrounds for Marlowe's *The Massacre at Paris*," *Modern Language Quarterly* 8 (1947), 151–73, and see his "François Hotman and Marlowe's *The Massacre at Paris*," *PMLA* 56 (1941), 349–68.

56. Sidney, *New Arcadia*, p. 492.

57. See Read, *Walsingham*, 2: 380–86, 389, 3: 1–48.

58. H. J. Oliver, "Introduction," in Christopher Marlowe, *The Massacre at Paris* (London: Methuen, 1968), p. 94.

59. Quoted in R. B. Wernham, *After the Armada: Elizabethan England and the Struggle for Western Europe, 1588–95* (Oxford: Clarendon, 1984), p. 146. See also Julia Briggs, "Marlowe's *Massacre at Paris*: A Reconsideration," *Review of English Studies* 34 (1983), p. 271, n. 38.

60. Marlowe attended the King's School in Cambridge with a William Lyly, who was the younger brother of John Lyly, author of *Euphues*; the elder Lyly appears to have had another brother named William as well. I have not been able to determine if either of these Williams was the diplomatic Lyly, but it is possible that Marlowe had an intimate source of intelligence for his assassination scene. See Urry, *Christopher Marlowe*, p. 102.

61. Oliver, p. lxiii. Urry, in *Christopher Marlowe* (pp. 2–3), points out that the Canterbury of Marlowe's childhood harbored many Huguenot refugees after 1572, some of whom may have circulated first-hand accounts of the massacre itself.

62. Wernham, "Christopher Marlowe," p. 345. Kuriyama (p. 357) suggests that Marlowe may have been spying on both noblemen for the Cecils—his statement that he was "very well known" to them may hint at this rather than simply laying claim to their patronage.

63. On the date of the play, see Oliver, p. lii.

64. Eccles, pp. 102–13; Henderson, "Messenger," p. 381; Urry, "Marlowe and Canterbury," 136.

65. Leech, p. 8.

66. Stephen Greenblatt, "The Cultivation of Anxiety: King Lear and His Heirs," *Raritan* 2 (1982), p. 103; Greenblatt's emphasis.

Chapter 4

1. *Ben Jonson [Works]*, 8: 25. Cited hereafter as Jonson. Compare Bacon's part in the Grays Inn revels of 1594, where the imaginary prince is told to "have care that your intelligence, which is the light of your state, do not go out, or burn dim or obscure": *Gesta Grayorum*, p. 28, in John Nichols, *The Progresses, & Public Processions, of Queen Elizabeth*, 2 vols. (London: Nichols, 1788), 2, 1594.

2. On authorship as a historically constructed function, see Foucault, "What Is an Author?," in *Language, Counter-Memory, and Practice*, ed. Donald F. Bouchard (Ithaca, N.Y.: Cornell University Press, 1977), pp. 113–

38; for a recent and compelling discussion in terms of sixteenth-century English writing, see Jonathan Crewe, *Trials of Authorship: Anterior Forms and Poetic Reconstruction from Wyatt to Shakespeare* (Berkeley: University of California Press, 1990), pp. 13–21. On Jonson and authorship, see Jonas Barish, *The Antitheatrical Prejudice* (Berkeley: University of California Press, 1981), pp. 132–45; Timothy Murray, "From Foul Sheets to Legitimate Model; Antitheater, Text, Ben Jonson," *New Literary History* 14 (1983), 641–64; and Joseph Loewenstein, "The Script in the Marketplace," in *Representing the English Renaissance*, ed. Stephen Greenblatt (Berkeley: University of California Press, 1988), pp. 265–78.

3. On the court and patronage in the early seventeenth century, see Smuts and Linda Levy Peck, "'For a King not to be bountiful were a fault,'" pp. 31–61. On its mechanism in action, see Peck, *Northampton: Patronage and Policy at the Court of James I* (London: George Allen & Unwin, 1982), chapters 2 and 3.

4. On the play's date, see Jonson, 1:43 n. 2; the first edition of *Volpone* is the quarto of 1607.

5. Jonson, 1: 139, 15; 11: 573–74.

6. Jonson, 11: 574.

7. This is my suggestion. For Shaa and Spencer, see Jonson, 1: 15–16.

8. For a recent discussion, see David Riggs, *Ben Jonson: A Life* (Cambridge, Mass.: Harvard University Press, 1989), pp. 72–76.

9. On "application" as a Renaissance term for a reading practice that links past to present, see Richard A. Burt, "'A Dangerous Rome': Shakespeare's *Julius Caesar* and the Discursive Determinism of Cultural Politics," in *Contending Kingdoms: Historical, Psychological and Feminist Approaches to the Literature of Sixteenth-Century England and France*, ed. Marie-Rose Logan and Peter L. Rudnytsky (Detroit: Wayne State University Press, 1991). Burt's argument that the "discourse of Rome" was a necessary language for the articulation of politics during the period complements my own.

10. Chambers, 1: 385n., 2: 206–7. It is not certain that the play was Shakespeare's, as is sometimes supposed.

11. Barish, p. 195. See also Chambers, 1: 253, and the rest of the volume. G. E. Bentley points out that the status of the players had improved by Jonson's time after the earlier Puritan attacks: *The Profession of Player in Shakespeare's Time* (Princeton: Princeton University Press, 1984), pp. 8–11.

12. Sidney, *New Arcadia*, p. 319.

13. Bakeless, 1: 84.

14. Barish, pp. 136, 139.

15. See Raymond Williams, *Marxism and Literature* (Oxford: Oxford University Press, 1977), pp. 45–54.

16. See Tony Bennett, *Formalism and Marxism* (London: Methuen, 1979).

17. Francis Barker, *The Tremulous Private Body* (London: Methuen, 1984), p. 26.

18. See the discussion of this passage by Annabel Patterson in *Censor-*

ship and Interpretation (Madison: University of Wisconsin Press, 1984), p. 53.

19. Jonson, 1: 37; Riggs, pp. 105–6.

20. Elias, *History of Manners*, p. 78.

21. La Boétie, pp. 90–91.

22. It may be significant that *Sejanus* seems to have had a following among the more educated during its first run, despite its unpopularity with the pit. In 1603 those connected with court circles may have been ahead of other spectators in appreciating the sort of intrigue all members of later Jacobean audiences seemed to enjoy. See Jonson, 1: 36n.

23. Alan Gilbert, "The Eavesdroppers in Jonson's *Sejanus*," *Modern Language Notes* 69 (1954), 164–68.

24. Christopher Ricks, "*Sejanus* and Dismemberment," *Modern Language Notes* 76 (1961), 301–8.

25. There may be a recollection in this passage of Juno's rival Io and her hundred-eyed jailer Argus, the parents of Cupid in Sidney's *Arcadia*.

26. On the monopoly of violence attained by early modern sovereignty, see Stone, *The Crisis of the Aristocracy*, pp. 96–134; on its inheritance by the early modern state, see Elias, *Court Society*, pp. 268–69, and *Civilizing Process*, p. 196.

27. See Jonson, *Sejanus* V. 75–81, 190–210, 236–66. This is a departure from Tacitus, who says that Sejanus affected humility before the world: *Annals* 4. 1, in *The Complete Works of Tacitus*, ed. Moses Hadas (New York: Modern Library, 1942), p. 144.

28. On disincorporation, see Lefort, p. 303. I borrow the notion of a spectral power from Goldberg, *James I*, p. 177. The "spectral" and absolutist readings are both present in his discussion of *Sejanus* and *Catiline*; while I incline to the former, I owe much to his reading throughout.

29. Gerhard Oestreich, *Neostoicism and the Early Modern State*, ed. Brigitta Oestreich and H. G. Koenigsberger (Cambridge, Eng.: Cambridge University Press, 1982), p. 6. Oestreich associated the promotion of *Romanitas* by humanists with "incipient absolutism," but I see it as part of a general statism that made absolutism possible while also suggesting the eventual replacement of the personal sovereign by the mechanisms of an abstract sovereignty.

30. On Jonson's debt to Lipsius's commentary as well as his edition, see Daniel Boughner, "Jonson's Use of Lipsius in *Sejanus*," *Modern Language Notes* 73 (1958), 247–55.

31. Goldberg, *James I*, p. 177; his emphasis.

32. See Agnew, pp. 128–29, who quotes Gosson. Agnew theorizes that actors were scapegoated for anxieties about social mobility under capital. His argument about the rise of a "placeless" or generalized market that encouraged "close observation" of people and manners (pp. 40–43, 83) parallels my account of the development of an idea of the abstract state in representations of court society.

33. Arthur F. Marotti, "The Self-Reflexive Art of Ben Jonson's *Sejanus*," *Texas Studies in Literature and Language* 12 (1970), 197–220.

34. See Montaigne, *Essais*, 3. 7, p. 920.

35. Compare Marotti, p. 206.

36. Foucault, *Discipline and Punish*, pp. 3–69.

37. On Jonson's reconstructive impulse in *Sejanus*, see Joseph A. Bryant, "The Significance of Ben Jonson's First Requirement for Tragedy: 'Truth of Argument,'" *Studies in Philology* 49 (1952), 195–213. An appreciation of this impulse need not impair a reading of his play in contemporary political terms more general than those of historical allegory, as I intend to demonstrate. Thomas Greene's discussion of Jonson's historical consciousness stresses its creativity: *The Light in Troy: Imitation and Discovery in Renaissance Poetry* (New Haven: Yale University Press, 1982), pp. 264–93.

38. A parallel between Tiberius and the elderly Elizabeth is suggested by Matthew H. Wikander, who sees both as weak: "'Queasy to be Touched': The World of Ben Jonson's *Sejanus*," *Journal of English and Germanic Philology* 78 (1979), 350, 356. On Tiberius and James, see Goldberg, *James I*, pp. 176–77, 184.

39. On Tacitus's reputation in the Renaissance, see Kenneth C. Schellhase, *Tacitus in Renaissance Political Thought* (Chicago: University of Chicago Press, 1976), esp. pp. 95, 133.

40. Pocock, p. 351. See also Peter Burke, "Tacitism," in *Tacitus*, ed. T. A. Dorey (New York: Basic Books, 1969), and Schellhase, *passim*. For Jonson's conventionally negative opinion of Machiavelli, see *Timber*, in Jonson, 8: 599.

41. Katherine Maus, *Ben Jonson and the Roman Frame of Mind* (Princeton: Princeton University Press, 1984), p. 4.

42. Geoffrey Hill, "The World's Proportion: Jonson's Dramatic Poetry in *Sejanus* and *Catiline*," in *Jacobean Drama*, Stratford-Upon-Avon Studies, 1, ed. John Russell Brown and Bernard Harris (London: Edward Arnold, 1960), p. 124.

43. According to Immanuel Wallerstein, "Absolutism was a rhetorical injunction, not a serious assertion. . . . We might better call the ideology 'statism.' Statism is a claim for increased power in the hands of the state machinery. In the sixteenth century, this meant power in the hands of the absolute monarch. . . . Nobody, then or now, took it or should take it as a description of the real world of the time." State power was identified with the monarch principally because "the various groups who controlled resources, felt that their class interests were better served politically by attempting to persuade and influence the monarch than by seeking their political ends in alternative channels of action": *The Modern World System*, vol. 1: *Capitalist Agriculture and the Origins of the European World-Economy in the Sixteenth Century* (San Diego: Academic Press, 1974), pp. 146–47.

44. John J. Enck, *Jonson and the Comic Truth* (Madison: University of Wisconsin Press, 1957), p. 177. See as well Goldberg, *James I*, pp. 196–97.

45. Geoffrey Hill, pp. 120, 127n.

46. The phrase is from Richard Dutton, *Ben Jonson: To the First Folio* (Cambridge, Eng.: Cambridge University Press, 1983), p. 128.

47. Goldberg, *James I*, p. 197.

48. Robert Ornstein, *The Moral Vision of Jacobean Tragedy* (Madison: University of Wisconsin Press, 1965), pp. 100–101.

49. Pocock, pp. 357, 360.

50. Nicolo Machiavelli, *Discourses* 1.11, in *The Portable Machiavelli*, ed. Peter Bondanella and Mark Musa (New York: Penguin, 1979), pp. 207–10.

51. William A. Armstrong, "Ben Jonson and Jacobean Stagecraft," in *Jacobean Drama*, pp. 52, 46. The effect of sudden darkness was probably created by the release of smoke through a trapdoor: see Herford and Simpson's note in Jonson, 10:127.

52. Marcus Tullius Cicero, *In Catilinam I–IV*, trans. C. Macdonald (Cambridge, Mass.: Loeb Classical Library, 1977), p. 41.

53. On Fulvia and Sempronia in *Catiline*, see Kathleen McLuskie, *Renaissance Dramatists* (Atlantic Highlands, N.J.: Humanities Press International, 1989), pp. 177–79.

54. Dutton, p. 129.

55. Jonson, 11:578.

56. Jonson, 1:40–41, 202; Riggs, pp. 127–32.

57. Barbara N. De Luna, *Jonson's Romish Plot: A Study of "Catiline" and Its Historical Context* (Oxford: Clarendon, 1967), pp. 134–35; on pp. 130–32 she gives a useful summary of past interpretations of Jonson's letter to Salisbury; Dutton, p. 144.

58. Riggs, pp. 127–32; Jonson, 1.41–42.

59. De Luna, p. 138. If Jonson was Salisbury's man in 1605 before the plot was discovered, why was another spy required to report on the supper party? It is possible, of course, that Salisbury had many agents in the field, of which Jonson was only one.

60. Cicero occupies roughly the same position as spymaster in *Catiline* that Salisbury held in 1605, but it would be wrong to hold with De Luna that Cicero "is" Cecil, or that the play is a carefully constructed "parallelograph" in which almost every person and event involved in the Powder Plot is represented in Roman dress. De Luna also argues that the language of the play, which dwells increasingly on the Catilinarians' plan to burn Rome to the ground, reflects the imagery of combustion and subterranean labor associated with the plotters after 1605. She mentions the "special significance" of words like "enginers" and "pioners" in *Catiline* (III. 760, 726). Yet engineering and undermining are part of a general metaphorics of espionage rather than an allusion to Guy Fawkes. The quarto version of *Sejanus* was first entered in the Stationers' Register in 1604, long before the Plot, and the "Argument" that Jonson prefixed to it similarly describes how Tiberius "underworketh" Sejanus through Macro (lines 31–32). The first act begins with Sabinus saying "No, SILIVS, wee are no good inginers" (I. 4). In *Catiline*, perhaps, the general significance of such metaphors merges with their topicality. See De Luna, p. 204, and *passim*; on "enginers" and "pioners," see pp. 215–16. Dutton (pp. 153–54) argues against such allegorizing.

61. For the term "double agency," see Goldberg, "Sodomy and So-

ciety," p. 373. In Jonson's case, more clearly than in Marlowe's, one can see the emerging author using doubleness to negotiate his identity with authority rather than simply accepting an imposed role.

62. Bryant, "*Catiline* and the Nature of Jonson's Tragic Fable," *PMLA* 69 (1954), 265–77.

Chapter 5

1. Horkheimer and Adorno, pp. 3–4; Bacon, *Works*, 8: 125. Future citations of Bacon's writings are included parenthetically within the text by volume and page numbers.

2. Horkheimer and Adorno, pp. 4, 6. Paolo Rossi has recently glanced disapprovingly at Horkheimer's and Adorno's comments on Bacon, but he does not provide an adequate context for the moments in Bacon that he cites against their reading. See "Ants, Spiders, Epistemologists," in *Francis Bacon: Terminologia e Fortuna nel XVII Secolo*, ed. Marta Fattori (Rome: Edizioni dell'Ateneo, 1984), pp. 246–47.

3. Elias frequently refers to "that *courtly rationality* which . . . played a no less important part, and at first an even more important one, than the urban-commercial rationality . . . in the development of what we call the 'Enlightenment' ": *History of Manners*, p. 281 (Elias's emphasis). For Foucault and the Frankfurt School, see Colin Gordon, "Afterword," in Foucault, *Power/Knowledge*, pp. 233–34.

4. James Spedding, *The Letters and the Life of Francis Bacon*, 10: 143, 8: 104–6, 252, 118, and *passim*. Future references to this multivolume documentary biography will be included within the text by volume and page numbers. See also Thomas Birch, ed., *Memoirs of the Reign of Queen Elizabeth*, 2 vols. (London: A. Millar, 1754), 1: 44.

5. Compare "In felicem memoriam Elizabethae," in Bacon, *Works*, 6: 314–15.

6. In what follows, Foucault's vocabulary will prove useful in exploring the micropolitical implications of the *New Atlantis*, but I have begun with Horkheimer's and Adorno's quotation of Bacon because their historical analysis of knowledge and politics in terms of the state is more concrete than Foucault's theorization of an anonymous "power." To reclaim Bacon for the history of state power in England in this way is to "reconstruct" him according to the principles of recent analysts of modernity such as Foucault and the Frankfurt School, but it is also to give some attention to Bacon's own self-construction as the custodian of a scientific intelligence that both supplants and supplements the political intelligence on which it is patterned. For an attempt to appropriate Bacon as the forerunner of a Protestant radicalism that was artisanal as much as bourgeois, and that posited a utopian sense of the collective good of society that transcended class interest, see Christopher Hill, *Intellectual Origins of the English Revolution*, corrected ed. (Oxford: Clarendon, 1980), pp. 85–130. There is much in Hill's reading that must be saved, but in general I feel that it is vulnerable to the sort of critique that Lawrence Stone launches against it

in *The Causes of the English Revolution*, p. 109. On the issue of the construction and appropriation of Bacon's texts today and in the seventeenth century, see Kathryn Flannery, "Models of Reading: Seventeenth-Century Productions of Bacon's Texts," *Assays* 5 (1989), 111–33. On a politicized reception theory in general, see Bennett, pp. 57–64; and John Frow, *Marxism and Literary History* (Cambridge, Mass.: Harvard University Press, 1986), pp. 170–206.

7. Arthur Collins, *Letters and Memorials of State in the Reigns of Queen Mary, Queen Elizabeth, King James*, 2 vols. (London, 1746; reprint, New York, 1973), 1: 362.

8. For a recent discussion of this device in the context of Bacon's own political career, see McCoy, *The Rites of Knighthood*, pp. 85–86. On patronage during Bacon's times see Smuts, esp. pp. 54–58. In the early Stuart period the court became increasingly urbanized; the great built their town houses around Whitehall, while their younger sons flocked to the Inns of Court, where some seriously pursued the law and others became the clients of courtiers. In the mid-Elizabethan period the young Bacon did both. By the 1590's, the groundwork of Stuart London's patronage system had already been laid; even the ambitious Bacon maintained his close connection with Gray's Inn. See Peck, " 'For a King not to be bountiful,' " pp. 31–61.

9. For a treatment of the first edition of the *Essays* in terms of the relationship between Bacon and Essex within the general political situation of the 1590's, see F. J. Levy, "Francis Bacon and the Style of Politics," reprinted in *Renaissance Historicism: Selections from English Literary Renaissance*, ed. Arthur Kinney and Dan S. Collins (Amherst: University of Massachusetts Press, 1987), pp. 146–67. Levy does not deal with espionage and courtly observation, but his discussion of patronage and his readings of particular essays have influenced my account below.

10. Bakeless, 1: 178.

11. Handover, p. 105.

12. Anthony Esler and Jonathan Marwil both assume that it was Anthony who first approached Essex, but it is difficult to understand why Francis would later claim to have made the first move in the document in which he dissociated himself from the treasonous earl. See Esler, *The Aspiring Mind of the Elizabethan Younger Generation* (Durham, N.C.: Duke University Press, 1966), p. 221; and Marwil, *The Trials of Counsel: Francis Bacon in 1621* (Detroit: Wayne State University Press, 1976), p. 72. I am very indebted to both of these books for my understanding of the Francis-Anthony-Essex triangle.

13. Birch, 1: 44.

14. For the details of the Lopez case, see Cecil Roth, *A History of the Jews in England*, 3rd ed. (Oxford: Clarendon, 1964), pp. 140–44, and Spedding, *Letters and Life*, 8: 271–88, 301.

15. For the suggestion that Francis first heard of Montaigne's *Essais* through Anthony, see Levy, p. 159.

16. Elias, *Court Society*, pp. 105–6n.

17. See Marwil, pp. 87–88.

18. Marwil (p. 89) parallels this passage with statements from a letter written by Bacon to Essex in 1593, but here as elsewhere he does not trace the influence of Bacon's intelligence experience on his writings. On Bacon's refusal to exalt friendship above clientage here, see both Levy, p. 164; and John C. Briggs, *Francis Bacon and the Rhetoric of Nature* (Cambridge, Mass.: Harvard University Press, 1989), p. 221.

19. The classic study of the later development of the *Essays* in terms of the systematization of such concerns within a science of human motivation is R. S. Crane's "The Relation of Bacon's *Essays* to his Programme for the Advancement of Learning," reprinted in Brian Vickers, ed., *Essential Articles for the Study of Francis Bacon* (Hamden, Conn.: Archon Books, 1968), pp. 272–92. For a counterstatement, see Lisa Jardine, *Francis Bacon: Discovery and the Art of Discourse* (Cambridge, Eng.: Cambridge University Press, 1974), p. 227, and chapter 13 in general. Jardine argues that the *Essays* retained their rhetorical and practical-political, albeit moral, character into the 1625 edition. She is correct, but I do not think this precludes their relation to Bacon's unfulfilled desire for a "human science" as well as a natural one.

20. Pocock, pp. 351–52.

21. See Marwil, pp. 160–61, and Judith Anderson, *Biographical Truth: The Representation of Historical Persons in Tudor-Stuart Writing* (New Haven: Yale University Press, 1984), p. 177.

22. Anderson, p. 177.

23. Kantorowicz, p. 382.

24. Karl Marx, *The Eighteenth Brumaire of Louis Napoleon*, trans. in *Surveys from Exile*, ed. David Fernbach (New York: Vintage, 1974), p. 146. Marx's general concern here with the illegitimate doubling of political leadership, and ultimately with the lack of any original sovereign legitimacy in the first place, is oddly anticipated in Bacon's *Henry VII*. It may also be significant that Louis Napoleon, like Henry, emerges as something of a spy king in Marx's account.

25. Anderson, pp. 181–83, 161, 179; see also Lisa Jardine, pp. 157–59. Jonathan Marwil (p. 132) argues plausibly that the purpose of the edition of 1612 "was to persuade James of his wisdom so that he might be employed as a counselor."

26. Timothy J. Reiss, *The Discourse of Modernism* (Ithaca, N.Y.: Cornell University Press, 1982), p. 189.

27. John Briggs, p. 173.

28. Ibid., p. 169.

29. On the medical bias of the *New Atlantis*, see Charles Webster, *The Great Instauration: Science, Medicine and Reform, 1626–1660* (London: Duckworth, 1975), pp. 249, 288–89; and Howard B. White, *Peace Among the Willows: The Political Philosophy of Francis Bacon* (The Hague: Martinus Nijhoff, 1968), pp. 148–49. On the connection between medicalization and an individualizing power, see Michel Foucault, *The Birth of the Clinic,*

trans. A. M. Sheridan Smith (New York: Vintage, 1975), *passim*; and *Discipline and Punish*, p. 185.

30. Foucault, *Discipline and Punish*, p. 189.

31. Greenblatt, *Renaissance Self-Fashioning*, pp. 29, 39. Greenblatt analyzes surveillance in *Utopia* in terms of honor and shame rather than knowledge and power.

32. Thomas More, *Utopia*, trans. Paul Turner (Harmondsworth: Penguin, 1965), pp. 84, 126, 78–79, 82.

33. Nevertheless, I cannot agree with Jerry Weinberger's rather ironic reading of Bensalemite hospitality. Weinberger sees the *New Atlantis* as a projection of the political problems of the new science as well as its advantages: see his "Introduction" to the Crofts Classics edition of Bacon's *Great Instauration and New Atlantis* (Arlington Heights, Ill.: Harlan Davidson, 1980). More recently, he seems to suggest that Bacon is parodying the ancient utopianism of Plato's *Republic*, *Critias*, and *Timaeus*, perhaps as part of an immanent critique of the secretive elements that remain within the modern science that he is helping to found: see his *Science, Faith, and Politics: Francis Bacon and the Utopian Roots of the Modern Age* (Ithaca, N.Y.: Cornell University Press, 1985), pp. 27–33. Bacon seems to me to be "thinking" social control and enlightened charity at the same time in a way that elides a self-critique: see John Briggs, p. 248, for a concluding argument about his paradoxical ability to do so. Briggs (pp. 172–73) also shows how Bacon's utopia maintains its distance from its Platonic precursors.

34. In the *Civitas solis* (1623), we are similarly told that the inhabitants of Tommaso Campanella's ideal scientific state possess "a knowledge of all languages, and that by perseverance they continually sent explorers and ambassadors [*exploratores*—which could also be translated 'spies'—*& legatos*] over the whole earth, who learn thoroughly the customs, forces, rules and histories of the nations, good and bad alike." See "The City of the Sun," trans. in *Ideal Commonwealths*, ed. Henry Morley (London, 1901; reprint, Port Washington, N.Y.: Kennikat Press, 1968), p. 149. For the Latin text, see *De civitate solis*, in Campanella's *Realis philosophiae epilogisticae* (Frankfurt, 1623; reprint in *Opera latina*, vol. II, Turin: Bottega d'Erasmo, 1975), pp. 422–23. And see Reiss, *Discourse of Modernism*, p. 179. As Howard B. White points out (p. 239), the Athenian in Plato's *Laws* would have his best possible state send out "observation missions" composed of men in their fifties to experience at first hand the legal customs of other cities, and to search out "certain divine human beings" whose advice might improve the laws of their land: *Laws* 951a–952b, in *The Laws of Plato*, trans. Thomas L. Pangle (New York: Basic Books, 1980), pp. 353–54.

35. Reiss observes that although we are not given a coherent picture of the state in the *New Atlantis*, "we can see that the 'political constitution' that was never written down as such is in fact already inscribed in the particular discursive order of which secrecy, willful hierarchy, and the power of the enunciating *I* are such essential elements": Reiss, *Discourse of Mod-*

ernism, p. 193. If the state seems hardly to exist for the Fathers, as Reiss maintains in the same place, this is because a conception of it as something that can exist apart from the body of the sovereign has not yet been clearly articulated in England in the early seventeenth century.

36. Some of these elements would be similarly combined in the career of the Baconian projector Samuel Hartlib during the Interregnum. He used his foreign contacts in the learned world to supply John Pym with political intelligence even before his series of proposals for an "Office of Address" that would provide scientific and economic news from abroad to the government. A little later he passed along information on affairs in Europe to the Council of State. During the 1650's, Hartlib recruited the diplomat Henry Oldenburg as both a scientific and political correspondent; Oldenburg built up his own intelligence system and became Hartlib's successor as an information broker in the age of the Royal Society. (See Webster, pp. 42, 74–75, 83, 501; Hartlib's plans for an "Office of Address" were more immediately influenced by Theophraste Renaudot's creation of a "Bureau d'addresse": Webster, p. 68.) The careers of Hartlib and Oldenburg demonstrate that scientific knowledge remained implicated in political intelligence in the wake of the *New Atlantis*. See also Hill, chapter 3, for the radical intentions behind such applications of Baconian ideas—radical intentions, I would add, that may have ended in the reactionary reinforcement of state power.

37. Goldberg, *James I*, chapter 2.

38. Ibid., pp. 43, 250 n. 50.

39. White (p. 226) remarks upon the absence of references to a king in the text.

40. That the England of Elizabeth and James was a properly absolutist state to begin with has been eloquently disputed by Sinfield, pp. 261–62.

41. On angelic intelligence, see Pocock, pp. 21–22.

42. The canopy may recall the so-called "Great Neech" in the south end of Inigo Jones's Banqueting House as it was during James I's reign. This mysterious structure, under or within which James sat, was possessed of a canopy or overhang constructed in part of gilded fretwork ribs. See John Charlton, *The Banqueting House, Whitehall* (London: Department of the Environment, 1983), pp. 5–6.

43. The phrase "masculine birth of time," Bacon's favorite version of the adage that "Truth is the daughter of Time," is also the title of a Latin work of 1603, which is translated by Farrington, pp. 61–72.

44. Coppélia Kahn, "The Absent Mother in *King Lear*," in *Rewriting the Renaissance*, ed. Margaret W. Ferguson et al. (Chicago: University of Chicago Press, 1986), p. 35.

45. Horkheimer and Adorno, p. 3. Nature was conventionally depicted as a cloaked or hidden figure in iconography; for a reading of the mother of the Feast in terms of mythological allegory elsewhere in Bacon's work, see White, pp. 173–74.

46. Alice Jardine, pp. 98, 99; see also pp. 139–40.

47. "The Order of receyveing Queen ELIZABETH in the Colledge

Churche of Westminster" (1597), and *Elizabetha Triumphans* (1588), p. 65, both in Nichols, vol. 2.

48. It is possible that the design of the Bensalemite dais also owed something to other structures with which Bacon may have been familiar. I have already mentioned the Banqueting House's "Great Neech." The Great Hall at Penshurst, one of the few remaining examples of a medieval hall in England, can be surveyed from an upper chamber that communicates with the dais below by means of a stone stairway. The chamber's window is an unobtrusive loophole, however, not a leaded window or conspicuous traverse. On Penshurst, see Malcolm William Wallace, *The Life of Sir Philip Sidney* (Cambridge, 1915; reprint, New York: Octagon, 1967), p. 19.

49. See Marwil, pp. 64–65, 85–86.

50. Foucault, *Discipline and Punish*, pp. 226, 227.

51. Horkheimer and Adorno, p. 42.

52. Ibid., p. 35.

References Cited

Agnew, Jean-Christophe. *Worlds Apart: The Market and the Theater in Anglo-American Thought, 1550–1750.* Cambridge, Eng.: Cambridge University Press, 1986.

Alban, J. R., and C. T. Allmand. "Spies and Spying in the Fourteenth Century." In *War, Literature, and Politics in the Late Middle Ages,* ed. C. T. Allmand. Liverpool: Liverpool University Press, 1976.

Anderson, Judith. *Biographical Truth: The Representation of Historical Persons in Tudor-Stuart Writing.* New Haven: Yale University Press, 1984.

Aristotle. *The Politics of Aristotle.* Trans. Ernest Baker. Oxford: Clarendon, 1948.

Armstrong, William A. "Ben Jonson and Jacobean Stagecraft." In *Jacobean Drama,* ed. John Russell Brown and Bernard Harris. Stratford-upon-Avon Studies, 1. London: Edward Arnold, 1960.

Bacon, Francis. *The Works of Francis Bacon.* Ed. James Spedding, R. C. Ellis, and D. D. Heath. 14 vols. London: Longman, Green, 1857–74.

Bakeless, John. *The Tragical History of Christopher Marlowe.* 2 vols. Cambridge, Mass.: Harvard University Press, 1942.

Baltrušaitis, Jurgis. *Anamorphic Art.* Trans. W. J. Strachan. Cambridge, Eng.: Chadwyck-Healey, 1977.

Barish, Jonas. *The Antitheatrical Prejudice.* Berkeley: University of California Press, 1981.

Barkan, Leonard. "Diana and Actaeon: The Myth as Synthesis." *English Literary Renaissance* 10 (1980), 317–59.

———. *Transuming Passion: Ganymede and the Erotics of Humanism.* Stanford: Stanford University Press, 1991.

Barker, Francis. *The Tremulous Private Body.* London: Methuen, 1984.

Beaujour, Michel. *Memoirs d'encre: Rhétorique de l'autoportrait.* Paris: Editions de Seuil, 1980.

Belsey, Catherine. "Disrupting Sexual Difference: Meaning and Gender in the Comedies." In *Alternative Shakespeares,* ed. John Drakakis. London: Methuen, 1985.

Benjamin, Jessica. "The End of Internalization: Adorno's Social Psychology." *Telos* 32 (1977), 42–64.

Bennett, Tony. *Formalism and Marxism.* London: Methuen, 1979.

Bentley, G. E. *The Profession of Player in Shakespeare's Time.* Princeton: Princeton University Press, 1984.

Birch, Thomas, ed. *Memoirs of the Reign of Queen Elizabeth*. 2 vols. London: A Millar, 1754.

Boas, Frederick. *Christopher Marlowe: A Biographical and Critical Study*. Oxford: Clarendon, 1940.

Borch-Jacobsen, Mikkel. *The Freudian Subject*. Trans. Catherine Porter. Stanford: Stanford University Press, 1988.

Boswell, John. *Christianity, Social Tolerance, and Homosexuality*. Chicago: University of Chicago Press, 1980.

Boughner, Daniel. "Jonson's Use of Lipsius in *Sejanus*." *Modern Language Notes* 73 (1958), 247–85.

Bourdieu, Pierre. *Outline of a Theory of Practice*. Trans. Richard Nice. Cambridge, Eng.: Cambridge University Press, 1977.

Bradbrook, Muriel. *The School of Night*. Cambridge, Eng.: Cambridge University Press, 1936.

Bray, Alan. *Homosexuality in Renaissance England*. London: Gay Men's Press, 1982.

———. "Homosexuality and the Signs of Male Friendship in Elizabethan England." *History Workshop Journal* 29 (1990), 1–15.

Bredbeck, Gregory W. *Sodomy and Interpretation: Marlowe to Milton*. Ithaca, N.Y.: Cornell University Press, 1991.

Briggs, John. *Francis Bacon and the Rhetoric of Nature*. Cambridge, Mass.: Harvard University Press, 1989.

Briggs, Julia. "Marlowe's *Massacre at Paris*: A Reconsideration." *Review of English Studies* 34 (1983), 257–78.

Brown, Frieda S. *Religious and Political Conservatism in the Essais of Montaigne*. Geneva: Droz, 1963.

Bruce, John, ed. *The Correspondence of Robert Dudley, Earl of Leycester . . . in the Years 1585 and 1586*. London: Camden Society, 1844.

Brush, Craig B. "Montaigne Tries out Self-Study." *L'Esprit Créateur* 20 (1980), 23–35.

Bryant, Joseph A. "The Significance of Ben Jonson's First Requirement for Tragedy: 'Truth of Argument.'" *Studies in Philology* 49 (1952), 195–213.

———. "*Catiline* and the Nature of Jonson's Tragic Fable." *PMLA* 69 (1954), 265–77.

Burckhardt, Jacob. *The Civilization of the Renaissance in Italy*. 2 vols. Trans. S. G. C. Middlemore. New York: Albert and Charles Boni, 1935.

Burke, Peter. "Tacitism." In *Tacitus*, ed. T. A. Dorey. New York: Basic Books, 1969.

Burn, Michael. *The Debatable Land: A Study of the Motives of Spies in Two Ages*. London: Hamish Hamilton, 1970.

Burt, Richard A. "'Tis Writ By Me': Massinger's *The Roman Actor* and the Politics of Reception in the English Renaissance Theatre." *Theatre Journal* 40 (1988), 333–46.

———. "'A Dangerous Rome': Shakespeare's *Julius Caesar* and the Discursive Determinism of Cultural Politics." In *Contending Kingdoms:*

Historical, Psychological and Feminist Approaches to the Literature of Six-teenth-Century England and France, ed. Marie-Rose Logan and Peter L. Rudnytsky. Detroit: Wayne State University Press, 1991, 16–19.

Camden, William. *Annales. The true and royal history of Elizabeth, Queen of England.* Trans. A. Darcie. London: H. Lownes, 1625.

Campanella, Tommaso. *De civitate solis.* In *Realis philosophiae epilogisticae.* Frankfurt, 1623. Reprint in *Opera latina*, vol. 2. Turin: Botega d'Erasmo, 1975. English trans.: "The City of the Sun." In *Ideal Commonwealths*, ed. Henry Morley. London, 1901; reprint, Port Washington, N.Y.: Kenikat Press, 1968.

Castiglione, Baldesar. *The Book of the Courtier.* Trans. Charles Singleton. Garden City, N.Y.: Doubleday, 1959.

———. *The Book of the Courtier.* Trans. Thomas Hoby. In *Three Renaissance Classics.* Ed. Burton A. Milligan. New York: Charles Scribners' Sons, 1953.

Chambers, E. K. *The Elizabethan Stage.* 2 vols. Oxford: Clarendon, 1923.

Chapman, George. *The Revenge of Busy D'Ambois.* In *The Plays of George Chapman: The Tragedies*, ed. T. M. Parrott. New York: Russell and Russell, 1961.

Charlton, John. *The Banqueting House, Whitehall.* London: Department of the Environment, 1983.

Cicero, Marcus Tullius. *In Catilinam I–IV.* Trans. C. Macdonald. Cambridge, Mass.: Harvard University Press, Loeb Classical Library, 1977.

Cleugh, James. *Chant Royal: The Life of Louis XI.* Garden City, N.Y.: Doubleday, 1970.

Cohen, Ed. "Legislating the Norm: From Sodomy to Gross Indecency." In *Displacing Homophobia: Gay Male Perspectives in Literature and Culture*, ed. Ronald R. Butters, John H. Clum, and Michael Moon. Durham, N.C.: Duke University Press, 1989.

Collins, Arthur, ed. *Letters and Memorials of State in the Reign of Queen Mary, Queen Elizabeth, King James.* 2 vols. London, 1746; reprint, New York: AMS, 1973.

Commynes, Philippe de. *The Memoires.* Ed. Samuel Kinser. Trans. Isabelle Cazeaux. Columbia, S.C.: University of South Carolina Press, 1969.

Connell, Dorothy. *Sir Philip Sidney: The Maker's Mind.* Oxford: Clarendon, 1977.

Crane, R. S. "The Relation of Bacon's *Essays* to His Programme for the Advancement of Learning." In *Essential Articles for the Study of Francis Bacon*, ed. Brian Vickers. Hamden, Conn.: Archon Books, 1968.

Crewe, Jonathan. *Trials of Authorship: Anterior Forms and Poetic Reconstruction from Wyatt to Shakespeare.* Berkeley: University of California Press, 1990.

De Luna, Barbara N. *Jonson's Romish Plot: A Study of "Catiline" and Its Historical Context.* Oxford: Clarendon, 1967.

Derrida, Jacques. "The Politics of Friendship." *The Journal of Philosophy* 85 (1988), 632–44.

Digges, Dudley, ed. *The Compleat Ambassador*. London: Thomas New-combe, 1655.

Dolet, Etienne. *De officio legati*. Trans. James E. Dunlap. *The American Journal of International Law* 27 (1933), 12–95.

Dollimore, Jonathan. "Transgression and Surveillance in *Measure for Measure*." In *Political Shakespeare*, ed. Jonathan Dollimore and Alan Sinfield. Ithaca, N.Y.: Cornell University Press, 1985.

————. *Sexual Dissidence: Augustine to Wilde, Freud to Foucault*. Oxford: Clarendon, 1991.

Duberman, Martin, Martha Vicinus, and George Chauncey, Jr., eds. *Hidden from History: Reclaiming the Gay and Lesbian Past*. New York: New American Library, 1988.

Dutton, Richard. *Ben Jonson: To the First Folio*. Cambridge, Eng.: Cambridge University Press, 1983.

Eccles, Mark. *Christopher Marlowe in London*. Cambridge, Mass.: Harvard University Press, 1934.

Enck, John J. *Jonson and the Comic Truth*. Madison: University of Wisconsin Press, 1957.

Elias, Norbert. *The Civilizing Process*, vol. 1, *The History of Manners*. Trans. Edmund Jephcott. New York: Pantheon, 1978.

————. *The Civilizing Process*, vol. 2: *Power and Civility*. Trans. Edmund Jephcott. New York: Pantheon, 1982.

————. *The Court Society*. Trans. Edmund Jephcott. New York: Pantheon, 1983.

Elizabeth I. *The Public Speaking of Queen Elizabeth*. Ed. George Rice, Jr. New York: Columbia University Press, 1951.

Elton, G. R. *Policy and Police: The Enforcement of the Reformation in the Age of Thomas Cromwell*. Cambridge, Eng.: Cambridge University Press, 1972.

————. "Tudor Government: The Points of Contact III: The Court." *Transactions of the Royal Historical Society* 26 (1976), 211–28.

Esler, Anthony. *The Aspiring Mind of the Elizabethan Younger Generation*. Durham, N.C.: Duke University Press, 1966.

Farrington, Benjamin. *The Philosophy of Francis Bacon*. Chicago: University of Chicago Press, 1964.

Foucault, Michel. *The Birth of the Clinic: An Archaeology of Medical Perception*. Trans. A. M. Sheridan Smith. New York: Vintage, 1975.

————. "What Is an Author?" In *Language, Counter-Memory, Practice*, ed. Donald F. Bouchard. Ithaca, N.Y.: Cornell University Press, 1977.

————. *Surveiller et punir: Naissance de la prison*. Paris: Gallimard, 1975. English trans.: *Discipline and Punish: The Birth of the Prison*. Trans. Alan Sheridan. New York: Vintage, 1979.

————. *Power/Knowledge: Selected Interviews and Other Writings*. Ed. Colin Gordon. New York: Pantheon, 1980.

————. "War in the Filigree of Peace: Course Summary." Trans. Ian Mcleod. *The Oxford Literary Review* 4 (1980), 15–19.

————. *The History of Sexuality*, vol. 1, *An Introduction*. Trans. Robert Hurley. New York: Vintage, 1980.

Flannery, Kathryn. "Models of Reading: Seventeenth Century Productions of Bacon's Texts." *Assays* 5 (1989), 111–33.

Frame, Donald M. *Montaigne's Discovery of Man*. New York: Columbia University Press, 1955.

————. *Montaigne: A Biography*. New York: Harcourt, Brace & World, 1965.

Freeman, Arthur. "Marlowe, Kyd, and the Dutch Church Libel." *ELR* 3 (1973), 44–52.

Freud, Sigmund. *The Standard Edition of the Complete Psychological Works*. 24 vols. Ed. James Strachey. London: Hogarth Press, 1953–74.

Friedrich, Hugo. *Montaigne*. Trans. Robert Rovini. Paris: Gallimard, 1968.

Frow, John. *Marxism and Literary History*. Cambridge, Mass.: Harvard University Press, 1986.

Gallagher, Lowell. *Medusa's Gaze: Casuistry and Conscience in the Renaissance*. Stanford: Stanford University Press, 1991.

Gilbert, Alan. "The Eavesdroppers in Jonson's *Sejanus*." *Modern Language Notes* 69 (1954), 164–68.

Gilbert, Arthur N. "Conceptions of Homosexuality and Sodomy in Western History." *The Journal of Homosexuality* 6: 1–2 (1980–81), 567–68.

Gilman, Ernest B. *The Curious Perspective: Literary and Pictorial Wit in the Seventeenth Century*. New Haven: Yale University Press, 1978.

Girard, René. *Violence and the Sacred*. Trans. Patrick Gregory. Baltimore: The Johns Hopkins University Press, 1979.

Goldberg, Jonathan. *James I and the Politics of Literature*. Baltimore: The Johns Hopkins University Press, 1983.

————. "Sodomy and Society: The Case of Christopher Marlowe." *Southwest Review* 69 (1984), 371–78.

————. "Colin to Hobbinol: Spenser's Familiar Letters." In *Displacing Homophobia: Gay Male Perspectives in Literature and Culture*, ed. Ronald R. Butters, John M. Clum, and Michael Moon. Durham, N.C.: Duke University Press, 1989.

Goldwell, Henry, ed. *A briefe declaration of the shows, deuices, speeches, and inuentions*. London: Robert Waldegrave, 1581.

Greenberg, David F. *The Construction of Homosexuality*. Chicago: University of Chicago Press, 1988.

Greenblatt, Stephen. *Renaissance Self-Fashioning: From More to Shakespeare*. Chicago: University of Chicago Press, 1980.

————. "The Cultivation of Anxiety: King Lear and His Heirs." *Raritan* 2 (1982), 92–114.

————. *Shakespearean Negotiations: The Circulation of Social Energy in Renaissance England*. Berkeley: University of California Press, 1988.

Greene, Thomas M. *The Light in Troy: Imitation and Discovery in Renaissance Poetry*. New Haven: Yale University Press, 1982.

———. "Dangerous Parleys—Montaigne's *Essais* 1:5 and 6." In *The Vulnerable Text: Essays on Renaissance Literature*. New York: Columbia University Press, 1986.

Greenlaw, Edwin A. "Sidney's *Arcadia* as an Example of Elizabethan Allegory." In *Anniversary Papers by Colleagues and Pupils of George Lyman Kittredge*. Boston: Ginn and Company, 1913.

———. "The Captivity Episode in Sidney's *Arcadia*." In *The Manly Studies in Language and Literature*. Chicago: University of Chicago Press, 1923.

Greville, Fulke. *The Life of Sir Philip Sidney*. Ed. Nowell Smith. Oxford: Clarendon, 1907.

Grün, Alphonse. *La vie publique de Montaigne*. Paris: Librarie d'Amyot, 1855.

Guicciardini, Francesco. *Maxims and Reflections (Ricordi)*. Trans. Mario Domandi. Philadelphia: University of Pennsylvania Press, 1972.

Handover, P. M. *The Second Cecil*. London: Eyre & Spottiswoode, 1959.

Harington, John. *The Letters and Epigrams*. Ed. M. E. McClure. Philadelphia: University of Pennsylvania Press, 1930.

Hebdige, Dick. *Subculture: The Meaning of Style*. London: Methuen, 1979.

Heinemann, Margot. *Puritanism and Theatre: Thomas Middleton and Opposition Drama Under the Early Stuarts*. Cambridge, Eng.: Cambridge University Press, 1980.

Henderson, Philip. "Marlowe as a Messenger." *The Times Literary Supplement*, June 12, 1953, 381.

Hill, Christopher. *Intellectual Origins of the English Revolution*. Corrected ed. Oxford: Clarendon, 1980.

Hill, Geoffrey. "The World's Proportion: Jonson's Dramatic Poetry in *Sejanus* and *Catiline*." In *Jacobean Drama*, ed. John Russell Brown and Bernard Harris. Stratford-upon-Avon Studies, 1. London: Edward Arnold, 1960.

Horkheimer, Max. "Montaigne et la fonction du scepticisme." In *Théorie Critique: Essais*. Ed. Luc Ferry and Alain Renault. Paris: Payot, 1978.

Horkheimer, Max, and Theodor W. Adorno. *Dialectic of Enlightenment*. Trans. John Cumming. New York: Continuum, 1972.

Hotson, Leslie. *The Death of Christopher Marlowe*. Cambridge, Mass.: Harvard University Press, 1925.

Howell, Roger. *Sir Philip Sidney: The Shepherd Knight*. London: Hutchinson, 1968.

Hoy, David Couzens. "Power, Repression, Progress: Foucault, Lukes, and the Frankfurt School." In *Foucault: A Critical Reader*, ed. David Couzens Hoy. Oxford: Basil Blackwell, 1986.

Hughes, Merrit Y. "Spenser and the Greek Pastoral Triad." *Studies in Philology* 20 (1923), 184–215.

———. *Virgil and Spenser*. Folcroft, Pa.: Folcroft Press, 1928.

Huguet, Edmond. *Dictionaire de la Langue Français de la Seizième Siècle*. Paris: Didier, 1946.

Human Figurations: Essays for Norbert Elias [no editor]. Amsterdam: Amsterdam Sociologisch Tijdschrift, 1977.

Jardine, Alice. *Gynesis: Configurations of Woman and Modernity.* Ithaca, N.Y.: Cornell University Press, 1985.

Jardine, Lisa. *Francis Bacon: Discovery and the Art of Discourse.* Cambridge, Eng.: Cambridge University Press, 1974.

Jay, Martin. *The Dialectical Imagination: A History of the Frankfurt School and the Institute of Social Research, 1923–1950.* Boston: Little, Brown, 1973.

Jonson, Ben. *Ben Jonson [Works].* Ed. C. H. Herford, Percy Simpson, and Evelyn Simpson. Oxford: Clarendon, 1947.

Kahn, Coppélia. "The Absent Mother in *King Lear.*" In *Rewriting the Renaissance,* ed. Margaret W. Ferguson, Maureen Quilligan, and Nancy J. Vickers. Chicago: University of Chicago Press, 1986.

Kahn, Victoria. "The Sense of Taste in Montaigne's *Essais.*" *Modern Language Notes* 95 (1980), 1269–91.

———. *Rhetoric, Prudence, and Skepticism in the Renaissance.* Ithaca, N.Y.: Cornell University Press, 1985.

Kantorowicz, Ernst H. *The King's Two Bodies: A Study in Mediaeval Political Theology.* Princeton: Princeton University Press, 1957.

Kimbrough, Robert, and Philip Murphy. "The Helmingham Hall Manuscript of Sidney's *The Lady of May,*" *Renaissance Drama* n.s. 1 (1968), 103–19.

Knapp, Jeffrey. "Elizabethan Tobacco." *Representations* 21 (1988), 27–66.

Kocher, P. H. "Contemporary Pamphlet Backgrounds for Marlowe's *The Massacre at Paris.*" *Modern Language Quarterly* 8 (1947), 151–73.

———. "François Hotman and Marlowe's *The Massacre at Paris.*" *PMLA* 56 (1941), 349–68.

Kuriyama, Constance Brown. "Marlowe's Nemesis: The Identity of Richard Baines." In *"A Poet and a filthy Play-maker": New Essays on Christopher Marlowe,* ed. Kenneth Friedenreich, Roma Gill, and Constance Brown Kuriyama. New York: AMS Press, 1988, pp. 343–60.

La Boétie, Etienne de. *Discours de la servitude volontaire.* Ed. M. Rat. Paris: Armand Colin, 1963.

Lacan, Jacques. *Ecrits: A Selection.* Trans. Alan Sheridan. New York: Norton, 1977.

———. *The Four Fundamental Concepts of Psycho-Analysis.* Trans. Alan Sheridan. New York: Norton, 1978.

Lawry, Jon S. *Sidney's Two Arcadias: Pattern and Proceeding.* Ithaca, N.Y.: Cornell University Press, 1972.

Leech, Clifford. *Christopher Marlowe: Poet for the Stage.* Ed. Anne Lancashire. New York: AMS Press, 1986.

Lefort, Claude. *The Political Forms of Modern Society: Bureaucracy, Democracy, Totalitarianism.* Ed. John B. Thompson. Cambridge, Mass.: MIT Press, 1986.

Levao, Ronald. *Renaissance Minds and Their Fictions.* Berkeley: University of California Press, 1985.

Levey, Michael. *The German School.* London: National Gallery, 1959.

Levy, F. J. "Francis Bacon and the Style of Politics." In *Renaissance His-*

toricism: Selections from English Literary Renaissance, ed. Arthur Kinney and Dan S. Collins. Amherst: University of Massachusetts Press, 1987.

Lowenstein, Joseph. "The Script in the Marketplace." In *Representing the English Renaissance*, ed. Stephen Greenblatt. Berkeley: University of California Press, 1988.

Lytle, Guy, and Stephen Orgel, eds. *Patronage in the Renaissance*. Princeton: Princeton University Press, 1981.

Machiavelli, Nicolo. *The Discourses*. In *The Portable Machiavelli*, ed. Peter Bondanella and Mark Musa. New York: Penguin, 1979.

Marlowe, Christopher. *The Complete Works of Christopher Marlowe*, 2nd ed. Ed. Fredson Bowers. Cambridge, Eng.: Cambridge University Press, 1973.

———. *Marlowe's Doctor Faustus, 1604–1616.* Ed. W. W. Greg. Oxford: Clarendon, 1950.

Marotti, Arthur F. "The Self-Reflexive Art of Ben Jonson's *Sejanus*." *Texas Studies in Literature and Language* 12 (1970), 197–220.

Marwil, Jonathan. *The Trials of Counsel: Francis Bacon in 1621*. Detroit: Wayne State University Press, 1976.

Marx, Karl. *The Eighteenth Brumaire of Louis Napoleon*. Trans. in *Surveys from Exile*, ed. David Fernbach. New York: Vintage, 1974.

Mattingly, Garrett. *Renaissance Diplomacy*. New York: Russell and Russell, 1970.

Maus, Katharine. *Ben Jonson and the Roman Frame of Mind*. Princeton: Princeton University Press, 1984.

MacCaffrey, Wallace T. "Place and Patronage in Elizabethan Politics." In *Elizabethan Government and Society*, ed. S. T. Bindoff, Joel Hurstfield, and C. H. Williams. London: Athlone Press, 1961.

———. *Queen Elizabeth and the Making of Policy, 1572–1588*. Princeton: Princeton University Press, 1981.

McCoy, Richard C. *Rebellion in Arcadia*. New Brunswick, N.J.: Rutgers University Press, 1979.

———. *The Rites of Knighthood: The Literature and Politics of Elizabethan Chivalry*. Berkeley: University of California Press, 1989.

McIlwain, C. H. *Constitutionalism Ancient and Modern*. Ithaca, N.Y.: Cornell University Press, 1958.

McLuskie, Kathleen. *Renaissance Dramatists*. Atlantic Highlands, N.J.: Humanities Press International, 1989.

Mennell, Stephen. *Norbert Elias: Civilization and the Human Self-Image*. Oxford: Basil Blackwell, 1989.

Meres, Francis. *Palladis Tamia*. London, 1598; reprint, New York: Scholars' Facsimiles, 1938.

Merleau-Ponty, Maurice. "Reading Montaigne." In *Signs*. Trans. Richard C. McClerry. Evanston, Ill.: Northwestern University Press, 1964.

Meyer, Arnold Oskar. *England and the Catholic Church Under Queen Elizabeth*. Trans. J. R. McKee. London, 1916; reprint, New York: Barnes & Noble, 1967.

Milton, John. *Areopagitica*. In *Complete Poems and Major Prose*, ed. Merritt Y. Hughes. Indianapolis: Odyssey, 1957.

Montaigne, Michel de. *Oeuvres complètes.* Ed. A. Thibaudet and M. Rat. Paris: Gallimard-Pléiade, 1962.

———. *Les Essais de Michel de Montaigne.* Ed. Pierre Villey. Paris: Presses Universitaires de France, 1965.

———. *The Complete Essays.* Trans. Donald M. Frame. Stanford: Stanford University Press, 1965.

Montrose, Louis Adrian. "Celebration and Insinuation: Sir Philip Sidney and the Motives of Elizabethan Courtship." *Renaissance Drama* n.s. 8 (1977), 24–30.

———. "Of Gentlemen and Shepherds: The Politics of Elizabethan Pastoral Form." *ELH* 50 (1983), 415–59.

———. "The Elizabethan Subject and the Spenserian Text." In *Literary Theory / Renaissance Texts*, ed. Patricia Parker and David Quint. Baltimore: The Johns Hopkins University Press, 1986.

More, Thomas. *Utopia.* Trans. Paul Turner. Harmondsworth: Penguin, 1965.

Murray, Timothy. "From Foul Sheets to Legitimate Model: Antitheater, Text, Ben Jonson," *New Literary History* 14 (1983), 641–64.

Myrick, Kenneth. *Sir Philip Sidney as a Literary Craftsman.* Lincoln: University of Nebraska Press, 1965.

Nashe, Thomas. *The Unfortunate Traveller.* In *The Works of Thomas Nashe*, vol. 2, ed. Ronald B. McKerrow. London: A. H. Bullen, 1904.

Nicholl, Charles. *A Cup of News: The Life of Thomas Nashe.* London: Routledge & Kegan Paul, 1984.

Nichols, John, ed. *The Progresses, & Public Processions, of Queen Elizabeth.* 2 vols. London: John Nichols, 1788.

O'Connor, John J. *Amadis de Gaule and Its Influence on Elizabethan Literature.* New Brunswick, N.J.: Rutgers University Press, 1970.

Oestreich, Gerhard. *Neostoicism and the Early Modern State.* Ed. Brigitta Oestreich and H. G. Koenigsberger. Cambridge, Eng.: Cambridge University Press, 1982.

Oliver, H. J. "Introduction." In Christopher Marlowe, *The Massacre at Paris.* London: Methuen, 1968.

O'Neill, John. *Essaying Montaigne: A Study of the Renaissance Institutions of Writing and Reading.* London: Routledge & Kegan Paul, 1982.

Orgel, Stephen. *The Illusion of Power.* Berkeley: University of California Press, 1975.

Ornstein, Robert. *The Moral Vision of Jacobean Tragedy.* Madison: University of Wisconsin Press, 1965.

Osborne, James M. *Young Philip Sidney, 1572–1577.* New Haven: Yale University Press, 1972.

Patterson, Annabel. *Censorship and Interpretation.* Madison: University of Wisconsin Press, 1984.

Peck, Linda Levy. *Northampton: Patronage and Policy at the Court of James I.* London: George Allen & Unwin, 1982.

———. "'For a King not to be bountiful were a fault': Perspectives on Court Patronage in Early Stuart England." *Journal of British Studies* 25 (1986), 31–61.

Plato. *The Laws*. Trans. Thomas L. Pangle. New York: Basic Books, 1980.

Pocock, J. G. A. *The Machiavellian Moment: Florentine Political Thought and the Atlantic Republican Tradition*. Princeton: Princeton University Press, 1975.

Queller, Donald E. *The Office of Ambassador in the Middle Ages*. Princeton: Princeton University Press, 1967.

Quilligan, Maureen. "Sidney and His Queen." In *The Historical Renaissance: New Essays on Tudor and Stuart Literature and Culture*, ed. Heather Dubrow and Richard Strier. Chicago: University of Chicago Press, 1988.

Read, Conyers. *Mr. Secretary Walsingham and the Policy of Queen Elizabeth*. 3 vols. Cambridge, Mass.: Harvard University Press, 1925.

———. *Mr. Secretary Cecil and Queen Elizabeth*. London: Cape, 1955.

———. *Lord Burghley and Queen Elizabeth*. London: Cape, 1960.

Regosin, Richard. *The Matter of My Book: Montaigne's Essais as the Book of the Self*. Berkeley: University of California Press, 1977.

Reiss, Timothy J. *The Discourse of Modernism*. Ithaca, N.Y.: Cornell University Press, 1982.

———. "Montaigne and the Subject of Polity." In *Literary Theory / Renaissance Texts*, ed. Patricia Parker and David Quint. Baltimore: The Johns Hopkins University Press, 1986.

Ricks, Christopher. "*Sejanus* and Dismemberment." *Modern Language Notes* 76 (1961), 301–8.

Rider, Frederick. *The Dialectic of Selfhood in Montaigne*. Stanford: Stanford University Press, 1973.

Riggs, David. *Ben Jonson: A Life*. Cambridge, Mass.: Harvard University Press, 1989.

Rigolot, François. "Montaigne's Purloined Letters." *Yale French Studies* 64 (1983), 145–66.

Ripa, Cesare. *Iconologia*. 3 parts. Padua: Donato Pasquardi, 1630.

Rossi, Paolo. "Ants, Spiders, Epistemologists." In *Francis Bacon: Terminologia e Fortuna nel XVII Secolo*, ed. Marta Fattori. Rome: Edizioni dell'Ateneo, 1984.

Roth, Cecil. *A History of the Jews in England*. 3rd ed. Oxford: Clarendon, 1964.

Sayce, Richard A. *The Essays of Montaigne: A Critical Exploration*. London: Weidenfeld and Nicolson, 1972.

Saslow, James. *Ganymede in the Renaissance: Homosexuality in Art and Society*. New Haven: Yale University Press, 1986.

Schaefer, David Lewis. *The Political Philosophy of Montaigne*. Ithaca, N.Y.: Cornell University Press, 1990.

Schellhase, Kenneth C. *Tacitus in Renaissance Political Thought*. Chicago: University of Chicago Press, 1976.

Schreber, Daniel Paul. *Memoirs of My Mental Illness*. Trans. Ida Macalpine and Richard A. Hunter. London: W. M. Dawson & Sons, 1955.

Sedgwick, Eve Kosofsky. *Between Men: English Literature and Male Homosocial Desire*. New York: Columbia University Press, 1985.

Shepherd, Simon. *Marlowe and the Politics of Elizabethan Theater.* Brighton: Harvester, 1986.

Shirley, John W. "Sir Walter Ralegh and Thomas Harriot." In *Thomas Harriot: Renaissance Scientist,* ed. John W. Shirley. Oxford: Clarendon, 1974.

———. *Thomas Harriot: A Biography.* Oxford: Clarendon, 1983.

Sidney, Philip. *The Poems of Sir Philip Sidney.* Ed. William Ringler. Oxford: Clarendon, 1962.

———. *The Prose Works of Sir Philip Sidney.* 4 vols. Ed. Albert Feuillerat. Cambridge, Eng.: Cambridge University Press, 1962.

———. *The Countesse of Pembrokes Arcadia.* [The *New Arcadia.*] Vol. 1 of *The Prose Works.*

———. *A Defence of Poetry.* Ed. Jan Van Dorsten. Oxford: Oxford University Press, 1973.

———. *Miscellaneous Prose of Sir Philip Sidney.* Ed. Katherine Duncan-Jones and Jan Van Dorsten. Oxford: Clarendon, 1973.

———. *The Countess of Pembroke's Arcadia (The Old Arcadia).* Ed. Jean Robertson. Oxford: Clarendon, 1973.

———. *The Countess of Pembroke's Arcadia (The New Arcadia).* Ed. Victor Skretkowicz. Oxford: Clarendon, 1987.

Sinfield, Alan. "Power and Ideology: An Outline Theory and Sidney's *Arcadia.*" *ELH* (1985), 259–77.

Smith, Bruce R. *Homosexual Desire in Shakespeare's England: A Cultural Poetics.* Chicago: University of Chicago Press, 1991.

Smuts, R. Malcolm. *Court Culture and the Origins of a Royalist Tradition in Early Stuart England.* Philadelphia: University of Pennsylvania Press, 1987.

Spenser, Edmund. *The Poems of Edmund Spenser.* Ed. J. C. Smith and E. de Selincourt. London: Oxford University Press, 1912.

———. *The Shorter Poems of Edmund Spenser.* Ed. William A. Oram, Einar Bjorvand, Ronald Bond, Thomas H. Cain, Alexander Dunlop, and Richard Schell. New Haven: Yale University Press, 1989.

Sprot, S. E. "Drury and Marlowe." *The Times Literary Supplement,* August 2, 1974, p. 840.

Starobinski, Jean. *Montaigne in Motion.* Trans. Arthur Goldhammer. Chicago: University of Chicago Press, 1985.

Stone, Lawrence. *An Elizabethan: Sir Horatio Palavicino.* Oxford: Clarendon, 1956.

———. *The Crisis of the Aristocracy, 1558–1641.* Oxford: Clarendon, 1965.

———. *The Causes of the English Revolution, 1529–1642.* London: Routledge & Kegan Paul, 1972.

Strong, Roy. *Splendour at Court: Renaissance Spectacle and Illusion.* Boston: Houghton Mifflin, 1973.

———. *The Cult of Elizabeth.* London: Thames and Hudson, 1977.

———. *Gloriana: The Portraits of Queen Elizabeth I.* London: Thames and Hudson, 1987.

Tacitus. *The Complete Works.* Ed. Moses Hadas. New York: Modern Library, 1942.

Tennenhouse, Leonard. *Power on Display: The Politics of Shakespeare's Genres*. London: Methuen, 1986.

Thompson, E. P. *The Making of the English Working Class*. Harmondsworth: Penguin, 1968.

Traub, Valerie. "Desire and the Difference it Makes." In *The Matter of Difference: Materialist Feminist Criticism of Shakespeare*, ed. Valerie Wayne. Ithaca, N.Y.: Cornell University Press, 1991.

Urry, William. "Marlowe and Canterbury." *The Times Literary Supplement*, February 13, 1964, 136.

———. *Christopher Marlowe and Canterbury*. London: Faber and Faber, 1988.

Waith, Eugene M. "Marlowe and the Jades of Asia." *Studies in English Literature* 5 (1965), 229–45.

Wallace, Malcolm William. *The Life of Sir Philip Sidney*. Cambridge, 1915; reprint, New York: Octagon, 1967.

Wallerstein, Immanuel. *The Modern World System*, vol. 1: *Capitalist Agriculture and the Origins of the European World-Economy in the Sixteenth Century*. San Diego: Academic Press, 1974.

Weber, Max. *The Theory of Social and Economic Organization*. Trans. A. M. Henderson and Talcott Parsons. New York: Free Press, 1964.

Webster, Charles. *The Great Instauration: Science, Medicine, and Reform, 1626–1660*. London: Duckworth, 1975.

Weinberger, Jerry. "Introduction." In Francis Bacon, *The Great Instauration and New Atlantis*. Arlington Heights, Ill.: Harlan Davidson, 1980.

———. *Science, Faith, and Politics: Francis Bacon and the Utopian Roots of the Modern Age*. Ithaca, N.Y.: Cornell University Press, 1985.

Wernham, R. B. "Christopher Marlowe at Flushing in 1592." *English Historical Review* 91 (1976), 344–45.

———. *After the Armada: Elizabethan England and the Struggle for Western Europe, 1588–95*. Oxford: Clarendon, 1984.

White, Howard B. *Peace Among the Willows: The Political Philosophy of Francis Bacon*. The Hague: Martinus Nijhoff, 1968.

Wikander, Matthew H. " 'Queasy to Be Touched': The World of Ben Jonson's *Sejanus*." *Journal of English and Germanic Philology* 78 (1979), 345–57.

Wilden, Anthony. "Par divers moyens on arrive à pareille fin: A reading of Montaigne." *Modern Language Notes* 83 (1968), 577–97.

Williams, Raymond. *Marxism and Literature*. Oxford: Oxford University Press, 1977.

Wraight, A. D. *In Search of Christopher Marlowe*. New York: Vanguard Press, 1965.

Zagorin, Perez. *The Court and the Country*. New York: Atheneum, 1969.

Index

In this index an "f" after a number indicates a separate reference on the next page, and an "ff" indicates separate references on the next two pages. A continuous discussion over two or more pages is indicated by a span of page numbers, e.g., "57–59." *Passim* is used for a cluster of references in close but not consecutive sequence.

Library of Congress Cataloging-in-Publication Data

Archer, John Michael.
   Sovereignty and intelligence : spying and court culture in the
English Renaissance / John Michael Archer.
       p. cm.
   Includes bibliographical references and index.
   ISBN 0-8047-2079-7 :
    1. English literature—Early modern, 1500–1700—History and
criticism. 2. Montaigne, Michel de, 1533–1592. Essais. 3. Courts
and courtiers in literature. 4. Kings and rulers in literature.
5. Espionage in literature. 6. Renaissance—England. 7. Spies in
literature. I. Title.
PR428.C64A74 1993
820.9′358—dc20   92–30593
                                                   CIP

This book is printed on acid-free paper ∞